Women and Sharia Law in Northern Indonesia

This book examines the life of women in the Indonesian province of Aceh, where Islamic law was introduced in 1999. It outlines how women have had to face the formalization of conservative understandings of sharia law in regulations and new state institutions over the last decade or so, how they have responded to this, forming non-governmental organizations (NGOs) that have shaped local discourse on women's rights, equality and status in Islam, and how these NGOs have strategized, demanded reform and enabled Acehnese women to take active roles in influencing the processes of democratization and Islamization that are shaping the province. The book shows that although the formal introduction of Islamic law in Aceh has placed restrictions on women's freedom, paradoxically it has not prevented them from engaging in public life. It argues that the democratization of Indonesia, which allowed Islamization to occur, continues to act as an important factor shaping Islamization's current trajectory; that the introduction of Islamic law has motivated women's NGOs and other elements of civil society to become more involved in wider discussions about the future of sharia in Aceh; and that Indonesia's recent decentralization policy and growing local Islamism have enabled the emergence of different religious and local adat practices, which do not necessarily correspond to overall national trends.

Dina Afrianty is a researcher at the Institute for Religion, Politics and Society, Australian Catholic University and affiliated with Syarif Hidayatullah State Islamic University, Indonesia.

Mukkuvar Women: Gender, Hegemony and Capitalist Transformation in a South Indian Fishing Community by Kalpana Ram 1991

A World of Difference: Islam and Gender Hierarchy in Turkey by Julie Marcus 1992

Purity and Communal Boundaries: Women and Social Change in a Bangladeshi Village by Santi Rozario 1992

Madonnas and Martyrs: Militarism and Violence in the Philippines by Anne-Marie Hilsdon 1995

Masters and Managers: A Study of Gender Relations in Urban Java by Norma Sullivan 1995

Matriliny and Modernity: Sexual Politics and Social Change in Rural Malaysia by Maila Stivens 1995

Intimate Knowledge: Women and their Health in North-east Thailand by Andrea Whittaker 2000

Women in Asia: Tradition, Modernity and Globalisation by Louise Edwards and Mina Roces (eds) 2000

Violence against Women in Asian Societies: Gender Inequality and Technologies of Violence by Lenore Manderson and Linda Rae Bennett (eds) 2003

Women's Employment in Japan: The Experience of Part-time Workers by Kaye Broadbent 2003

Chinese Women Living and Working by Anne McLaren (ed) 2004

Abortion, Sin and the State in Thailand by Andrea Whittaker 2004

Sexual Violence and the Law in Japan by Catherine Burns 2004

Women, Islam and Modernity: Single Women, Sexuality and Reproductive Health in Contemporary Indonesia by Linda Rae Bennett 2005

The Women's Movement in Post-Colonial Indonesia by Elizabeth Martyn 2005

Women and Work in Indonesia by Michele Ford and Lyn Parker (eds) 2008

Series Editor's foreword

The contributions of women to the social, political and economic transformations occurring in the Asian region are legion. Women have served as leaders of nations, communities, workplaces, activist groups and families. Asian women have joined with others to participate in fomenting change at micro and macro levels. They have been both agents and targets of national and international interventions in social policy. In the performance of these myriad roles women have forged new and modern gendered identities that are recognisably global and local. Their experiences are rich, diverse and instructive. The books in this series testify to the central role women play in creating the new Asia and re-creating Asian womanhood. Moreover, these books reveal the resilience and inventiveness of women around the Asian region in the face of entrenched and evolving patriarchal social norms.

Scholars publishing in this series demonstrate a commitment to promoting the productive conversation between Gender Studies and Asian Studies. The need to understand the diversity of experiences of femininity and womanhood around the world increases inexorably as globalization proceeds apace. Lessons from the experiences of Asian women present us with fresh opportunities for building new possibilities for women's progress the world over.

The Asian Studies Association of Australia (ASAA) sponsors this publication series as part of its on-going commitment to promoting knowledge about women in Asia. In particular, the ASAA Women's Forum provides the intellectual vigour and enthusiasm that maintains the Women in Asia Series (WIAS). The aim of the series, since its inception in 1990, is to promote knowledge about women in Asia to both academic and general audiences. To this end, WIAS books draw on a wide range of disciplines including anthropology, sociology, political science, cultural studies, media studies, literature and history. The series prides itself on being an outlet for cutting-edge research conducted by recent PhD graduates and postdoctoral fellows from throughout the region.

The series could not function without the generous professional advice provided by many anonymous readers. Moreover, the wise counsel provided by Peter Sowden at Routledge is invaluable. WIAS, its authors and the ASAA are very grateful to these people for their expert work.

Lenore Lyons (The University of Sydney)
Series Editor

Women and Sharia Law in Northern Indonesia

Local women's NGOs and the reform of Islamic law in Aceh

Dina Afrianty

Routledge
Taylor & Francis Group

LONDON AND NEW YORK

First published 2015
by Routledge

2 Park Square, Milton Park, Abingdon, Oxfordshire OX14 4RN

711 Third Avenue, New York, NY 10017

Routledge is an imprint of the Taylor & Francis Group, an informa business

First issued in paperback 2017

British Library Cataloguing in Publication data

A catalogue record for this book is available from the British Library

Library of Congress Cataloguing in Publication data
Afrianty, Dina, author.
    Women and Sharia law in Northern Indonesia: local women's NGOs and the
    reform of Islamic law in Aceh / Dina Afrianty.
        p.   cm. – (ASAA women in Asia series; 41)
    Includes bibliographical references and index.
    1. Women–Legal status, laws, etc.–Indonesia–Nanggroe Aceh Darussalam.
    2. Women (Islamic law)–Indonesia–Nanggroe Aceh Darussalam.
    3. Non-governmental organizations–Indonesia–Nanggroe Aceh
    Darussalam.   I. Title.
    KNW2935.A33A37 2015
    346.598'110134–dc23
    2014034937

ISBN: 978-1-138-81936-8 (hbk)
ISBN: 978-0-8153-6240-1 (pbk)

Typeset in Times New Roman
by Out of House Publishing

Contents

Introduction

Background

A photo that circulated in September 2005 in local and national media of an Acehnese woman giving her non-Acehnese military boyfriend a passionate open-mouthed kiss in front of a battalion of the Indonesian army getting ready to leave the war-torn province following the peace agreement with the Free Aceh Movement (GAM) shocked Acehnese men and women (*Tempo interaktif* 2005). The Acehnese were in disbelief, wondering what could have gone wrong with a fellow Acehnese Muslim woman to violate the strong religious principle of not showing affection or being in close proximity with the opposite sex. To many Acehnese, the incident was a disgrace to Aceh's *adat* and the Islamic tradition that they strongly uphold. The authorities were upset that the woman violated and undermined the sharia law that has been formalized since 2002. For many Indonesians, who live outside Aceh, we wondered how many lashes the couple would get for violating the law. Fortunately, they escaped the rattan cane.

This incident provided an opening for sharia activists to push the local government to implement sharia law more seriously. They also demanded that the government not discriminate between anyone who violates the law. They believe that total implementation of Islamic law would save Acehnese women from any further wrongdoing. This incident legitimizes the spirit of the sharia activists that women should be the central focus in their attempt to Islamize society.

This book is about the lived experiences of Acehnese women in the Indonesian province of Aceh who live under Islamic law. The enforcement of Islamic law has subjected women's sexuality, bodies and religiosity. The Acehnese women respond to it by mobilizing for change, shaping local discourse on women's equality and status, promoting equality, women's civil and political rights and demanding law reform within an Islamic framework. The arrival of international development agencies, foreign and national NGOs has helped Acehnese women to become familiar with Western/international feminist discourse on gender equality, women's civil and political rights and social justice. With Islam and tradition strongly entrenched in the identity of Acehnese women, they insist on the need to reread and reinterpret the sources of Islamic law in reforming Islamic law. Acehnese women talk about equality and their rights in Islam, learn about women's role in the history of Aceh, discuss, debate and argue, making equality and women's rights in Islam their daily conversation.

Acehnese women are not alone. Along with many other Indonesian women, their behaviour and sexuality have increasingly been targeted by those who want to revive Islamic values. Islamic political parties and other Muslim groups established after the 1998 *Reformasi* are at work with the agenda of returning the society back to Islam. In this project, Muslim politics put women's bodies, status and roles subject to the contestation of what is right and wrong according to Islam. The decentralization policy introduced by the Indonesian government in 1999 provides regional authorities with the power to introduce regulation that is inspired by religion, in particular Islam. A number of provinces and districts around Indonesia have enacted religiously inspired regional regulations or PERDA (Peraturan Daerah) *syari'at*. Up to 2008, about 52 out of 470 districts and municipalities enacted 78 religious regulations or PERDA (Bush 2008, 176). The desire to promote *adat* (local customs) and the idea to return to Islam are the key source of values believed to be behind the formation of social norms implemented into PERDA. This religiously inspired PERDA regulate public morality to diminish social problems, from prostitution, gambling and alcohol consumption to the regulation of women's behaviour and what women can and cannot wear. In some cases, they also regulate sexual mores.[1] Sadly, it is only when Indonesia democratizes that women are being criminalized for not following Islamic dress code.

Indonesian women use various means to challenge this. They use democratic openings to engage in political and social activism to express their political views.[2] Indonesia's cultural and social structure still places constraints on women to participate in formal politics such as being elected to political office. In the last three democratic general elections, in 1999, 2004 and 2009, women's representation in the parliament has remained at around 16–18 per cent, while the number of women voters is counted to be around 51 per cent of the total voters. Women then use various alternatives by organizing into social movements to express their socio-religious and political views. They get involved in various efforts from religious organizations to many other forms of voluntary organizations aimed at transforming society, from the grassroots to those at higher levels of society.

Politicians and male religious authority figures use Islam to justify the attempts to limit women's freedom and status. This has prompted Muslim women take the initiative to promote the need to have more gender-sensitive reinterpretations of Islamic texts. Muslim women's groups and other Muslim organizations at the national level developed connections with international feminist groups, as well as receiving support from Western sources and building alliances with modernist Muslim men scholars since the 1990s. They build alliances with male Muslim reformists to pioneer the discourse on the need to contextualize Islamic texts and emphasize their egalitarian messages (Bowen 1998, 2003; Feener 2007; Robinson 2007). These male and female Muslim reformists are educated in *pesantren*[3] or traditional Islamic educational institutions and received higher education from the modernized State Institute of Islamic Studies or IAIN system, giving them religious credentials to reform Islamic teachings.[4]

It is thus tempting to see similar developments that have occurred at the local level, which is in Aceh, where Islamic law is formalized into the regional regulation. This book will show how Muslim women and male Muslim reformists at the local level are moved and influenced by the movements at the national level. This book in particular addresses the following specific research question. First, how Acehnese women respond to the implementation of Islamic law. Second, how women activists understand their status in Aceh's culture and how they perceive the gender relations in Aceh's society. Third, it questions how religious Acehnese women activists reconcile their understanding of gender equality and women's rights with those of Western/international values. This book does not aim to examine the attempts by Islamic jurists in Aceh to shape Islamic legal doctrine, as it is not intended to show the development of Islamic jurisprudence. It is, however, an initial attempt to identify how women activists of local women's NGOs in Aceh have responded to the formalization of Islamic law and how they mobilize for change.

Conceptual framework

The lived experience of women living under Islamic law has prompted women to mobilize for change. Women use the available social, religious and political opportunities to promote changes and advance women's interests in society. The implementation of Islamic law that occurs along with the political reform has significantly affected the way women respond to sharia law. Islamic law has negatively affected women's mobility; however, this book will show that women are able to find ways to actively promote change. Discrimination, humiliation and marginalization do not stop women from finding avenues to promote policy changes and transform the religious society by making these subjects part of their conversations.

One of the aims of this book is to show that women's participation in public cannot be seen just from their participation in formal politics, such as involvement in political parties or in the bureaucracy. In studying women and politics, as Waylen suggests (1996a, 7–8), we should consider three things. First, 'politics does not have the same impact on women as it does on men', because women are considered to belong to domestic sphere and therefore out of way of state interference. Second, the political process often affects gender relations. Third, women often participate as political subjects in political activity in different ways to men.

Many of us who are not Acehnese may quickly take pity on the Acehnese women's lived experience. We hear stories of women being humiliated in public for not wearing proper Muslim dress or for being in close proximity with the opposite sex on a regular basis, which may lead some of us to think how powerless Acehnese women are. The question we should ask then is how Acehnese women react to these practices and what avenues women use to stop the practices. Indonesians have long believed in the bravery of Acehnese women, with national heroines such as Tjut Nyak Dien who fought against Dutch colonial occupation.

The Acehnese have not just been silent victims of sharia law. Siapno's (2002, x) ethnographic work during the military conflict, which focused on rural Acehnese women, provides evidence that rural Acehnese women, despite the depiction of being powerless and victimized, have, in fact, formulated 'their agency in a complex interplay of indigenous matrifocality, Islamic beliefs, practices and state violence'. This demonstrates that Acehnese rural and poor women were able to show 'women's political subjectivity by creating spaces beyond conventional and institutional practices of doing politics' even when spaces for them were limited. The Acehnese are widely perceived as pious and strong believers of Islam. The question is how, as Muslim believers, Acehnese women deal with and challenge the restrictions and limitations imposed on them, which are said to be derived from Islamic teachings.

Scholars working on women and politics in the Third World have reminded us of the need to acknowledge that women should not be seen as homogeneous and unitary or that they experience a common oppression thus seeing them as passive victims (Waylen 1996b). Likewise, seeing Third World women as different to women in the First World, mainly because they are non-Western, will result in ignoring the agency of Third World women. This is in line with what Mohanty (1991, 56) has suggested, namely that Third World women do not tend to be seen as agents of their own destiny, but as victims.

I reflect on Saba Mahmood's work (2005) in looking at women's piety movements in Egypt. She offers a different way to understand women's agency in a society that imposes oppressive regulations derived from Islam against women. Mahmood does not see the absence of resistance to oppressive norms as an absence of agency. Looking at women in the mosque movement in Egypt, women's activities have in fact a profoundly transformative effect in the social and political field. The activities of the Acehnese, as this book shows, reveal how women engage with the state and the religious authority in making their attempt to create change while maintaining their religiosity.

Gender and politics

The study of women and their political participation has not received enough attention, especially within political science literature (Waylen 1996; Afshar 1996; Beckwith 2000; Jacquette 2001). This is because women's political participation is considered 'marginal or non-existent', partly due to the minimal role that women have played in political leadership or in the established political institutions, and also because political parties, legislatures and executives are dominated by men, which pushed women to confine themselves to the private or domestic spheres (Afshar 1996, 1; Waylen 1996, 7).[5] However, political decentralization has paved the way for more activism and participation of women, as politics becomes more diffuse, allowing new forms of participation. From Latin America to the Middle East, women mobilize to promote social and political changes (Alvarez 1990; Basu 2010).

Women's increased mobilization and activism have shifted the focus within the study of women and politics from focusing only on women's political behavior in conventional politics such as women's voting behavior and their participation in formal politics, to women's engagement in community actions, social movements and other forms of mobilized struggles (Beckwith 2000, 431). This shift happens, according to Beckwith, because women are increasingly more active in public spaces. Studies of women and politics have begun to give more emphasis to women's movements, women's activism in NGOs and women's mobilization. Studies of political democratization in Latin America, for example, demonstrate how women's movements play significant roles during the initial breakdown of authoritarian regimes, through to the process of democratic consolidation (Alvarez 1990). Likewise, Waylen (1994, 328) discussed how popular movements including women's movements play an important role in the transition to democracy.

Women can act either on an individual basis or by joining a movement or organization to exercise their political participation. Women's movements and the vitality of women's NGOs are important components in the process of democratization (Jacquette 2001). The presence of women's movements and women's organizations is one indicator of how democratic transition has progressed. The trajectory of women's movements and women's organizations are important indicators of how well the institutions are working on the ground so that women's political participation affects democracy and gender analysis can contribute to a deeper understanding of democratic transitions (Jacquette 2001, 111).

Based on this conceptual understanding, I frame my book as a study of women and political participation by looking at women's activism within women's movements and women's organizations or NGOs. The implementation of Islamic law in Aceh is the product of political process, and the way it is implemented will therefore relate to local and national politics. This, in turn, also affects women and gender relations. What makes the implementation of Islamic law in Aceh unique is that the implementation occurs within the wider framework of Indonesia's democratization. This is not found in other places where the implementation of Islamic law is often applied by authoritarian administrations or where no democratic mechanisms are available. Acehnese women mobilize into women's movements and work with women's NGOs to exercise their agency in the public sphere.

Women's movements and women's NGOs

Literature on women's movements has acknowledged the difficulty of strictly defining what should be considered to be 'women's movements'. Ferree and Mueller (2004, 577), for example, define women's movements as a process of women's mobilization based on appeals to women both as a constituency and as an organization. Women's movements bring women's political activities to empower women to challenge limitations to their roles, and create networks among women that enhance women's ability to recognize existing gender relations as oppressive and in need of change. Women's movements are far-reaching expressions of women's agency and activisms and they are defined by their constituencies, that is women, and address a variety of goals (Basu 2010, 4). Women's movements are in many ways inspired by feminist movements whose goals are to challenge gender equality, but different in a way that the constituents of the movements can also include men (Krook 2012, 4)

Women's movements in the late twentieth century are categorized as 'fluid, diverse, fragmented, sporadic, issue-oriented and autonomous, employing different ideological thought and strategies' (Gandhi and Shah cited in Bystydzienski and Sekhon 1999, 11). Women's movements encompass a great variety of organizations from women's NGOs to other groups or actions, many of which 'emerge in response to the needs of and are firmly anchored in local communities'. Likewise, Margolis (1993, 379) argued that every women's movement follows a distinctive course, developing its unique agenda in response to local circumstances.

There has been academic discussion on the difference of women's movements and women's organizations or NGOs. Based on her observations in Latin American countries, Alvarez (1999, 185–186) differentiates NGOs from women's movements. According to her, NGOs are run by specialized, paid and professional staff, with only a small number of volunteers. In terms of funding, NGOs obtain the support of international or national donors. They engage in pragmatic and strategic planning which aims to influence public policy. Unlike NGOs, women's movements are largely made up of volunteers, who are sporadic participants rather than 'staff'. They also have more informal organizational structures and operate on smaller budgets. Women's movements and their actions are guided by 'more loosely defined, conjectural goals or objectives'. Based on this discussion, I categorize women's movements in Aceh as encompassing all kinds of women's activism, including activities of women's Muslim organizations, women's NGOs and women members of religious groups, whose work and interests centre on promoting human rights and women's rights.

There have been a number of scholarly works that have discussed the roles of NGOs in the process of democratization in Indonesia (Eldridge 1989, 1995, 2005; Hadiwinata 2002; Aspinall 2009). This literature, however, lacks information on the role of Muslim women's organizations in particular. Women scholars such as Susan Blackburn, Saskia Wierenga, Kathryn Robinson, Rachel Rinaldo, Suzanne Brenner and Elizabeth Martyn, have, however, sought to fill this gap. Blackburn (2004, 2) mentioned a tendency to overlook the role of women's NGOs in the literature of political democratization, which may be because women's organizations are seen as unrepresentative. That is, it is not clear which women are being represented by women's NGOs, and whose interests women's movements represent. This view derives from understanding that women have different gender interests due to differences in ethnicity, class and religion (Cooke 2000). Despite being perceived as unrepresentative, and despite their limitations, women's NGOs should be considered important because they provide insights into the perceptions and feelings of certain groups of people (Blackburn 2004, 2).

Studies on Indonesia's women's movements and women's NGOs mostly look at the activities of women's organizations based in Java or in Jakarta (Martyn 2005; Rinaldo 2002). Martyn (2005, 13) fears that the tendency to focus only on national-based women's organizations can create 'an elite and Java/Jakarta bias' in understanding women's movements in Indonesia. She is concerned that these studies are then used as a model to characterize women's NGOs' experiences across the country, while women's voices and experiences in other regions of Indonesia are silenced or neglected. It is for this reason that this book seeks to examine the emergence and development of women's movements and activities of women's NGOs in Aceh. Given Aceh's history, and its position within the history of Indonesia's nation-building, the development of Aceh NGOs should be scrutinized.

Local women's NGOs are not only present in Aceh, but also in places like Jakarta, Tangerang regency in Banten province, Cianjur and Tasikmalaya in West Java and in Sulawesi, Kalimantan and Sumatra, where norms derived from Islamic law have been introduced as local regulations or PERDA. However, Aceh has been the only place where local women's NGOs have received such extensive support from both national and international networks, allowing massive interaction between the local and international NGOs.

Islam, militarism, economic exploitation, violence and the recent natural disasters have all had significant impacts on women's lives in Aceh. This has generated a sympathetic response from both national and international communities to local women's NGOs. The failure of the state's structure following the massive loss of its officials because of the tsunami on 26 December 2004 is another factor that has prompted donors and international organizations to work with local NGOs to deliver services and humanitarian assistance. Zuckerman and Greenberg (2004, 76) observe that in post-conflict areas there is a need to guarantee that:

> Within the process of transition women are given the right to participate in policy making and resource allocation, to benefit equally from public and private resources and services and to build gender-equitable society for lasting peace and prosperity.

Post-conflict rehabilitation, post-tsunami reconstruction and the implementation of Islamic law created a favourable environment for the proliferation of NGOs in Aceh, which then led to the establishment of women's movements.

The Media Center Aceh (Aliansi Jurnalis Aceh) reports that around 225 national/local organizations or NGOs have been established since April 2005. Other than these local NGOs, about 326 international NGOs came and worked in post-tsunami Aceh. This proliferation of NGOs has led many Acehnese to believe that Aceh is experiencing an 'NGO-ization' of society alongside '*syari'ah*-ization'. Almost 70 per cent of these NGOs are reported to work on issues related to women.

This book contributes to the debate within the literature assessing the work of NGOs. Edwards and Hulme (1996) describe NGOs as a 'magic bullet' within the development process. However, recent literature on NGOs has begun to question whether NGOs really represent the interests of the grassroots when they act as lobby groups to influence public policy. This debate emerges from NGOs' failures to address the needs of the people in various places. Critics believe that NGOs have increasingly moved towards extending the agenda of capitalism, through Western donors and international organizations (DeMars 2005). Hamami (2000, 27) for example, explains that NGOs in the Gaza Strip have failed to play a role as catalysts of social change since they failed to challenge the continued 'Arafatization' of Palestinian political life and have been unable to mount a single sustained campaign against expanding Israeli control over Palestinian land. As a result, Hamami argues that these NGOs are merely seen as 'fat-cats' that exploit donor funds for their own enrichment, at the cost of an increasingly destitute population. In another region, Helms (2003) demonstrates that the work of local women's NGOs in post-conflict Bosnia have been controlled by their donors' interests. Women's NGOs in Bosnia have been unable to carry out programmes based on their own assessments of the needs of the Bosnian people. According to Helms, although donors claim to be promoting a diverse and healthy civil society for Bosnia, they actually introduce local women's NGOs to new values that do not always resonate with local needs. This hampers the work of local women's NGOs to fulfil the needs and expectation of the local people. This is because in Bosnia, Helms further argues, international donors force their own formula on gender discourse by excluding the indigenous, religious and ethnic identities of the local women. Similar cases have been seen in other post-conflict crises. In Afghanistan, for example, local women's NGOs that partner with international NGOs are forced to practise 'template' solutions that fail to take into account the local social and cultural contexts (Barakat and Wardell 2002, 910).

These discussions reinforce the argument that in many places local women's NGOs are confined by the interests of their donors, leading to a failure of NGOs to address the interests and problems of their societies. This can be understood, as local NGOs are challenged by the need to maintain non-profit status but, on the other hand, have to gain financial support in order to run their offices. They cannot rely on keeping their work voluntary, since they are also increasingly forced to be professional and accountable.

Given the matters discussed above, this book also consider how the study of local women's NGOs' responses to the implementation of Islamic law can shed light on how interactions between local women's NGOs and international donors affects local NGOs' programmes and activities. The book also assesses whether local women's NGOs have acted as the machinery of international institutions and fulfilled the agendas of foreign donors in responding to the implementation of Islamic law. In doing so, I examine Kandiyoti's (1995, 4) argument that the agenda of international institutions and foreign NGOs is to promote policy changes in increasingly conservative societies, especially relating to the role of women.

The research

The data for this research comes from an ethnographic approach. It is based on analysis of primary and secondary resources in both Indonesian and English. The primary data for this book was obtained through in-depth interviews, field notes and journal writings from participating in participant-observations during six months of fieldwork in Banda Aceh. I interviewed activists from local, national and international NGOs. Acehnese women and men from various backgrounds, such as students, villagers, academics and others, are also included in my interviews. Many of my interviewees requested that their identity not be revealed, and this is reflected in the anonymized references to interviewees used in this book in some cases.

As there are many local women's NGOs in Banda Aceh, I chose to focus only on those whose programmes and activities are confined to issues related to the implementation of Islamic law. In post-reconstruction Aceh, there are many other local women's NGOs who work to provide support to fulfil women's basic needs and healthcare. I obtained the name of local women's NGOs from a handbook published by the Women's Empowerment Bureau or Biro Pemberdayaan Perempuan (BIRO PP) in 2006, which compiled a list of women's NGOs in Aceh after the tsunami. This compilation includes information on their establishment and the work they are doing.

Conducting research in Aceh at that time was quite challenging. Many foreign NGOs, international donors, and foreign consultants and international researchers were also in Aceh conducting their own research and implementing development programmes. The Acehnese were overwhelmed by 'research' as they talked to a large number of researchers, interviewing them to gather information. Doing fieldwork in Aceh was also challenging as many Acehnese were very traumatized by all the events they have endured, the military conflict and tsunami. Under such circumstances, skilled research adopting a careful approach is needed so that objectives can be achieved without inconveniencing subjects

The positive side of doing research while Aceh was inundated by donors was that many of these organizations organized seminars, training or workshops on women's issues and Islamic law. I attended more than five seminars on this subject and several other small and close discussions between activists, which allowed me to listen and talk not only with NGO activists who organized the events, but also with speakers and participants from different areas in Aceh.

The secondary data in this book includes archival materials, including local newspapers, research reports carried out by various international and national NGOs, and previous studies on Aceh. It is difficult, however, to find articles or books writing on Acehnese women, local women's NGOs or the Acehnese women's movement. My interviews, field notes and observations try to capture and generate firsthand experiences and data through this ethnographic approach. In analysing the data and observations thus generated, I tried to take into account the following issues. First, the way Acehnese women in various social classes observe Islam as their religion, including to what extent factors like education, economic and socio-religious backgrounds affect the way Acehnese women observe and incorporate Islamic teachings into their behaviour and their interactions within families and societies. Second, how women in general respond to the perceived victimization of women by Islamic law. In analysing this, I seek to uncover the backgrounds of women's organizations that make Aceh's women's movements, their institutional capacities and the socio-educational, political and religious backgrounds of activists within these organizations. Understanding this has helped me uncover the objectives of women's organizations and their approaches. The establishment and activisms of local women's organizations also needs to be looked at within the context of the socio-economic and political background of Aceh. Third, the professionalism of women's organizations by looking at how local women's organizations run their activities and programmes. I also examine how local women's NGOs deal with international agencies and foreign donors, especially in their efforts to generate financial support. I chose MISPI as my case study, because it has been successful in delivering its programmes to the wider Acehnese women community, and because of its ability to engage with the religious authority and the government bureaucracy.

The ethnographic field

I focused my research only in the capital city of Nanggroe Aceh Darussalam Province, Banda Aceh.[6] I choose to focus my research here, because it is where most local, national and international organizations have their offices. Focusing on Banda Aceh also allowed me to directly observe the interaction of local activists with national-based and international activists. As the capital city, Banda Aceh is the centre of the reconstruction and rehabilitation processes in post-tsunami and post-conflict Aceh. It is not hard to see foreign people walking around the central market in the city. The four-wheel-drive vehicles of many international institutions and NGOs, such as the UN (United Nations), UNICEF (United Nations Children Fund), Oxfam, UNDP (United Nations Development Programs), GTZ (the German Technical Cooperation, aid agency), the Red Cross and Save the Children, dominate the main roads of Banda Aceh. These international organizations and foreign NGOs employ foreign expatriates as well as Indonesian nationals.[7] This situation during my research was a great contrast to what Aceh looked like during the conflict, when it was hard for foreigners to get access. Internet cafes and Western food chains were scattered across every corner of the city, making Banda Aceh into a small international town.

My first visit began by attending the First International Conference of Aceh and Indian Ocean Studies (ICAOS), held on 24–27 February 2007.[8] This event provided me with the opportunity to meet Acehnese scholars and activists, as well as dozens of scholars from international institutions working in Aceh. The variety of issues discussed over the three days informed me of the recent social, economic, political and religious developments, as well as the history of Aceh. The conference was held at the Swiss Bell hotel,[9] the first four-star hotel to be built after the tsunami. The conference was funded by the Bureau of Reconstruction and Rehabilitation (BRR), which spent about 1.7 billion Indonesian rupiah (IDR) to support this conference, a fact that later led to mass demonstrations outside the hotel.

The arrival of foreigners and other Indonesian nationals in Aceh created new social settings. The presence of foreign NGOs and international institutions has changed the socio-religious and traditional values of the Acehnese, while boosting Aceh's economy. Some Acehnese people complained and worried about the future of Aceh when all the money goes away. With money from international donors and foreign NGOs, the inflation rates in Aceh have increased significantly. By 2005, the inflation rate reached 41.5 per cent, the highest compared to previous years. In 2006, it decreased to 9.54 per cent but rose again to 11 per cent in 2007, still higher than the national inflation rate of 6.7 per cent. This high inflation led to a rise in consumer prices and services (Furqon 2008; Kasim 2008). Acehnese and NGO workers from other parts of Indonesia call the rocketing prices 'NGO prices', or '*harga* NGO', implying that the increasing prices were the result of the arrival of foreigners working for international NGOs, and, of course, their money.[10]

This new economic setting posed particular challenges in living in Aceh. Accommodation was in high demand as the result of the arrival of foreign workers and non-Acehnese Indonesian nationals. Not only that, the price of rental accommodation was soaring, exceeding even the average price of rental accommodation in Jakarta. In the city area, the cost of renting one bedroom in a shared house could reach almost IDR 3 million per month, equal to AUD\$ 353. By comparison, in Jakarta, the capital city of Indonesia, the rental for similar types of accommodation would only be IDR 750,000, or about AUD\$ 90.[11] For those who work for international NGOs this is not expensive, because their salaries are about five to ten times more than those of NGO workers in Jakarta. One official from a foreign embassy in Jakarta told me that a foreigner who works at an international NGO in Aceh receives approximately IDR 90 million, or about AUD\$ 11,250, per month. This was not surprising to me, because I knew that a university student who works casually as a guide for international workers could get paid almost IDR 12 million per month, or about AUD$ 1,500, comparable to the salary of an experienced professional manager in Jakarta. One of my informants, a volunteer sent by her university in Jakarta, said that she received IDR 16 million for working at an Australian-based NGO immediately after she finished her assignment as a volunteer. She therefore refused to return to Jakarta, because she could earn lots of money working in Aceh. An Acehnese activist informed me that she plans to send her parents to perform the *Hajj*, the pilgrimage to Mecca, which costs about IDR 35 million, or AUD$ 4,118, because her income skyrocketed once she began working with an international NGO.

The arrival of foreigners has also changed the attitudes of the Acehnese to academic work. Siapno (2007) noted that the huge amount of money poured into Aceh has affected the attitudes of academics and students in Aceh. University students are more interested in attending seminars, training or joining a research team than attending classes at university. Similarly, academics spend much of their time as researchers at international NGOs or as consultants for foreign organizations. Students chose to do this instead of attending class because of the relatively high financial compensation available. One informant, a student at the Law Faculty at Syiah Kuala University, told me that if she gets invited to be a participant in a seminar or training she receives IDR 400,000 (equal to AUD$ 48) per day, which is about half the money she receives from her parents every month, and each seminar usually lasted for two to three days (interview, Banda Aceh, 10 March 2007). Their lecturers also tell similar stories. One junior academic at IAIN Ar-Raniry told me that by being involved in research conducted by foreign institutions she earned about IDR 40 million per month, approximately two years of her salary as a lecturer at IAIN (interview, Banda Aceh, 20 February 2008).

It was not only students and academics who financially benefited from the NGO-ization in Aceh. People in the market and teachers at schools also benefit. One high school teacher in Banda Aceh told me she was once asked to answer a questionnaire by an NGO (interview, Banda Aceh, 20 March 2007). After answering all the questions, which took her less than an hour, she was given an envelope with IDR 75,000 (almost AUD$ 9). She said that her school was visited three times in one week by three different NGOs conducting surveys. Each time she received an envelope containing almost the same amount of money. By contrast her weekly salary might only be IDR 200,000 or about AUD$ 23.

Some Acehnese, however, resented the changes that took place during Aceh's reconstruction period. One local woman activist based in Lhoksemauwe blamed the international donors for changing social attitudes among the Acehnese (interview, Banda Aceh, 12 March 2007). She said that the Acehnese have changed their perception of their own environment, since foreign donors and international bodies such as the UN introduced the 'cash for work' programme immediately after the tsunami. This programme introduced the Acehnese to a system where people get paid for any kind of work they do, including cleaning their own gardens, their own houses and their own village or mosque. According to her, this created a perception among the Acehnese that they are entitled to receive money for their participation in any activity. She is therefore not surprised that people now demand payment for their involvement in research or surveys.

As the Acehnese are, in fact, inundated by surveys and research, an Acehnese man who worked for Oxfam reminded me that conducting research during this period of time is not easy (interview, Banda Aceh, 14 January 2008). He also mentioned how the money issue has changed Acehnese attitudes. He is concerned that some Acehnese may have not really told the truth when asked about their experiences. According to him this is because many Acehnese feel tired of being questioned. He referred to the giant billboard posted at Simpang Lima, the very centre of the city of Banda Aceh, which says:

Data itu Mahal: Membangun Tanpa Data Merpuakan Pekerjaan yang sia-sia untuk itu Bantulah Petugas Statistik Dengan Memberikan Data yang Benar. [Data is expensive. To build without data is a useless job. Therefore, help the statistician by providing the right data.]

The research positioning

Conducting research in a place where sharia is formalized offers unique challenges. As a female and Muslim researcher, the implementation of Islamic law presented another issue that I needed to deal with. Ziba Mir-Hosseini (1998, 45–46) believes that every researcher who is doing research on gender in Islam needs to clearly state her or his position on the issues. She is aware that for Muslim researchers, doing research on gender in Islam may make the researchers 'feel at ease' because they see Islam as part of their identity, their way of life, their culture and their value system. At the same time, Muslim researchers may also find that they are in a painful and ambiguous relationship, because according to Mir-Hosseini (1998, 46), 'It is not easy to distinguish the personal from the political, what we see from what we want to see, while claiming that we have retained academic impartiality'.

I grew up in a pious Muslim family, and I am aware that my argument about the Acehnese women and their agency in reforming Islamic law may be influenced by my personal experience. My lived experience being a daughter of a pious Muslim family has not hindered me from feeling the freedom to express my views on various issues, however, as Muslim woman, I am aware of the discriminatory practices found in many Muslim communities that impede women's liberation and freedom to choose, including in places like Aceh. My experience of being a female teenager who grew up during Indonesia's authoritarian and militaristic administration meant that I did experience discrimination against women in Indonesia, albeit caused by the state's gender policy. Therefore, I agree with Kandiyoti (1995), who has argued that it is a gross generalization to say that Muslim women are oppressed because of their religion. In her opinion, when analysing women's lack of freedom in many

Muslim societies it is necessary to consider whether encounters by Muslim societies with colonialism and post-colonial nation-building projects may have contributed to women's subjugation (Kandiyoti 1995, 23–24).

I am not ruling out the argument that Acehnese women may lose access to freedoms and to participate in politics as Islamic law is implemented. But I was also keen to see how Aceh's transition to democracy, which is taking place within the context of a broader democratization in Indonesia, allowed Acehnese women to participate in politics, including by influencing government policy in the implementation of Islamic law.[12] Having friends with Acehnese backgrounds, I understand they have strong opinions about their religion. I was convinced that Acehnese women, in fact, have the ability to manoeuvre effectively within the spaces that are available to them to engage in policy-making, as can be seen from the making of some *Qanun* in Aceh.[13]

Despite my position towards this research, I encountered challenges as how I should position myself as regards the subjects of my research. Unlike female research students from abroad, as an Indonesian and a Muslim I must abide by Islamic law.[14] Muslim clothing is one of my major concerns, as it is heavily regulated under Islamic law in Aceh. Although I have been wearing Muslim dress for more than 15 years and have covered my hair, I still fear that my understanding of what constitutes Muslim dress is not the same as that subscribed to by many Acehnese. I heard, for example, that it is not acceptable for women to wear trousers in Aceh, while I have often worn trousers and still saw myself as following Islamic norms. I considered the issue of how I should dress while undertaking research for my book to be an essential one, as Wolf (1996, 8) has argued that entering fieldwork is always difficult and may pose particular challenges for women because of their gender identity. Women are more likely to conform to local gender norms, which may create difficulties and dilemmas for feminist researchers. Thus, I tried to make sure that I followed Acehnese women's practices in wearing Muslim clothing, as I did not want this issue to jeopardize my research and lead the Acehnese to form 'negative' impressions of me.

I was also aware of the problems that I might encounter by developing relationships with the subjects of my research. Harding and Norberg (2005) have pointed out that during fieldwork a researcher must negotiate her power and knowledge with the informant. I was aware that the Acehnese women activists who are the subject of my research might attempt to define or steer my project for several reasons, and indeed, in my first encounters with women activists, I found it challenging to position myself and my research. One of the senior activists asked me why as a non-Acehnese I researched about women in Aceh. When she found out that I am originally from West Sumatra, she asked me why I did not conduct research on Minangkabau women in West Sumatra as sharia-derived PERDA have also been introduced in this region. I also found that my identity as a Minangkabau woman did not make it easier for me to gain acceptance, although I had thought it would give me some advantage, due to the cultural and religious proximity between Aceh and Minangkabau.

One Acehnese sociologist, however, explained to me that many Acehnese resent the Minangkabau, because some feel Islam developed faster in West Sumatra than in Aceh, where the Acehnese believe it first penetrated Sumatra (interview, Banda Aceh, 17 March 2007). Later, the Acehnese had to travel to West Sumatra to gain Islamic education from modern Islamic educational institutions.[15]

Another activist posed the question of why I was interested in looking at women under Islamic law, as many other foreign researchers have already done similar research. This activist was particularly troubled by the fact that those who write about women and Islamic law have no attachment to Islam, and no experience living under Islamic values, so she doubted that their work can really reflect reality. I am not Acehnese and I have no experience living under either conflict or Islamic law. These two factors created perceptions among the local activists, that I lacked adequate knowledge to approach my research. Finally, my identity as an international student who is doing a PhD based on a scholarship provided by a Western country added to the perception of the Acehnese that my research was deliberately arranged or manipulated by my university, that is 'the West'. Two of my informants even bluntly asked me if my project was part of the agenda of the West to contradict Islamic law and universal women's rights.

However, I did hear some other informants enthusiastically express their interest and argue that there was a real need to conduct research on the issues I was addressing. One activist stated that by being a Muslim myself, my research outcome might be different from similar research conducted by others [foreign researchers]. Many women expressed their concern over media reports that they felt judged Islam as being an oppressive religion. As a Muslim, I can understand these views. Having lived in a Western country, I have encountered incidents and heard comments that tend to grossly generalize Islam as a religion that spreads only oppression, hatred and violence.

For my interview, I followed what Frankenberg (1993, 30) has identified as 'dialogical method'. I shared some information about my own life, particularly about juggling motherhood and studying. The fact that I was an Indonesian Muslim woman who has pursued a PhD in Australia with an Australian Government Scholarship also helped make them interested in me. The younger Acehnese women activists asked me the 'tricks' and 'tips' to win a scholarship, while the older Acehnese asked if their daughters or sons could also get a scholarship to study in Australia. I also discussed with some of my informants my position within the broader discussion of Islam, gender and the Western perspectives on these two issues. All these things finally made me feel like I had earned the respect of my respondents, and I could see that they started to believe that I am 'part of them', or at least not hostile to them. Kirsch (2005, 2164) reveals that it is important for researchers to be able to create a friendly relationship with their interviewees. She argues, 'the more successful [one is] at forming [a] close relationship with interviewees, the more likely they [are] to reveal personal thoughts or feelings'.

At the beginning, I intended that my research would deal with two local women's NGOs as case studies. However, when I returned to Aceh for the second time, from December 2007 to March 2008, I decided to only look at MISPI or Mitra Sejati Perempuan Indonesia (True Partner of Indonesian Women). I learned from activists within Aceh's civil society, both female and male, that MISPI has a leading role in activism within the context of the implementation of Islamic law. I had already met MISPI leaders and activists when I had visited their office, and had developed acquaintances with them. During my second visit I expanded my range of informants to include not just women and male activists, but also the Head of Provincial Government's Kantor Dinas Syari'at Islam or Office of Islamic Sharia, members of parliament, women judges, and other government officials. With people at MISPI I continued to develop a friendly working relationship, as I spent most of my time at their office. I sometimes shared lunch with them, a tradition that seemed to be common among them. This enabled me to observe conversations on various issues, from how they have to juggle work and domestic chores, how they see family structure in Islam, to dealing with participants at their workshops or seminars, and dealing with donors. During my two field-work visits, MISPI conducted various training on issues related to women and Islamic law. This was very helpful, as I could sit in on the events and try to make conversation with the participants. It also enabled me to observe the way NGO training programmes facilitate Acehnese women and men to have their say and conversation in a public forum.

Over a total of six months in Banda Aceh, I lived in three different places, which I later realized equipped me well to understand the everyday lives of the Acehnese in dealing with issue of Islamic law. During my first visit, I stayed at the house of Soraya Devi, the friend of a colleague in Jakarta. Soraya and I quickly became friends ourselves. She is a very open-minded and easy-going person. Born in Medan, Soraya spent most of her teenage years in West Sumatra, as her parents sent her to study at the Diniyah Putri[16] in Padang Panjang. When I arrived Soraya had just been elected as the new head of Women's Center or Pusat Studi Wanita (PSW)[17] at the IAIN or the State Institution of Islamic Studies, Ar-Raniry in Banda Aceh. This fact in some ways helped me develop my networks among women activists. Her house in Lampriek is only three kilometres away from the governor's offices and other official buildings.

During my second visit, I choose not to stay at Soraya's house, because I thought I should experience something different. This time I chose to live with Sukma,[18] an NGO worker from Jakarta who first came to Aceh a week after the tsunami, as a volunteer for Muhammadiyah, a modernist Muslim mass-based organization. She rented a small house with two other Acehnese students from Meulaboh and Aceh Selatan in Blang Krueng, a village close to the Darussalam area.[19] The house that Sukma lived in was a new house built by an international NGO to replace village houses swept away by the tsunami. This area is close to the Krueng Aceh River and was totally destroyed by the tsunami. Sukma told me that the owner of the house refused to live in the new house, because it could not accommodate their big family. Instead, the family leased their new house and rebuilt their old one. This is very common.[20] I was told that many of the owners choose to rent their new houses out not only because they are not happy with the new house, but also because they could make money by doing so. I even heard that some chose to stay in the temporary shelters built after the tsunami and rent their houses to generate income.

During the last month of my second visit I moved to the female student dormitory near the campus complex of IAIN Ar-Raniry. I lived with about 20 female students who studied both at IAIN Ar-Raniry and Syiah Kuala University. These students were mostly in their early twenties, originating from different areas in the province. Having constant interaction with them helped me better understand the feelings and perceptions of young people about what was happening in Aceh, including perceptions of the implementation of Islamic law. Most of these students had grown up under severe military conflict. While previous studies on Aceh indicate that due to the history of conflict, the Acehnese resent Jakarta, I found these young Acehnese were, in fact, obsessed with Jakarta, including its pop culture. They perceived Jakarta as a place where they could achieve their dreams and many times I heard how they dreamt of the opportunity to go there. I observed that these young Acehnese have social rituals whereby, after their morning prayer, they turn on their stereo sets, playing Indonesian or Western pop songs. Their fashion styles and clothing were similar to teenagers in other places in Indonesia who match their *jilbab* with skirts and t-shirts and even tight t-shirts and tight blue jeans. At the same time, these female students were also obsessed with reading Islamic popular fiction, which was booming at that time in Indonesia. They discussed the famous *Ayat-ayat Cinta*, or *Love Verses*, a novel written by an Islamist that promotes polygamous marriage.

Organization of the book

The book consists of seven chapters. The Introduction sets out the theoretical and conceptual framework of women's political participation though NGOs and women's movements.

Chapters 1 and 2 discuss the lived experiences of Muslim women in Muslim societies that experience Islamic revivalism, including in Indonesia and how they negotiate often patriarchal and restricting legal and social norms justified as derived from Islam, Islamic law or sharia. With a particular focus on Aceh, it shows how Islamic law was introduced and how it has been enforced in a way that discriminates against women. The introduction of sharia law made Islam a public discourse in Aceh, as the local elites seek a form of sharia that conforms with Acehnese *adat* and culture, and many women concerned to prevent this also resulted in a weakening of their position.

Chapter 3 sets out the historical context of the emergence and development of women's movements in Aceh: the military conflict, the Boxing Day tsunami and the introduction of Islamic law.

Chapters 4 and 5 look at the dynamics of women's movements and the work of women's organizations in challenging the interpretation of Islam and demanding government and religious authority to reform sharia law.

The concluding chapter discusses the dominant discourses of women's NGOs and women activists and the roles their work plays in influencing public policy-making, increasing public awareness of women's issues and framing Acehnese visions of Islamic feminism, women's political participation and sharia.

Notes

1 Salim (2006, 126) classified these PERDA into three categories, in terms of the issue that they try to address. The first relates to public morality and social problems such as prostitution, gambling, alcohol consumption. The second relates to the need to have religious skills and obligations, which include the ability to read the *Qur'an*, paying *zakat* or religious alms-giving. The third relates to religious symbolism in particular regulation of Muslim clothing. However, Bush (2008, 3) argues that of the three categories offered by Salim, only categories two and three embrace Islamic values, while the first is more about general moral issues familiar in the teachings of other religions.
2 A number of studies have been undertaken on this, including by Brenner (2005), Rinaldo (2006) and Blackburn (2008).
3 The *pesantren* is a traditional Islamic educational institution where students come to learn the *Qur'an*. The name '*pesantren*' is Javanese, but in other regions in Indonesia, people use different terms, but with similar meanings. In West Sumatra, for example, they are called *surau*, while in Aceh *Dayah*. For further accounts of the origin of *pesantren* see Dhofier (1990, 1999), Ricklefs (1993) and Azra *et al.* (2006).
4 The IAIN are the nationally based Islamic Higher Educational Institutions under the Ministry of Religion. In its early establishment, IAIN trained young Muslim men and women to teach in Islamic education in both public and private schools and to work at the Ministry of Religion. Currently there are about 14 IAIN scattered in provinces around Indonesia. The first IAIN was established in 1960 in Yogyakarta, followed by Jakarta. IAIN offer Islamic studies such as Islamic Law, Islamic Theology, Islamic History and Islamic Education. In recent developments, some IAIN, led by IAIN Syarif Hidayatullah in Jakarta, have transformed into State Islamic Universities (UIN), which offer not only Islamic knowledge but also other 'conventional' (non-Islamic) sciences. For more detail on the history of the establishment of IAIN see Mudzhar (2003) and Meuleman (2002).
5 Waylen (1996, 7–8) argued that the public and private split which underlies Western liberal democracy and liberal democratic theory has largely influenced the study of gender and politics.
6 The name of the province was changed from the Special Province of Aceh (Daerah Istimewa Aceh) to become Nanggroe Aceh Darussalam (NAD) Province following the enactment of the Special Autonomy Law for the Special Region of Aceh No. 18/2001. In 2006, the name was changed back to 'Aceh' by the Law on Governing Aceh (LOGA). Aceh consists of 15 districts.
7 McCulloch (2005, 2) observes that there are at least four main ethnic groups in the province of Nanggroe Aceh Darsussalam. They include the Acehnese, the Gayonese, the Alas and the Tamiang. There are also other smaller ethnic groups such as the Ulu Singkel, Kluet, Aneuk Jamee and the Simeulue. All these ethnic groups have their own language and distinct cultural traits. In the city of Banda Aceh,

it is hard to differentiate who belongs to certain ethnic groups. However, ethnic background can be influential in the public sphere. In another account, Hurgronje (1906, 178) elaborated the belief of many Acehnese that the population in the area were the descendants of three ethnic groups; the Arabs, the Persians and the Turks. During my fieldwork, I heard many Acehnese explain that ACEH itself stand for Arab, Chinese, Europe and Hindia (for India). To justify this belief they refer to the physical differences that can be seen in the population of Aceh: some have lighter skin like the Europeans and the Chinese, while others have dark skin and curly hair like some Arabs and people from South Asia. In this research I did not categorize the Acehnese women activists by their ethnic backgrounds because, as my observation reveals, the activists try not to use ethnic tags, as it can cause uneasiness.

8   The conference was organized jointly by the Asia Research Institute at the National University of Singapore and the Agency for Reconstruction and Rehabilitation of Aceh and Nias (BRR). The Indonesian president established the BRR in April 2005, following the Boxing Day tsunami on 26 December 2004. It has responsibility to oversee the reconstruction and rehabilitation of Aceh and Nias Island. At the end of the conference, which was officially closed by the Ministry of Research and Technology, a research centre was established. The Governor of Aceh, the BRR, the Syiah Kuala University and the IAIN Ar-Raniry will support the creation of the research centre (*Serambi Indonesia*, 28 February 2007).

9   When I returned at the end of 2007 the hotel's name had been changed to the Hermes Hotel.

10 In terms of Aceh's economy, Panggabean (2003) argued that the war in Aceh left the province with low economic production. Aceh contributed only 2.2 per cent in 2002 to Indonesia's GDP, which was less than it did in 1990, when contributions reached 3.6 per cent.

11 At the time of my research, the exchange rate for AUD$ 1 was around IDR 8,500.

12 I am aware of the continuing debate over the compatibility of Islam and democracy. One group believes that Islamic culture is inhospitable to democracy, while others see a compatibility between Islam and democracy. Among the latter group is, for example, Hefner (2000). His observation reveals the civil character of Islam. He argues, for example, that Islam in Indonesia has played a crucial role in promoting democracy, as can be seen from Indonesia's history and its socio-cultural politics. In particular, he refers to the Muslim mass-based organizations of Muhammadiyah, a modernist Muslim organization (established in 1912) and Nahdhlatul Ulama, a traditionalist organization (established in 1926), that have both been crucial in keeping Islam from being politicized.

13 I discuss attempts by some Acehnese women to change the regulations in Aceh in Chapter 4.

14 During my fieldwork I met three other female PhD students from Western countries. According to the *Qanun*, as non-Muslims they are not obliged to follow the Islamic law; however, some of them chose to cover their hair by wearing a scarf or simply draping a shawl over their shoulders. One of them told me she felt more comfortable wearing scarf, especially when she has to meet religious leaders.

15 See for example Morris (1985, 87), who discusses how teachers at Madrasah (Islamic school) established around Aceh in the mid-1930s obtained middle-level religious school and teacher training from Islamic educational institutions in West Sumatra. For similar accounts, see also Bowen (2003) on the role of West Sumatran Muslims in propagating the modernist Islamic teachings in the Gayo highlands, Central Aceh. In addition, Ricklefs (2001, 206) has shown that Muslims in West Sumatra had initiated the first major reform to Islam under the Padri Movement.

16 Diniyah Putri is the first modern Islamic education institution designed to accommodate women. It was established in 1923 by Rahmah El-Yunusiah. See Afrianty (2006).
17 Pusat Studi Wanita (PSW) was created during the 1980s. All public universities are required to have PSW. This institution was first established in 1989. In its early years, there were only 16 PSW across the country but, this increased to 101 in 2002, including 14 PSW at Islamic higher educational institutions under the Ministry of Religion. In the 1999 Broad Outlines of the State Policy or Garis-Garis Besar Haluan Negara, it was mentioned that the women's empowerment programme aims at promoting equality and gender justice, prosperity and protection to children in the family, nation and society. In the Profile of Women's Studies Center in Indonesia published in 2002 by the Ministry of Women's Empowerment, it was written that the institutions will serve as a catalyst to facilitate and initiate the process of socialization, and advocacy in developing and empowering women and children (Ministry of Women's Empowerment 2002).
18 Many Indonesians use only one name.
19 Other friends later told me that Blang Krueng used to be called 'daerah hitam' or black area, an area where GAM militias lived. The tsunami swept away most of the villages in the area.
20 The poor quality of the new houses built by NGOs, especially those built by BRR, has become a public joke among the Acehnese. They call their houses 'Rumah BRR', with 'BRR' said to mean 'Bangun Rumah Rusak' or 'building a damaged house' or 'building ruins'. This is because people found many of their windows frames or doorframes cannot be open or are damaged. Many said that if they can open the window they would not be able to close it or vice versa. Many Acehnese claim the best housing complex for tsunami victims was built by the Turkish government, in Lamphu'uk village, Lhok Nga, Aceh Besar.

References

Afrianty, Dina 2006, 'Transformasi Pendidikan Islam di Sumatera Barat', in Jajat Burhanudin and Dina Afrianty (eds), *Mencetak Muslim Modern: Peta Pendidikan Islam Indonesi*, Raja Grafindo Persada, Indonesia, pp. 23–44.

Afshar, Haleh 1996, *Women and Politics in the Third World*, Routledge, London.

Alvarez, Sonia E. 1990, *Engendering Democracy in Brazil, Women's Political Movements in Transition Politics*, Princeton University Press, Princeton.

Alvarez, Sonia E. 1999, 'Advocating Feminism: The Latin American Feminist NGO-Boom', *International Feminist Journal of Politics*, vol. 1, issue 2, pp. 181–209.

Aspinall, Edward 2009, *Islam and Nation: Separatist Rebellion in Aceh, Indonesia*, Stanford University Press, California.

Azra, A., Afrianty, Dina and Hefner, Robert 2007, 'Pesantren and Madrasa, Muslim Schools and National Ideals in Indonesia', in Robert Hefner and Muhammad Qasim Zaman (eds), *Schooling Islam, the Culture and Politics of Modern Muslim Education*, Princeton University Press, Princeton, pp. 172–198.

Barakat, Sultan and Wardell, G. 2002, 'Exploited by Whom? An Alternative Perspective on Humanitarian Assistance to Afghan Women', *Third World Quarterly*, vol. 23, issue 5, pp. 909–930.

Basu, Amrita 2010, *Women's Movements in Global Era: The Power of Local Feminism*, Westview Press, Boulder.

Beckwith, Karen 2000, 'Beyond Compare? Women's Movements in Comparative Perspective', *European Journal of Political Research*, vol. 37, pp. 431–468.

Blackburn, Susan 2004, *Women and the State in Modern Indonesia*, Cambridge University Press, Cambridge.

Blackburn, Susan 2008, 'Indonesian Women and Political Islam', *Journal of Southeast Asian Studies*, vol. 39, issue 1, pp. 83–105.

Bowen, John R. 1998, 'Qur'an, Justice, Gender: Internal Debates in Indonesian Islamic Jurisprudence', *History of Religions*, vol. 38, issue 1, pp. 52–78.

Bowen, John R 2003, *Islam, Law and Equality in Indonesia: Anthropology of Public Reasoning*, Cambridge University Press, United Kingdom.

Brenner, Suzanne 2005, 'Islam and Gender Politics in Late New Order Indonesia', in Andrew C. Wilford and Kenneth M. George (eds), *Spirited Politics: Religion and Public Life in Contemporary Southeast Asia*, Cornell University Southeast Asia Program, Ithaca, NY, pp. 93–118.

Bush, Robin 2008, 'Regional Sharia Regulations in Indonesia: Anomaly or Symtom?', in Greg Fealy and Sally White (eds), *Expressing Islam: Religious Life in Politics in Indonesia*, ISEAS, Singapore, pp. 174–191.

Bystydzienski, J.M. and Sekhon, J. (eds) 1999, *Democratization and Women's Grassroots Movements*, Indiana University Press, Bloomington.

Cooke, Miriam 2000, 'Multiple Critique: Islamic Feminist Rhetorical Strategies', *Nepantia: Views from South*, vol. 1, issue 1, pp. 91–110.

DeMars, E. William 2005, *NGOs and Transnational Networks: Wildcard in World Politics*, Pluto Press, England.

Dhofier, Zamakhsyari 1990, 'Traditional Islamic Education in the Malay Archipelago, its Contribution to the Integration of Malay World', *Indonesia and the Malay World*, vol. 19, no. 53, pp. 19–34.

Dhofier, Zamakhsyari 1999, *The Pesantren Tradition: The Role of Kyai in the Maintenance of Traditional Islam in Java*, Arizona State University, Arizona.

Edwards, M. and Hulme E. (eds) 1996, *Beyond the Magic Bullet: NGO Performance and Accountability in Post-Cold War World*, Kumarian Press, West Hartford.

Eldridge, Philip 1989, *NGOs in Indonesia: Popular Movement or Arm of Government?*, Center for Southeastern Asian Studies, Monash University, Clayton, Victoria, Australia.

Eldridge, Philip J. 1995, *Non-Government Organizations and Democratic Participation in Indonesia*, Oxford University Press, Kuala Lumpur.

Eldridge, Philip 2005, 'Non-Governmental Organizations and Democratic Transition in Indonesia', in Robert P. Weller (ed.), *Civil Life, Globalization and Political Change in Asia: Organizing Between Family and State*, Routledge, London and New York, pp. 148–167.

Feener, Michael 2007, *Muslim Legal Thought in Modern Indonesia*, Cambridge University Press, Cambridge.

Ferree, Myra Marx and Mueller, Carol 2004, 'Feminism and the Women's Movement: A Global Perspective', in David A. Snow, Sarah A. Soule and Hanspeter Kriesi (eds), *Blackwell Companion to Social Movements*, Blackwell Publishing, USA.

Frankenberg, Ruth 1993, *White Women, Race Matters: The Social Construction of Whiteness*, University of Minnesota Press, Minneapolis.

Furqon, Hafas 2008, 'Ekonomi Aceh and runtutan Inflasi', *Aceh Institute*, available at: http://web.acehinstitute.org/OPINI/EKONOMI/161.html (accessed 20 February 2008).

Hadiwinata, Bob S. 2002, *The Politics of NGOs in Indonesia: Developing Democracy and Managing a Movement*, RoutledgeCurzon, London and New York.

Hamami, Rena 2000, 'Palestinian NGOs since Oslo: From NGO Politics to Social Movements?', *Middle East Research and Information Project*, no. 214, pp. 16–19.

Harding, Sandra and Norberg, K. 2005, 'New Feminist Approaches to Social Science Methodologies: An Introduction', *Signs*, vol. 31, issue 3, pp. 2009–2015.

Hefner, Robert 2000, *Civil Islam: Muslims and Democratization in Indonesia*, Princeton University Press, Princeton.

Helms, Elissa 2003, 'The Nation-ing of Gender? Donor Policies, Islam and Women's NGOs in Post-War Bosnia-Herzegovina', *Anthropology of East Europe Review*, vol. 21, issue 2, available at: http://condor.depaul.edu/~rrotenbe/aeer/v21n2/Helms.pdf (accessed 20 January 2008).

Hurgronje, Snouck C. 1906, *The Acehnese*, trans. A.W.S. O'Sullivan, vol. I, E Leiden, E.J. Brill.

Jacquette, Jane S. 2001, 'Women and Democracy: Regional Difference and Contrasting Views', *Journal of Democracy*, vol. 12, no. 3, pp. 111–125.

Kandiyoti, Deniz 1995, 'Reflections on the Politics of Gender in Muslim Societies: From Nairobi to Beijing', in Mahnaz Afkhami (ed.), *Faith and Freedom: Women's Human Rights in the Muslim World*, Syracuse University Press, United Kingdom, pp. 19–32.

Kasim, Syurkani Ishak 2008, 'Menatap Ekonomi Aceh, antara harapan Investasi dan Inflasi Tinggi', *Aceh Institute*, available at: http://web.acehinstitute.org/OPINI/Ekonomi/37.html (accessed 20 February 2008).

Kirsch, Gesa E. 2005, 'Friendship, Friendliness and Feminist Fieldwork', *Signs: Journal of Women in Culture and Society*, vol. 30, no. 4, pp. 2163–2172.

Krook, Mona Lena 2012, 'Women, Gender, and Politics: An Introduction', in Mona Lena Krook and Sarah Childs (eds), *Women, Gender and Politics: A Reader*, Oxford University Press, New York.

McCulloch, Lesley 2005, 'Aceh: Then and Now', in Sophie Richmond (ed.), *Report: Minority Rights Group International*, Minority Rights Group International, pp. 1–40.

Mahmod, Saba 2005, *Politics of Piety: The Islamic Revival and the Feminist Subject*, Princeton University Press, Princeton.

Margolis, Diane R. 1993, 'Women's Movements around the World: Cross-Cultural Comparisons', *Gender and Society*, vol. 7, no. 3, pp. 379–393.

Martyn, Elizabeth 2005, *The Women's Movement in Post-Colonial Indonesia*, RoutledgeCurzon, London and New York.

Meuleman, Johan 2002, 'The Institute Agama Islam Negeri at the Crossroads: Some Notes on the Indonesian State of Islamic Studies', in Johan Meuleman (ed.), *Islam in the Era of Globalization; Muslim Attitudes towards Modernity and Identity*, RoutledgeCurzon, London, pp. 281–298.

Ministry of Women's Empowerment 2002, 'Profil Pusat Studi Wanita Se-Indonesia; Laki-laki dan Perempuan Memang Beda, Tetapi tidak Untuk Dibeda-bedakan', Jakarta, Indonesia.

Mir-Hosseini, Ziba 1998, 'Rethinking Gender: Discussion with Ulama in Iran', *Middle East Critique*, vol. 7, no. 13, pp. 45–59.

Mohanty, Talpade Chandra 1991, 'Under Western Eyes: Feminist Scholarship and Colonial Discourses', in Chandra Mohanty, Ann Russo and Lourdes Torres (eds), *Third World Women and the Politics of Feminism*, Indiana University Press, USA, pp. 51–80.

Morris, Eric 1985, 'Aceh: Social Revolution and the Islamic Vision', in Audrey R. Kahin (ed.), *Regional Dynamics of the Indonesian Revolution: Unity from Diversity*, University of Hawaii Press, Honolulu, pp. 83–110.

Mudzhar, Atho 2003, 'Sejarah Singkat IAIN', *DITPERTAIS Departemen Agama RI*, available at: www.ditpertais.net/ttgiain.asp (accessed 10 March 2010).

Panggabean, Martin P.H. 2003, 'War in Aceh, its Economic Impact', *Viewpoints*, Institute of South East Asian Studies, Singapore, May, available at: http://web.iseas.edu.sg/viewpoint/mpmay03.pdf (accessed 8 June 2007).

Ricklefs, M.C. 1993, *A History of Modern Indonesia since c.1300*, , Macmillan, Houndmills.

Ricklefs, M.C. 2001, *A History of Modern Indonesia since c.1200*, Palgrave, Basingstoke.

Rinaldo, Rachel 2002, 'Ironic Legacy: The New Order and Indonesian Women's Group', *Outskirts*, November/December, vol. 10, available at: www.chloe.uwa.edu.au/outskirts/archive/vol.10 (accessed 3 August 2009).

Rinaldo, Rachel 2006, 'Feminism in Uncertain Times: Islam, Democratization and Women Activists in Indonesia', *Globalization Conference*, University of Chicago.

Robinson, Kathryn 2007, 'Islamic Influences on Indonesian Feminism', in Tony Day (ed.), *Identifying with Freedom: Indonesia After Soeharto*, Berghahn Books, New York and Oxford, pp. 39–48.

Siapno, Jacqueline 2002, *Gender, Islam, Nationalism and the State in Aceh: The Paradox of Power, Co-optation and Resistance*, Routledge, London.

Siapno, Jacqueline 2007, 'Precarious Reconstruction(s), Contested Development(s): Decolonizing Gender Discourse (s) and Reading Competing Islamist Presentations and Re-presentations in Aceh', *First International Conference of Aceh and Indian Ocean Studies*, Banda Aceh, Indonesia, 24–27 February 2007, available at: www.ari.nus.edu.sg/docs%5CAceh-project%5Cfull-papers%5Caceh_fp_jacquelinesiapno.pdf.

Tempo interaktif 2005, 'Pangdam Aceh Minta Maaf karena Prajuritnya Cium gadis', 25 September, available at: http://tempo.co.id/hg/nasional/2005/09/25/brk,20050925-67069,id.html (accessed 20 January 2006).

Waylen, Georgina 1994, 'Women and Democratization: Conceptualizing Gender Relations in Transition Politics', *World Politics*, vol. 46, no. 3, pp. 327–354.

Waylen, Georgina 1996a, 'Analysing Women in the Politics of the Third World', in Haleh Afshar (ed.), *Women and Politics in the Third World*, Routledge, London, pp. 8–25.

Waylen, Georgina 1996b, *Gender in Third World Politics*, Lynne Rienner Publishers, Boulder.

Wolf, Diane L. 1996, *Feminist Dilemma in Fieldwork*, Westview Press, Boulder.

Zuckerman, Elaine and Greenberg, Marcia 2004, 'The Gender Dimensions of Post-conflict Reconstruction: An Analytical Framework for Policymakers', *Gender and Development*, vol. 12, issue 3, pp. 70–82.

1 Women's movements in Muslim societies

Introduction

Muslim societies are defined both as societies living under codified Islamic law, or in secular countries where Islam is used by the rulers and religious authority to justify their political interests (Gellner 1981; Fluer-Lobban 2004; Eickelman and Piscatori 1996). The common assumption is that women in Muslim societies continue to face obstacles in exercising their freedom and having their rights respected. The tendency is then to generalize that all Muslim women are subjects of oppression and experience discrimination. Muslim women from the Middle East, North Africa, Malaysia and Indonesia are perceived to be constantly struggling against systematic disadvantages, as they continue to be discriminated against by the law and social practices (Badran 1995; Fluer-Lobban 2004). Spatial segregation for women, children and forced marriage, women's limited mobility, female circumcision, the prohibition against women marrying men from different faiths and the practice of veiling are believed to be burdensome for Muslim women.

The Western view of Islam as an oppressive religion has been time and again challenged by not only feminists in the West but also Muslim women and male reformist Muslim scholars. Islam has been one of the religious traditions that are often the subject of the feminist agenda. Mahmood (2005) sees this also as the result of the contentious relationship between Muslim societies and the West, with Islamic movements in many Muslim societies continuing to challenge secular liberal politics. Afshar (2008) argues that the portrayal by non-Muslims of Muslim women is influenced by 'Orientalism', a term coined by Edward Said in the late 1970s. This has contributed to the creation of a constructed image, which perceives Muslim women as 'others' primarily because they live by the laws of the land and under the regulation of their kin and community (Afshar 2008, 413). These images of Muslim women, however, need to be seen in the context that women's lives are the result of the long and dynamic interaction that Muslim countries have historically had with the West (Afshar 2008, 413).

An-Na'im (2008a) suggests that in order to better understand the experience of Muslim women who live under social norms and legal regulations based on

Islam, one needs to understand that Islam is not immune to the interests of the state. Similarly, Kandiyoti (1995, 21) observes that the experiences of Muslim women need to be examined within women's lived contexts, including the political regimes, economic systems and diverse histories of the relationships between the state, society and imperial powers. It is imperative to consider the political and historical trajectories of Muslim society in assessing women's suffering, rather than looking only at 'religio-political' ones (Abu-Lughod 2002, 784). For example, encounters between Muslim societies and Western imperialism exacerbated the centrality of women in politics in Muslim societies (Kandiyoti 1995, 20–21). Another example is how state-led post-independence nation-building projects and development have further advanced the subordination of women in the post-colonial Muslim worlds (Kandiyoti 1995, 23–24). Shaheed (1994, 998) made a similar point that in this situation political actors [male] attempted to gain political pre-eminence by justifying their legal, social and administrative formulations of Islam, which have disadvantaged women's autonomy and self-actualization. In sum, gender construction in many Muslim worlds needs to be seen as the result of ideological contestation from colonialists, nationalism and socialism (Mojab 2001, 128).

This chapter locates this research within the broader literature on women's movements, the struggle of Muslim women in Muslim societies.

Women in Muslim societies

Women in the Middle East and North Africa might be ones that experience the most hardship, as discrimination against women has been institutionalized (Moghadam 2009, 10). In Saudi Arabia, women are banned from driving. In Egypt, women suffered from massive sexual harassment and the practice of genital mutilation and many women are trafficked, making Egypt the worst country to violate women's rights (BBC 2013). Other than that, the practice of forced child marriage is still very common in North African countries, such as in Yemen. Upon presenting the US State Department Award for International Women of Courage to seven female activists from various countries at the State Department on 11 March 2009, US Secretary of State Hillary Rodham Clinton praised the courage of a 12-year-old girl, Reem Al-Numery, who was forced by her family to marry her 30-year-old cousin, in challenging Yemeni legal authority (Clinton 2009). Despite her young age, Reem was considered fit to get married and to become a wife. When she filed for divorce, the court required her to provide consent from her father, because it considered her too immature to make such a decision on her own. Only with the consent of her father would the court approve her plea. Child marriage is seen as part of Yemeni culture and tradition. Economic difficulties often used to be reason for this practice, as parents no longer have responsibility for their daughters once they get married.

Likewise, in Sudan, a female journalist, Lubna Ahmed Hussein, was arrested while at a restaurant with 12 female colleagues on 3 July 2009 in

Khartoum. She was arrested for wearing 'indecent' clothing, because she wore trousers. Under Islamic law in Sudan, Lubna faced 40 lashes and a fine of 250 Sudanese pounds, which is about AUD$ 122, if the court found her guilty (*Sudanese Tribune* 2009).[1] In Malaysia, officers caught a mother, Kartika Sari Dewi Shukarnor (also a part-time model), drinking beer in a hotel lobby in December 2007 (*Bernama* 2009). She pleaded guilty in the Kuantan Syariah High Court on 11 July 2008. The court ordered that she receive six lashes and pay 5,000 Malaysian ringgit, about AUD$ 1,644.[2] On 9 February 2010, three Malaysian Muslim women were caned after being found guilty by the Kuala Lumpur Syariah High Court for having sexual relations outside marriage, or adultery (*The Malaysian Insider* 2010). In Indonesia, about a dozen Acehnese women have also been caned since 2005 for failing to uphold the newly-implemented Islamic law.[3] Another Indonesian woman, Lilis Lindawati, was falsely accused in Tangerang district in Banten province of being a prostitute, as she was caught out alone at night without being in the company of her immediate kin, and with a makeup compact and a lipstick in her bag (*The Jakarta Post* 2006).[4] The above incidents are the result of rigid application of Islamic law as it is purportedly divine (Bowen 1996, 12).

Of all these practices, veiling is often depicted as a symbol of women's oppression. Muslim feminists have argued, however, that to see veiling mainly as a form of oppression is simplistic and sometimes even totally misleading (Abu-Lughod 1993; Parker 2008; Mahmood 2005; Robinson 2009). These relegated understandings of Muslim women with veiling derive from a failure to understand that there are some practices found in Muslim societies that should be seen as a matter of women's choice (Afshar 2008, 413). Women choose to veil because they perceive it as their choice and a responsibility to their earlier commitment to being followers of Islam (Mernissi 1991; Mahmood 2001; Anwar 2001). Many Muslim women believe, for example, that certain parts of their bodies are *awra*[5] and should not be seen by men, except their husband and immediate kin, such as brothers and fathers.

Abu-Lughod (2002) denounced the portrayal that 'women of cover', or those who choose to wear chador, have no freedom.[6] She discussed how Bedouin women in Egypt voluntarily cover their faces with the 'black head cloth' when they are in front of older and respected men. Women perform this act because of their deep commitment to being 'moral' and to give 'a sense of honour' to their family. In a similar vein, Brenner (1996), Robinson (2009), Smith-Hefner (2007) and Ong (1990) emphasize the importance of not seeing the practice of veiling as a form of religious oppression. In her recent observations, Mahmood (2001, 214) reveals that Egyptian Muslim women who become part of the mosque movement perceive veiling as 'a critical marker' of their identity and part of the process of becoming a pious Muslim.[7]

Scholars, however, have acknowledged the continuing oppression and discrimination against women and the poor in Muslim societies. Muslim feminist scholars such as Mir-Hosseini (1996, 629) question, for example, why women who live under Islamic law are treated as second-class citizens, and have to live under men's domination, if justice and equality are believed to be intrinsic principles of Islam and sharia.[8] It is believed that inequality and dis-crimination against women in Muslim societies appear because Islam is used as the source of power of the male elites (Mernissi 1991). The fact is that men have the ability to manipulate the *Qur'an*, which is then used 'to legitimate men's egoistic, highly subjective and mediocre view of culture and society' (Mernissi 1991, ix). Gender inequality in Muslim societies appears because the version of Islamic law that is being applied is the product of the interpret-ations of male jurists who are the sole authority to interpret Islamic texts and their interpretation, in most cases, 'goes contrary to the very essence of divine will as revealed in the sacred texts of Islam' (Mir-Hosseini 2003, 20).

At the heart of the discussion on women in Muslim societies is sharia and ideas of Islamic law. In looking at Muslim women's experiences in Muslim societies, there is a need to assess if inequality and discrimination are in fact generated from sharia. It is therefore the objective of the next section to con-sider how sharia should be understood in the context of this discussion.

Sharia and Islamic law

Scholars working in the field of sharia and Islamic law have attempted to offer varied understandings of sharia and Islamic law (Schacht 1964; An-Na'im 2008a, 2008b; Tucker 2008; Salim 2006; Mir-Hosseini 2006; Bowen 1996). Schacht (1964, 1) argued that 'sharia' refers to Islam as a religion, because sharia is indeed 'the core and kernel of Islam'. Sharia is thus generally understood as 'religious law' because many believe that it includes religion, morality and law (Salim 2006, 21–22; An-Na'im 2008a, 3). Muslims believe that sharia offers 'totality' and is 'eternal' and 'derived from God's revelations in the form of *Qur'anic* verses and *Hadith* (the sayings of the Prophet)' (An-Na'im 2008a, 245; Salim 2006). Similarly, Mir-Hosseini (2006, 632) argues that sharia carries with it the 'totality of God's will as revealed to the prophet Muhammad'. Mir-Hosseini (2003, 21) therefore argues that sharia inherently calls for justice, freedom and equality.

Based on the understanding that sharia is divine law, Muslim women scholars and male reformists believe that sharia cannot limit women's free-dom or discriminate against women, as that would be contrary to divine will (Mernissi 1991; Ahmed 1999; Wadud 1999). To Muslim women scholars it is the methodological approaches that were used in the eighth and ninth centur-ies that have generated interpretations of that divine law that disadvantage women (Mernissi 1991; Ahmed 1999; Wadud 1999). Thus, the central argu-ment in this discourse is that the practice of interpretation requires a specific methodology to determine what interpretations are accepted as authoritative formulations of sharia. An-Na'im (2008a, 13), for example, argues that while the *Qur'an* and *Hadith* cannot be changed, there could always be 'consen-sus around new interpretative techniques or innovative interpretations of the *Qur'an* and *Sunna*'.

This interpretive process is known as *Fiqh*. Mir-Hosseini (2006, 632) defines *Fiqh* as the 'science of jurisprudence which is part of the human endeavour to discern and extract legal rules from the sacred sources of Islam that includes *Qur'an* and the *Sunna* or *Hadith* (the practice of the prophet)'. She argues that while sharia is 'sacred, universal and eternal', *Fiqh* is 'human and like any other system of jurisprudence, it may change over time'. Thus, she contends that if there is discrimination and oppression towards women, it is not the result of sharia, but derives from patriarchal interpretations of sharia which can and must be challenged or overruled. On the other hand, *Fiqh*, she argues, is 'nothing more than human understanding of the divine will that is sharia'. To her, it is:

> This transcendental ideal which condemns all relations of exploitation and domination that underpins Muslim women's quest and critique of patriarchal constructions of gender relations, which are to be found not only in the vast corpus of jurisprudential texts but also in the positive laws that are claimed to be rooted in the sacred texts.

Similarly Bowen (1996, 13) defines *Fiqh* as 'the very human interpretative art of fitting a narrow range of sharia to the world'. According to Bowen *Fiqh* practice is 'supposed to be socially and culturally variegated, taking into account custom as well as circumstance'. Thus, the making of religious law is, according to him, a cultural interpretation in which judges and lawmakers make choices for or against human rights, social tolerance or gender equality. Likewise, Hooker (2008, 1), in a discussion of sharia in Indonesia, argued that in the modern nation-state, Islamic law is the result of a process of state's selection, 'the practice of taking from the classical legal thought' performed by the state based on the political circumstances of the time and place of the state. Thus, Islamic law (in the sense of *Fiqh*) is not divine and, in fact, changes along with the social and political circumstances of the particular society.

Political struggles of women in Muslim societies

The previous discussion demonstrates the belief shared by Muslim women scholars and reform-minded Muslims that women's lived experiences in the Muslim societies are the result of the interpretation of Islamic texts, turned by rulers into legal doctrine. They also believe that the patriarchal nature of the society results in the patriarchal character of sharia. Patriarchy is 'the power men had accorded themselves, irrespective of class, to make rules and to impose their rules on women to keep them subordinate' (Badran 1995, 1). Reforming legal system is central in the struggle of Muslim women and male Muslim reformists to challenge traditional interpretations of Islamic texts and deconstructing norms and values in Muslim societies. Mernissi (1991, ix) suggests that one way of dismantling this order is by reconstructing the text through rereading the sources of Islamic law.

This understanding forms the basic character of Muslim women's political struggles. The limited opportunity women enjoy to participate in formal politics has prompted them to find alternative ways. Muslim women and some male Muslims seek to promote justice and equality in society within an Islamic framework. They believe that Islam guarantees equality between men and women (Mir-Hosseini 1996; Badran 2002; Ahmed 1999; Wadud 1999; Othman 2006; Anwar 2001; Muzzafar 2006).[9] In doing this, Muslim women and men go directly to the Islamic texts in their effort to find the egalitarian messages of Islam (Badran 2002, 4).[10] However, since it is the ruler of the state who defines and interprets Islam to be used both as an ideology of the state and as a religion of the people, women activists promote the need for the society to understand what constitutes sharia or Islamic law and that Islamic law is a product of the laws created by rulers to regulate the lives of Muslim societies. Women activists learn that although discrimination occurs under the institutionalization of Islamic law, they do not direct their criticism towards its sources, the *Qur'an* and *Hadith*.

Thus, Muslim women and Muslim reformers attempt to dismantle the product of these interpretations by calling for a rereading of the Islamic scriptures. They believe that gender inequality in Muslim societies derives from 'inner contradictions between ideals of the sharia and the social norms of Muslim cultures' (Mir-Hosseini 2003, 21). Thus, if there is discrimination and oppression towards women, it is not the result of sharia, but derives from patriarchal interpretations of sharia, which can, and must, be challenged or overruled (Mir-Hosseini 2006, 632). As believers in Islam, Muslim women are committed to find liberation, truth and justice from within their own faith. As one activist from Malaysia, Zainah Anwar (2001, 227), puts it, Muslim women like her are convinced that Islam allows and grants women the right to:

> Reclaim their religion, to redefine it, to participate in and contribute to an understanding of Islam, how it is codified and implemented – in ways that take into consideration the realities and experience of women's lives today.

This path of struggle by women in the Muslim world to address inequality and injustices is described as 'Islamic feminism'. 'Islamic feminism' can be defined as a feminist discourse and practice articulated within an 'Islamic paradigm' (Badran 2002, 1). Islamic feminism believes that the struggle for equality within Islam should be based on rereading and reinterpreting the *Qur'an* and *Hadith* in order to produce feminist interpretations of sharia. It seeks justice, equality and women's rights directly from the *Qur'an*, from the totality of their existence (Badran 2002, 1). Muslim feminists seek to find justice and equality by focusing on *Fiqh* knowledge. As Mernissi (1991, viii) argues:

> Muslim women can walk into the modern world with pride, for full participation in the political and social affairs without the drive of imported western values, but from within the true part of the Muslim tradition.

Islamic feminists have also acknowledged the fact that the Islamic law being implemented in Muslim societies tends to be misogynist, gender-biased and discriminatory against women because, according to Afshar (2008, 422), the interpretation has been dominated by conservative male *Ulama*.[11] The result is that hundreds of verses are narrowly interpreted to confine the role of women in the family and in Islam.[12] But in the late nineteenth century, women began to question the reading and interpretation of the *Qur'an* and, in particular, matters strongly related to women's interests and gender relations (Afshar 2008, 423). Those of this view believe that a reinterpretation of Islamic texts will reduce restrictions on women and create more equal gender relations in Muslim societies.[13] Yet, it is not easy for women and modernists alike to reread and reinterpret the *Qur'an* and *Hadith*, as attempts made by women are immediately seen as a threat to both formal and informal social authority, which is mostly comprised of men (Afshar 2008, 423). Muslim women believe that Islam teaches the moral and spiritual equality of men and women as expressed in *Qur'anic* verses.

Islamic feminism gained wider public attention in the 1990s following growing interest in the West in the lived experiences of women and Islam (Mojab 2001, 124). In Egypt, alternative voices among Muslim women in Egypt emerged at that time, articulating female subjectivity within what is called 'a native vernacular, Islamic discourse', apart from the dominant feminist voice affiliated with Western and secular tendencies (Ahmed 1992, 174). Looking more broadly in the Middle East, Badran (2005, 8) argued that Islamic feminism has appeared at a moment of late post-colonialism and a time of deep disaffection over the inability of the Middle East nation-states to deliver democracy and foster broad economic prosperity.

Islamic feminism has sparked debate among both Muslim scholars and Western feminists, for whom even the term 'Islamic feminism' is an oxymoron (Cooke 2000; Abu-Lughod 2002; Moghadam 2002). Not all Muslim women feminists agree that Islamic feminism is the only path that Muslims can choose in attempting to reform Islamic legal system or to advance women's rights in Muslim society. Tohidi (2003, 136), for example, observes that in Iran the right-wing conservative and the expatriate leftist secularists considered Islam and feminism mutually exclusive.[14] In her article, Tohidi also cites an observation made by Abou-Bakr regarding Islamic feminism. According to Abou-Bakr (cited in Tohidi 2003, 136), promoting Islamic feminism to achieve equality and justice means that other Muslims who do not engage with Islamic teachings are considered to be outside the circle of Islamic feminists. Despite the debates, Tohidi (2003, 143) still perceives Islamic feminism to be an alternative discourse within wider feminist discourse. For her, what matters is how the Islamic feminist movement is able to promote and contribute to the empowerment of women, tolerance and cultural pluralism.

Cooke (2000, 93–94) offers another view of Islamic feminism. She argues that women who choose to work within the framework of Islamic feminism prefer to work 'within the system', since they can engage in public debates and directly challenge those who claim to speak on behalf of women. Thus, Cooke tries to understand the binary of Islamic feminism by looking at it as women's double commitment: on one hand commitments to their faith, and, on the other, a commitment to women's rights in both the public and domestic sphere. As a result, she perceives Islamic feminism as a new and complex self-positioning that demonstrates women's multiple 'belongings'. Cooke (2000, 95) thus defines Islamic feminists as:

> Whenever Muslim women offer a critique of some aspects of Islamic history or hermeneutics and they do so with and/or on behalf of all Muslim women and their rights to enjoy with men full participation in a just community, I called them Islamic Feminists. This label is not rigid, rather it describes an attitude and intention to seek justice and citizenship for Muslim women.

By being Islamic feminists, Muslim women feel that they continue to belong to their religious community while also pursuing activism on behalf of, and with, other women. Similarly, in order for women to reclaim their rights and justice in Islam and under its laws, Muslim women must be actively engaged with the project of interpretation of texts and laws (Othman 2006, 339).

This section has demonstrated that the path taken by Muslim women activists in dealing with injustices and discrimination is typically framed within Islamic values, and the political struggle of many Muslim women activists can therefore be defined as an 'Islamic feminism'. The next section turns to consider in more detail the form of the struggles taken by Muslim women to promote gender equality and women's rights in Muslim societies.

Women's movements in Muslim societies

The awareness of Muslim women of inequality and limited access to justice compared to their male counterparts is the result of Muslim encounters with Western values through, for example, education. Muslim women activists and male Muslim reformists in the Middle East have become increasingly aware that much of the contemporary formulation of Islamic law based on the ninth-century compilation of Islamic jurisprudence was heavily influenced by the patriarchal thinking and views of that period (Badran 2002, 4). Similarly, Muslim women's awareness of their identity and rights is part of a historical process by which women and men continue to appropriate their identity within this process (Afkhami 1995, 3–4). It is difficult to ignore the influence of the feminist movement in the West on Muslims' awareness of their rights, as shown by the women's movement in Egypt in the early twentieth century (Badran 1991; Ahmed 1992). In other Muslim countries, women's movements seeking greater equality only materialized in the late nineteenth century (Badran 2003; Kandiyoti 1995).

Studies of women's movements indicate that women began to organize into movements as they became modernized (Ahmed 1992; Brenner 1995). Women's encounters with modernization indeed bring betterment for women's status. The number of literate women continues to increase as education becomes more accessible. Women are able to achieve higher education, which later enables them to engage in public affairs. Some women have even enjoyed political leverage in their communities. Women become active participants in social, economic and political fields, but they are at the same time challenged by the surviving patriarchal social structure. Some Muslim men see women's wider engagement in public affairs as a threat to their authority, both at home and in public (Ong 1990). As a result, they demand that women retreat from public space and return to their 'domestic' tasks. This phenomenon should be seen as a result of the Islamic resurgence and its challenge to modernity which then led to the emergence of feminist activism (Anwar 2001, 227).

To counter this move, Muslim women form themselves into women's groups. Muslim women associate within women's groups to challenge traditional authorities and their use of religion to justify women's subordination. In Iran, women began to organize into autonomous groups in 1905. In Turkey and Egypt women's movements emerged in 1908 and in 1920 respectively (Ahmed 1992; Paidar 1996). In Iran, women's movements began in the form of individual struggle before the establishment of women's groups. Since it began with individual struggle, the struggle did not seek power or attempt to democratize the patriarchal social and economic system. Rather, these individual struggles addressed women's resentment under the oppressive domination of men and demanded fairness in the way they were treated (Mojab 2001, 125). It was only later in their development that women's movements in Iran began to fight against the conservative practices of religion. However, at this time, they did not yet accept ideas of Western feminism, so their outlook and motivations were primarily based on Islam, making it an indigenous struggle (Mojab 2001, 126, 128).

In the 1970s, Iran experienced a growing Islamization of society and women responded by forming movements to struggle for gender equality and justice. These movements were 'Islamic', since they held Islam as the only authentic, indigenous road to gender equality and justice (Mojab 2001, 130). During this period, women's movements emerged as a response to growing conservatism, which provoked women's awareness of their rights within Islam. This awareness later manifested in various forms of women's activities developed together with the 'new religious thinking movement', which emerged in the late 1980s. The 'new religious thinking movement' in Iran was led by Abdolkarim Soroush, and attempted to address the use of sharia/Islam to justify the state's ideology that regulates the private lives of individuals (Mir-Hosseini 2006, 637).

Islamic feminist movements, such as that which emerged in Iran, have also appeared in other countries in the Middle East. Women's movements in the Muslim world, especially in the Middle East and North Africa, consist largely of women with professional backgrounds such as lawyers, writers, educators, civil servants and business women (Moghadam 2009, 12). At least seven forms of women's groups currently exist in the Middle East and North African countries. These include service or charitable organizations, official or state-affiliated women's organizations, professional associations, women's studies centres, women's rights, or feminist organizations, non-governmental organizations working on women's and development issues, and worker-based or grassroots women's groups (Moghadam 1998, 2003). These groups of women have played a highly vocal and visible role in pushing for family law reform. They prioritize their struggles to change laws on personal status so that women can have their rights and equality in the family. Their campaigns include criminalization of domestic violence (including honour crimes), equality of nationality rights and greater opportunities for political and economic participation. To advance their causes, women's organizations also initiate research, advocacy and lobbying directed at government institutions, religious leaders, the media and international organizations. In pursuing their goals, women activists pursue different platforms, incorporating ideas ranging from universal human rights, global women's rights, to Islamic feminist agendas. They appeal to their governments to align their domestic policies with international conventions, such as CEDAW[15] (the Convention on the Elimination of All Forms of Discrimination against Women) and the Beijing Platform for Action (Kandiyoti 1995).

In many other Middle East and North African countries, women's rights groups have been pushing for women's empowerment through legal reforms. They demand better employment opportunities and access to wider political participation. In Morocco, women's rights organizations build coalitions with progressive elements in government and society (Moghadam 2009, 13–14). They use Islamic sources to defend their case for a more contemporary interpretation of sharia, and expect that this can be used to frame new family laws and to justify women's inclusion in national development. Moroccan women's movements have the advantage of receiving sympathetic support from the government as the result of women's activists' ability to build linkages with researchers and policy-makers. This proves to be effective in pursuing legal reform and promoting progressive social change (Moghadam 2009, 14).

In Nigeria, human rights and women's rights activists employ multiple and intersecting discourses, including Islamic feminism, human rights, democracy and progressive religious discourse to advance their cause. These discourses complement each other and can help advance the agenda of women's rights, gender and social justice (Badran 2008, 174). Badan observes that Nigeria, which is a secular country, has a number of both Muslim and Christian women's organizations, and all these women's organizations employ a variety of different frameworks in approaching women's problems. Some Muslim women choose to work within an Islamic framework, while others employ multiple frameworks with reference to international norms or secular feminism. Though working in a different framework, these two kinds of women's organizations are increasingly converging on one common concern that touches on issues including women's rights, state and society. This can be seen following the famous *zina* (sexual activities outside marriage) cases in Nigeria. They involved two women, Safiyatu Husseini and Amina Lawal, who were sentenced to death by stoning for committing *zina* in 2002 (Badran 2008, 173). Their death sentences galvanized Nigerian women and human rights activists from different ideological backgrounds to seek gender justice (Badran 2008, 183). Women rights and human rights activists defended the rights of these two women and pursued public advocacy to make an appeal to the High Sharia court. Following these pressures, the High Sharia court finally set the two women free. This event was an important contribution to the 'ongoing project of Islamic Feminism' in Nigeria (Badran 2008, 174).

Muslim women's movements that operate within an Islamic framework have also begun to appear in Muslim countries in Asia such as in Indonesia and Malaysia. Like the struggle of Muslim women in the Middle East, in order for Muslim women in Southeast Asia to advocate reform and demand change of the laws, they need to engage in the project of interpretation of texts and laws. Muslim feminist scholars such as Norani Othman, for example, are adamant that Muslim women need to continuously engage with Islamic issues, challenge the male monopoly on the interpretation of Islamic texts, and maintain their struggle against patriarchal religious authority (Othman 2006, 340). Othman also highlights the need for women's activists to form coalitions and alliances to work with progressive and democratic Muslim intellectuals and scholars.

In the case of Malaysia,[16] 'women and the family have been defined and redefined in the concepts, policies, and practices circulated by the state and by resurgent Islam' (Ong 1990, 258). The *Ulama* and the government have also introduced a rigid interpretation of Islam and hindered open discussion of religion. Thus, the struggle for gender equality in Malaysia begins with challenging the conservative religious establishment, such as the *Ulama* (religious authorities) and the government (Othman 2006, 346–347). The biggest challenge for women activists in Malaysia is that they have to challenge conventional conservative understandings that the doors to *ijtihad* (independent and innovative legal reasoning) are closed, except for *Ulama* with a traditional religious education. On this view, other Muslims do not have the right to speak on or question any matter pertaining to Islam. This situation is exacerbated by the fact that only a very small number of Muslims in Malaysia are willing to critically engage in religious discussion.

Another depressing fact for women's activists in Malaysia is that many Malaysian Muslims lack the willingness to question the details of any bill enacted by government, many of which are said to be derived from Islam (Othman 2006, 346). This is because the state has systematically set a measure that questioning 'sharia-derived bills' will lead to accusations of being 'against Islam'. Martinez (2006, 261) has also made similar observations, claiming that middle-class Malay Muslims are 'unwilling' to address any issues affecting Muslim women for fear of being labelled 'less Islamic' or 'insulter of Islam'.

This public mood was then used by political leaders to gain political mileage from Islamic voters.

This situation has led women's movements in Malaysia to employ two strategies to fight for women's rights (Othman 2006, 347). The first is to fight against the patriarchal culture embedded within the society, which has become a source of bias or discrimination against women. The second is to fight against the use and adoption of Islam by the state to justify gender-biased or discriminatory and misogynist policy and regulation in society. While pursuing these two strategies, women activists in Malaysia seek the support of progressive Muslim scholars and intellectuals who have authority on religious knowledge, to reinterpret Islamic sources. Muslim women activists in Malaysia also seek to introduce gender discourse to politicians and members of religiously conservative groups and the Islamist political parties.

One women's organization that has played a significant role in promoting gender equality within the Islamic framework in Malaysia is Sisters in Islam. Sisters in Islam (SIS) is committed to advancing women's rights, as well as human rights in general, within an Islamic framework (Saeed 2004, 96–97). This organization was established in 1993 from what began as women's study group. Its leaders come from well-educated backgrounds and most have a law degree. SIS engages in public advocacy and provides education for women to help them understand their rights within Islam. The establishment of SIS arose from concerns over the injustices that women experienced under the implementation of Islamic law (Anwar 2001, 228). As indicated above, the founders of SIS were previously lawyers who became part of the sharia subcommittee of the association of women lawyers looking into problems with Islamic family law. According to Hefner (2001, 242–243) the establishment of SIS in Malaysia is:

> A result of dynamic development following the global politics which enhanced the legitimacy of increasingly high-profile Muslim feminist organizations who have worked to bring about reforms in the Islamic courts and other Islamic institutions so as to improve the legal options and overall living standards of Muslim women.

As demonstrated, Muslim women activists organize themselves into organizations and involve themselves in women's movements in attempts to advance women's status and to promote legal reforms and social transformation in society. It shows that in their struggle women strategize their movement by developing networks and coalitions with male religious authorities and the reform-minded Muslims, as seen in the case of Iran, Morocco and Nigeria. Women's movements have also demonstrated the ability to engage in their struggle for equality within Islamic frameworks, and within the broader discourse of democracy and human rights.

The next section discusses the emergence and development of women's organizations, women's NGOs and women's movements in twentieth-century

Indonesia. Although Indonesia is not an Islamic state, Islam has been an important element in shaping national politics. Thus, the discussions above are relevant to understanding Indonesia's women's movements.

Muslim women's movements and women's NGOs in Indonesia

Indonesia is not an Islamic state but a secular republic.[17] However, with almost 90 per cent of the population identifying themselves as Muslims, Islam continues to influence Indonesian politics.[18] As the major religion, Islam also plays its role in framing gender relations in Indonesian society. As with women in other Muslim countries, Indonesian women also need to deal with various issues such as seclusion from the public sphere, child forced marriage, the practice of polygamous marriage, the difficulty for women to divorce, inequality in inheritance, and the recent movement of forcing women into veiling and wearing proper Muslim dress.

Indonesia's Muslim women's movements emerged during the twentieth century and appeared alongside nationalist movements (Blackburn 2004; Martyn 2005; Soetjipto 2005; Robinson 2009; Suryochondro 2000).[19] At an individual level there are famous names like Raden Ajeng Kartini (1879–1904),[20] a daughter of an aristocratic family in Java who was later depicted as a symbol of the emergence of Indonesian feminism for her struggle to liberate Javanese women from traditional Javanese and Islamic patriarchal practices, which included polygamy, forced marriage and limited access for women to education (Sadli 2002, 84; Blackburn 2001; Robinson 2009). Other Indonesian females fought against colonialism in the early twentieth century, such as Acehnese heroines Tjut Nyak Dien and Cut Mutia. These, according to Martyn (2005, 30–31), symbolized 'women's strength' and 'active Indonesian womanhood'.

In the early twentieth century, individual women such as Dewi Sartika from West Java and Rahmah El-Yunusiah from West Sumatra struggled for women's equality through educational institutions. These two women founded schools for women in their areas. Inspired by the struggle of Kartini, Dewi Sartika built a school as her way to liberate women through education. In Padang Panjang, West Sumatra, Rahmah El-Yunusiah established the first Islamic school dedicated to women only (Afrianty 2006, 23–24). The establishment of this school was intended to 'modernize' women by embodying the spirit of Islam in education (Robinson 2009, 41). Rasuna Said, another woman from West Sumatra, contributed to women's empowerment in the realm of politics through her activism in journalism (Jahroni 2004, 602). Rasuna Said sought to advance women's status based on Islam and nationalism through her activism as the leader of PERMI or Persatuan Muslimin Indonesia (Indonesian Muslim Union), which was founded in 1930 (Blackburn 2008, 87).

Indonesian Muslim women's movements developed further through the establishment of various women's organizations (Soetjipto 2005, xxi–xxii; Robinson 2009; Blackburn 2004). 'Putri Merdiko' (Independent Women) in Batavia is considered to be the first women's organization struggling for women's emancipation (Suryochondro 2000, 227). It provided scholarships for indigenous women to go to school. Other organizations were also found in other areas throughout Indonesia such as 'Pawiyata Wanita' (1915) in Magelang, 'Wanita Hado' (1915) in Jepara, 'Wanita Soesila' (1918) in Pemalang, and 'Poetri Sejati' in Surabaya. On other islands of the archipelago, Soetjipto (2005) has noted that 'Keradjinan Amai Satia' in Minangkabau was also established in 1914. Kartowirjono (1977, 5) has suggested that women's organizations in that period were based either on the spirit of regionalism (*kedaerahan*) or of religion.

Indonesia's women's movements consolidated when women gathered at the First Women's Congress held on 22 December 1928 in Yogyakarta, which in modern Indonesia is celebrated as Mother's Day. The congress led to the creation of Indonesia's Women's Union or Perikatan Perhimpunan Indonesia (PPI). The congress was successful in outlining three requests, including a demand for the government to provide a *penghulu* (celebrant) to explain the meaning of conditional divorce following the marriage contract or *nikah*; a demand for an increase in the number of girls' schools; and a call for the government to provide support for widows and orphans of civil servants (Kartowirjono 1977, 6; Burhanuddin and Fathurrahman 2004, 42; Robinson 2009, 43). These demands were approved by the government during the Second Women's Congress in 1929, when the union also changed its name to Perserikatan Perhimpunan Istri Indonesia (PPII), or the Federation of Indonesian Wives Organization (Robinson 2009, 44; Blackburn 2004). One interesting development was that PPII declared itself part of Indonesia's national movements, and based its movements on the 'spirit of nationalism' (Kartowirjono 1977, 6; Blackburn 2004, 19; Suryochondro 2000, 228). In 1935, the PPII changed its name back to Kongres Perempuan Indonesia or Indonesian Women's Congress and in 1946, it became Kongres Wanita Indonesia or KOWANI (Suryochondro 2000, 228).

The establishment of PPII was followed by the creation of 'Isteri Sedar' in 1932, which consisted of women with different views from those at PPII (Burhanuddin and Fathurrahman 2004, 42). To 'Isteri Sedar' (Aware Women) the Women's Congress was too heavily focused on family issues, and not enough on social issues. 'Isteri Sedar' suggested that Indonesian women's movements should be directed towards more public issues and not just confined to family issues and religion. These two women's groups also held slightly different views on polygamy. Istri Sedar radically opposed polygamy, arguing that Islam inherently forbids a man to take another wife, while PPII acknowledged that Islam indeed allows polygamy, but that difficult requirements make it impossible for Muslim men to have a polygamous marriage (Burhanuddin and Fathurrahman 2004, 42; Martyn 2005, 42).[21]

Polygamy remains a contested issue among Indonesian Muslims. Although the majority of Indonesian Muslims believe that polygamy is allowed in Islam, they also understand that Islam places very strict requirements on this practice, which are difficult for Muslim men to fulfil, financially and emotionally. The majority of Indonesian Muslims, therefore, do not respect those who practice polygamy. Polygamy in Indonesia is generally regarded as 'morally reprehensible' (Butt 1999, 126). A recent example involved the famous Islamic preacher A.A. Gym, or Abdullah Gymnastiar, leader of the famous Daarut Tauhid pesantren in Bandung, West Java, who had long given a weekly sermon on national television. He reportedly took a second wife on November 2006. He publicly announced this, and argued that in doing so he was following the teaching of the *Qur'an*. The news immediately sparked national debate among Muslims. It reignited the tension between Islamists, who strongly believe that men can practice polygamy, and those who have the opposite view (Nurmila 2007, 107). Despite the theological debate, A.A. Gym had to accept that his decision to take a second wife damaged his reputation and popularity. His popularity fell drastically and the national television channel no longer broadcasts his sermons. His business is reportedly going bankrupt and many Muslim women no longer wish to listen to him.[22] This incident drew the attention of Muslim women activists. They have not only challenged the theological basis of polygamy but also argue that it has a negative impact, especially for the psychological development of children.

Throughout its history, Indonesia's Muslim women's movements have not only engaged in discourse on social and religious issues but have also played roles within the nationalist struggle for Indonesia to be independent. During the Dutch colonial period Indonesian Muslim women were heavily involved in the nationalist struggle, both through their affiliation with Islamic political parties, such as Sarekat Islam, or through women's movements (Blackburn 2008, 85). The establishment of women's wings within mass-based Muslim organizations make Islamic women's organizations an important element in the broader women's movements (Burhanuddin and Fathurrahman 2004, 11).

The modernist Muslim organization Muhammadiyah, for example, created Aisyiah in 1917 to emphasize the need for women's education. Muhammadiyah believes that women must be given better access to education in order to modernize the society (Jahroni 2005, 602). Aisyiyah shared the agenda of secular organizations of promoting secular education for women and encouraging women to participate more in public life (Robinson 2009, 41). Among the activities of Aisyiyah were establishing women's mosques, *Qur'anic* reading groups and publishing religious pamphlets and magazines. Following Muhammadiyah, another modernist Muslim organization, PERSIS (Persatuan Islam) established its women's wing, PERSISTRI, in December 1936, to equip women with religious guidance (Jamhari and Ropi 2003, 31). In 1946, the traditional Muslim mass-based organization NU (Nahdhlatul Ulama) established its women's wing organization, Muslimat NU. It provides women of NU backgrounds with skills and knowledge seen as important for women. These women's wings of the Muslim organizations are still very active and their establishment demonstrates how Islam as a religion has framed the character of Indonesia's women's movements (Vreede-de Stuers 1960, cited in

Chudzaifah 2007, 68). The establishment of Muslim women's organizations has led Indonesia's women's movements into both religious and non-religious camps (Blackburn 2004, 12).

The nature of the struggle of Indonesian women's movements is also shaped by the political development in post-independence Indonesia. Indonesia's women's movements were then framed, energized and constructed by two dominant paradigms: nationalism and development (Blackburn 2001, 12). The variety and diversity of strategies and platforms of women's organizations are the result of how women's movements have developed over the years and are reactions to the social, economic, religious and political constraints that surround it (Blackburn 2004, 12).

Under Suharto's authoritarian government from 1966 to 1998, the development of Indonesia's women's movements was subject to the state's gender ideology. Scholars observe that the New Order administration aimed to 'domesticate' Indonesian women through its gender policies (Tiwon 2000; Suryakusuma 1996; Robinson and Bessell 2002; Brenner 2005; Wierenga 2002; Blackburn 2004). Suryakusuma (1996) eloquently argues that the New Order's gender policy was centred on 'state-Ibuism', an official policy to return women to the roles of wife and mother. Through this ideology, the state forced women's organizations to adopt the definition of women as 'appendages and companions to their husbands, as protectors of the nation, as mothers and educators of their children, as housekeepers, and as members of Indonesian society' (Suryakusuma 1996, 101). Wierenga (2005, 2) notes that this gender policy was built upon women's social, political and sexual subordination.

The domestication of women under the New Order government was intended to secure 'family stability', because it believed that the family has to serve as a building block for social and political stability and national development (Brenner 2005, 95). The 1993–1998 GBHN or Garis Besar Haluan Negara (General Outlines of State Policy), for example, defined women's roles in development as to make efforts 'to materialise a healthy, prosperous and happy family ... within the framework of the development of the complete Indonesian human' (Tiwon 2000, 73). This policy led to the enactment of the Marriage Law 1/1974. The Marriage Law does not only allow polygamy within the limit set by Islamic orthodoxy, but it also entrenched women's position as 'dependent housewives' (Wierenga 2005, 2; Katjasungkana and Wierenga 2003, 65). The Marriage Law 1/1974 also discriminates against women because it obliges them to accept polygamy in cases where the Religious Court permits a man to take another wife (Blackburn 1999, cited in Nurmila 2007, 76).[23]

However, according to Suryochondro (2000, 232) the passing of the Marriage Law 1/1974 should, in fact, be seen as one of the major achievements of the women's movements in Indonesia. According to her, the new law was a response to women's constant pressure on the government over the issue of divorce, polygamy and child marriage.[24] Likewise, Soewondo (1977, 285) argued that Law 1/1974 was the result of the joint efforts made by women organizations to improve the position of women in marriage and divorce.

The majority women's organizations saw Law 1/1974 as a step forward to improve the status of women. Katz and Katz (1978, 309–314) observe that the Marriage Law was effective in decreasing the number of divorce cases and polygamous marriages. In addition, although the law has not totally stopped parents from arranging the marriages of their children, the number of child marriages has decreased (Katz and Katz 1978, 314).

Women's organizations under the New Order had a limited range of thinking on how to change society's views on gender (Blackburn 2004, 9). This is because autonomous women's organizations and women's representative bodies were dissolved immediately after the New Order took office, and turned into 'wives' organizations, installed at all government offices (Sen 1999).[25] Wives of civil servants were obliged to join Dharma Wanita to support their husband's work.[26] Dharma Wanita turned to be a state institution to promote New Order's model of womanhood as supporters of their husbands' careers and as procreators and educators of children (Budianta 2002, 36). At the village level, women were organized into PKK (Family Welfare Guidance), through which many of the government's family welfare measures were delivered.[27] This institution was committed to the 'five duties' assigned by the government to women, which included roles as wife and mother. As part of the machinery of the New Order, the PKK was successful in reaching out to women nationwide, from remote village areas to those in the urban cities. One of its more famous programmes was *Posyandu* (integrated health service centres) for women in the village. In the *Posyandu*, young mothers regularly bring their babies to be weighed and obtain nutritional meals, such as its famous green bean porridge.

Despite the New Order's extensive attempts to curb women's movements and to systematically domesticate Indonesian women, some women established women's organizations. The political setting surrounding the establishment of women's movements in the 1980s was the result of a massive industrialization and modernization project promoted by the New Order. As Brenner (2005) demonstrates, despite political subordination of women, the New Order was, in fact, relying on women to join its massive industrialization project, which necessarily gave women access to join the workforce. New Order policies indeed brought betterment to women, as education become increasingly accessible, literacy rates for females improved, the middle class expanded, and standards of living rose (Brenner 2005, 97). As a result, Indonesia witnessed an increasing number of women who managed to enter the white-collar, middle-class professional jobs as women moved into higher education (Sen 1999). With higher education, women become more aware of their rights.

The increased awareness of women's rights and gender issues, especially in public spaces, was not only the result of women's increased attainment of education but also the result of the New Order's dependence on global financial institutions that demanded that the government take into account gender issues in its development policies from the early 1980s (Sen 1999). As a result, Indonesia witnessed increased gender awareness among bureaucrats. In the early 1990s, for example, the New Order government required all public universities to establish Women's Studies Centres (Pusat Kajian Wanita). The University of Indonesia established its graduate programme on Women's Studies (Kajian Wanita) in 1992, and eight years later Hasanuddin University in South Sulawesi established a similar programme (Sadli 2002, 80–81). There were about 70 women's studies centres in 27 provinces in Indonesia in 1997 (Suryochondro 2000, 237). These centres received support from the Minister of Women's Role (Menteri Peranan Wanita), the Ministry of Education and Culture (Menteri Pendidikan dan Kebudayaan) and the Ministry of Home Affairs (Menteri Dalam Negeri) in their efforts to improve the status of women.

At the level of civil society, new women's non-government organizations (NGOs) began to emerge in the early 1980s, and continued to grow until the 1990s. They consisted of women who were not only wives and mothers but also working-class women, middle-class professional women, and democrats within government and semi-government institutions (Sen 1999). These women's groups that emerged under repressive authoritarian rule played a key role in bringing down Suharto in 1998.[28]

Women's entrance to the labour force, modernization and industrialization were the causes of the changing of social norms within family and social structure. While men and women's attitudes towards family and their society were changing, it was only women's changing lifestyles that were being scrutinized. Women were blamed for neglecting their roles at home as mothers, daughters and wives. They were accused of spending too much of their time pursuing their career outside their homes. Women's increasing demands for greater freedom, power and autonomy became sources of tension in society, especially among more conservative Muslim communities (Brenner 2005, 98). This development led to what Brenner called the emergence of a revivalist movement in the late 1980s. Similarly, Kandiyoti (1995, 23) argues that the call for a return to Islam is a result of failed promises of 'post-independence developmentalism', signified by the broader trends of Westernization, consumerism and changing gender relations in the family.

Indonesia women's movements began a new chapter as Islamic resurgence gained supporters during the 1990s. The Islamic resurgence that began in the early 1990s awakened Muslim women and reform-minded Muslims to the need to introduce women's rights in Islam, because of the Islamist claim that Islam requires women to dedicate their lives only to domestic roles, becoming obedient wives and dedicated mothers (Hasyim 2009).[29] Muslim conservatives felt that Western values have impinged on the life of Indonesian Muslims, eventually turning Muslims from reorienting their lives away from the upholding of Islamic moral standards, to upholding values coming from the West (Brenner 2005, 1998). Aside from returning women to the domestic sphere, women are also continuously reminded, and sometimes forced, to cover their hair and to wear appropriate Muslim clothing. Discourse on polygamy has also resurfaced, reminding Muslim women that allowing their husbands to take another wife is seen by conservatives as part of observing Islam.

Reformist Muslims, both male and female, have responded to these developments which then contributed to the emergence of a new feminist discourse (Doorn-Harder 2007; Feener 2007; Bowen 2007; Robinson 2009; Wierenga 2005, 5). They were prompted to become familiar with major concepts used by Muslim feminists in other parts of the world, such as 'patriarchy' and 'women's rights'. Indonesian Muslim feminist discourse is then built upon the idea of the reform of interpretation religious texts, in particular those that use gender-sensitive terms, such as patriarchy and equality. Activists look to international norms on women's rights, for example the Convention on the Elimination of all Forms of Discrimination against Women (CEDAW), and the Beijing Platform for Action. Muslim activists believe that the universal principles of women's rights do not contradict those entrenched in the basic principles of Islam. These developments are also a result of literature produced by feminist Muslim scholars such as Fatima Mernissi, Amina Wadud, and Asghar Ali Engineer, which have been circulated widely since being translated into the Indonesian language (Robinson 2007; Doorn-Harder 2007; Jamhari and Ropi 2003).

Muslim activists and scholars have also long expressed the need for a contextualized interpretation of Islamic texts to counter conservative moves among Indonesian Muslims (Marcoes-Natsir and Meuleman 1993; Bowen 2003; Feener 2007; Robinson 2007). They discussed this matter during a seminar organized by the Indonesian-Netherlands Cooperation in Islamic Studies (INIS) on *Wanita Islam Indonesia dalam Kajian Tekstual dan Kontekstual* (Indonesian Muslim Women in Textual and Contextual Analysis) in Jakarta from 2 to 5 December 1991. The Muslim men and women scholars and activists who participated in this forum were educated in a range of Islamic institutions from traditional *pesantren* to the State Institutes for Islamic Studies (IAIN). Women academics working at women's centres in 14 IAIN throughout Indonesia also participated, along with representatives from various Muslim organizations. The seminar discussed a range of issues, from the position of women in Islamic texts (*Qur'an*, *Hadith* and *Fiqh*) and in the Indonesian legal system, to the history and the development of Muslim women's organizations in Indonesia. At the end of the seminar, it was agreed that there was a need to reveal the egalitarian spirit of Islamic texts so that patriarchal tendencies might be eradicated (Marcoes-Natsir and Meuleman 1993, xii–xiii).

P3M, or Perhimpunan Pengembangan Pesantren dan Masyarakat,[30] or the Society for Pesantren and Community Development, an NGO based in Jakarta, was a pioneer of this new activism. Under the leadership of Masdar F. Mas'udi, it introduced the rereading of Islamic teachings and the reinterpreting of the sources of Islamic law, the *Qur'an* and *Hadith*. Mas'udi published a book on *Islam dan Hak-Hak Reproduksi Perempuan* (Islam and Women's Reproductive Rights) in 1997. This book is an attempt to reveal the rights of women in Islam, in particular, women's reproductive rights (Arimbi 2009, 68). The publication of the book inspired many Muslim women to begin discussion on women's reproductive rights, which was previously considered controversial.

With most of its activists being from a Nahdlatul Ulama (NU)[31] background, P3M designed its activities to transform the *pesantren* curriculum to enable students to gain better understanding of social and religious issues, including discussing the teaching of Islam concerning women (Doorn-Harder 2007, 33). In 1995, it initiated a programme called *fiqh an-nisa* (or *Fiqh* on women), later named FN-P3M (Marcoes-Natsir 2002, 194; Bruinessen and Wajidi 2006, 25). P3M's initiative to change the *pesantren*'s perspective on the role of women began by addressing texts used widely by the *pesantren* community that have been the source of negative opinions against women, including the *Kitab Uqud-al-luj-jayn fi bayan huquq al-zawjayn* (or *Kitab uqud*) written in 1874 by Ibn Umar al-Nawawi al-Jawi (Doorn-Harder 2007, 34).[32] This text deals with the rights and duties of married women and Muslim activists considered it gender-biased, as it focused heavily on issues concerning women's ritual purity; women's obligation to veil; and women's smaller share than men in inheritance, while ignoring matters such as women's rights to work, the social status of widows, and women's participation in education, politics and the economy (Bruinessen 1990b, 236; Bruinessen 1995, 182, cited in Doorn-Harder 2007, 35–36).

As part of its strategy, P3M included male Muslim scholars who have a strong knowledge of Islam and a *pesantren* background. This strategy was adopted because it was believed that it would be easier for P3M's new ideas to be accepted by traditional communities if male Muslim scholars introduced them (Hasyim 2009). In later developments, Islamic organizations and NGOs continue to promote equality by engaging male Muslim scholars (Robinson 2007, 41–42). They include Kyai Husein Muhammad,[33] Faqihuddin Abdul Kodir, Lutfi Fathullah and Marzuki Wahid, all of whom are strongly based in *pesantren* and are familiar with traditional Islam. From the academic milieu, Nasaruddin Umar, a professor of *Fiqh* Science of the State Islamic University Syarif Hidayatullah Jakarta and Director for Islamic Affairs in the Ministry of Religion, developed academic discourse on gender in Islam. He has published books on *Argumen Kesetaraan Jender: Perspektif Al-Qur'an* (Argument for Gender Equality: Qur'anic Perspective) and *Qur'an untuk Perempuan* (*Qur'an* for Women) (Robinson 2007, 42; Arimbi 2009, 68). They combined both Western-based and Islamic methodology in reading the Islamic texts to reveal a different interpretation, that is, one that protects the rights of women.

Following P3M, these Muslim activists also begin to critically read other classical religious texts taught at *pesantren*, known as *Kitab Kuning* or the 'yellow books'.[34] These texts contain *Fiqh* knowledge, mostly written in Arabic. The *Kitab Kuning* are the main reading materials for all *pesantren* students, which are strongly influenced by misogynist perspectives and patriarchal character, and hence are heavily gender-biased (Hasyim 2009).

In recent years, a number of similar feminist Muslim organizations began to emerge in Java, such as Rahima, Puan Amal Hayati, Fahmina, Rifka An-Nisa and Balqis, all of which are involved in trying to deconstruct gender discourse within the *pesantren* tradition. These organizations chose Arabic words for their names as part of the strategy to gain the acceptance of *pesantren* and other traditional communities. In 1997, a group of progressive men and women activists, mostly graduates of the State Institute for Islamic Studies (IAIN), formed a 'Forum Kajian Kitab Klasik Islam' (Forum for the Study of Classical Islamic Texts) (Doorn-Harder 2007, 37). With different educational backgrounds including sociology, anthropology, Islamic law, theology and gender specialists, activists at this forum sought to construct a less gender-biased and more balanced interpretation of classical Islamic texts (Marcoes-Natsir 2002, 194).

Musdah Mulia is a prominent Muslim woman feminist. A professor of *Fiqh* Science of the State Islamic University Syarif Hidayatullah Jakarta, she is also a member of the Indonesian Human Rights Commission or KOMNAS HAM. Other leading figures include Lies Marcoes Natsir, Sinta Nuriyah (the wife of former Indonesian President K.H. Abdurrahman Wahid), Ciciek Farha, Badriyah Fayumi and Ruhaini Dzuhayatun. All are well-known Muslim women feminists who have actively worked on deconstructing Islamic patriarchal thought. Most of them are also graduates of the State Institute of Islamic Studies (IAIN).

International women's networks

The earlier section demonstrated how women's movements and women activists in Muslim societies form their struggles to promote the status of women. Although women activists indicate that their struggles are based on Islam, women's movements in the Muslim societies cannot be separated from global feminist movements. This section discusses how the local struggles of women's movements are influenced by their encounters with international women's networks.

Women's rights issues have become part of the agenda of the international community, signified by the emergence of transnational movements for women's human rights during the 1980s and 1990s (Hesford and Kozol 2005). Women from different regions in the world gathered at the International Conference on Human Rights in Vienna, Austria, in 1993. There, they agreed that the human rights of women and girls are an absolute, essential and insep-arable part of universal human rights. Following this, several international declarations have been issued in which women from different parts of the world have condemned human rights violations, including ethnic cleansing, forced pregnancies, systematic sexual violation of women in armed conflict and domestic violence. This statement was strengthened during the Fourth International Women's Conference in Beijing in 1995, which, again, empha-sized that women's rights are human rights. International lobbying on 'women in development' has put pressure on governments to recognize the role of women in combating literacy, poverty and high birth rates.

Global feminist movements have not been without obstacles. Debate has already appeared, for example, over the idea of 'liberating' other women based on international standards, as if all women are perceived to have similar experiences and hence need only one uniform solution to inequalities and justice. This debate found resonance for example in 2003, when Barbara Bush, former First Lady of the United States, declared that US military intervention in Afghanistan was an attempt to 'liberate' Afghan women. The US media reported this by posting pictures of women taking off their *burqas* following the US military intervention in Afghanistan (Hesford and Kozol 2005, 3–13). The military intervention was thus hailed as a liberating force for Afghan women, on the premise that getting rid of the Taliban will free Afghan women from oppression. To this, Abu-Lughod (2002, 784) strongly denounces the use of Muslim women by the military or state to justify their acts. In the case of Afghan women, Abu-Lughod insists that women's oppression in Afghanistan has to be seen in the larger historical and political contexts of Afghanistan since the Cold War.

Debate over women's human rights has led to the debate regarding the universality of women's rights. Mayer (1995, 176) discussed two positions on women's human rights, the universalists and the cultural relativists.[35] The universalist believes that human rights is universal, so that all humans share the same rights. On this view, the universality of women's human rights means that the international community has the right to judge by reference to international standards such as CEDAW. On the other hand, the cultural revivalists argue that there are no legitimate cross-cultural standards for evaluating the treatment of rights issues. The proponents of cultural revivalism argue that 'Western condemnation of discrimination against women in particular regions reflects insensitivity, ethnocentricity and that it is produced by cultural imperialism' (Mayer 1995, 176).

With this in mind, women's human rights discourse within a transnational feminist framework has paid attention to the need to acknowledge the power differentials and inequalities that shape geopolitical alignments and the global movement of goods, people and capital (Hesford and Kozol 2005, 7). Ong and Peletz (1995, 1–2) also assert that attention needs to be given to the fact that women's issues cannot be separated from ideologies of religion, ethnicity, nationhood and the process of development, which all shape women's experience and identity. These have, accordingly, resulted in the diverse construction of women's lives and gender in all societies, including in Muslim societies.

Despite these debates within the global women's movement, Basu (1995) demonstrates that women's movements at the global level have affected the way local women activists formulate their political struggles. Kandiyoti (1995, 24) mentions that 'the framework for policy interventions affecting women and local women's movements has been set by both local measures and complex set of international influences'. Official feminist rhetoric has been dispensed to local movements through international bodies such as donors and international government agencies (Kandiyoti 1995, 25).

Women living under Islamic law created a transnational organization called Women Living under Muslim Laws (WLUML) in 1984. The creation of WLUML is a move to respond to events in which women, Islam and laws are involved. There are three basic understandings that underline the creation of WLUML (Shaheed 1994, 1995). First, Muslim women have similar experiences to women who live in non-Muslim societies, as both live in societies that have essentially patriarchal structures. Thus, Muslim women should not be seen as the only victims. Like non-Muslim women, Muslim women are also active social agents who are able to deal with both state and religion. Second, Muslim women are not homogeneous since women undergo different lived experiences. Third, the diversity of Muslim societies has created diverse feminist responses, ranging from the secular to the theological, to approaches that try to mix both. The creation and existence of WLUML is evidence of a serious attempt to form linkages which cut across diverse contexts, and that the alliance among Muslim women is not a singular path but ranges from secular feminism to Islamic feminism (Kandiyoti 1995, 26). WLUML has engaged in advocacy and lobbying work around questions of laws and their implementation, issuing alerts and circulating petitions on behalf of women suffering (Badran 2008). The women who initiated WLUML were secular feminists and human rights advocates who used international discourses and familiarized themselves with the various legal discourses (including religious jurisprudence) found in the societies where they operated.

Studies of transnational women's movements reveal that the intersection of local and transnational movements has allowed the transmission of knowledge and awareness of women's rights (Ferree 2006; Afkhami 1995). This has been facilitated by networks of various international institutions with local women's organizations and women's NGOs. Hopkins and Patel (2006, 426) analyse the challenges faced by international NGOs working on gender equality issues in Muslim contexts. These challenges include the need for international organizations to acknowledge that individuals in the Muslim communities have multiple, intersecting identities, some of which are owned and others which are perceived. Second, international institutions need to carefully understand aspects of religious fundamentalism, discrimination and stereotyping. This demonstrates that the struggle of local women's NGOs in Muslim societies is also related to international movements seeking to advance women's rights.

Conclusion

Muslim women activists see the inequality and repression they experience as a result of how Islam has been used by the rulers and religious elites, rather than something caused directly by the Islamic texts, the *Qur'an* and *Hadith*, themselves. This understanding leads Muslim women activists to approach gender inequality by looking at new interpretations of the Islamic religious texts. This strategy is known as 'Islamic feminism' and gained currency in the 1990s.

Through this framework, Muslim women activists do not see Islam as a stumbling block for women, but rather as a basis for women to assert equality with men and to be treated fairly. Women and male reformists in Muslim societies mobilize and refer to 'Islamic feminism' as they see it as the most realistic approach to fight against conservative religious authority, restrictive social attitudes and global pressures. As shown in this chapter, feminist Muslims who are part of women's movements use a range of different strategies, including collaborating with male religious authority, in their attempts to reform legal Islamic doctrines and social norms. They also incorporate their understanding of Islamic texts within a wider discourse on human rights and democracy. This chapter also showed that the emergence of Islamic feminism in Muslim societies is a response to three interrelated sets of domestic, national and global pressures.

The chapter provides a comparative analysis on the experience of women mobilizing into NGOs and creates movements in Muslim countries to challenge the move towards pushing back women from public life. The next chapter discusses the history behind the application of Islamic law in Aceh and that it is the result of both local and national politics in Indonesia. It discusses how Acehnese society in general has responded to it and debated about it. This will demonstrate that the application of legal Islamization has not gone uncriticized within Acehnese society.

Notes

1 It was reported that ten out of 13 women were found guilty and received ten lashes and paid a fine of 250 Sudanese pounds. Ms Hussein worked for the UN, which gives her impunity in Sudan, however she chose to challenge Islamic law in Sudan by appealing to the sharia court. See Copnall (2009) and BBC (2009).

2 The Malaysian National News Agency, *Bernama* (1 April 2010) reported that Kartika Sari Dewi Shukarnor was finally ordered by the Sultan of Pahang to do three weeks' community service at a welfare home in Kuantan, instead of undergoing the caning punishment.

3 See Chapter 2 for a discussion on the implementation of Islamic law and how it has negatively affected women. Acehnese women have been caned for being in violation of *Qanun* 14/2003 on Khalwat or illicit sexual relations outside marriage, and *Qanun* No. 13/2003 on Maisir or gambling. There has been no exact record of how many women have been caned. The first caning for women was on August 2005 in Biereuen district. Sumardoni (2009) noted that in 2005 four women were caned and, in 2006, three more were caned for violating Islamic law.

4 The Tangerang district enacted a Regional Regulations or PERDA No. 8/2005 on banning prostitution. However, the definition of prostitution was broad, and it includes all women's activities at night. For more detail on the effect of recent Islamization and the enactment of a series of PERDA in Indonesia see Bush (2008), Chandraningrum (2006) and Crouch (2009).

5 Ahmed (1992, 116) wrote that the word *awra* is 'one of those words with complicated layered meanings and range of possible referents'. According to her its meaning includes 'blind in one eye'; 'blemished defective'; 'the genital area'; 'generally parts of the body that are shameful and must be concealed'; 'women's bodies'; and 'women's voices'. Lorius (1996, 518) defines *awra* as 'shame', meaning men and women have to guard their private parts. In the dictionary of Indonesian Islam, Federspiel (1995, 25) defines *aurat* or *awra* as 'the body part of the human body that is to be covered when a person is outside the confines of the family'.

6 In her article 'Do Muslim Women Really Need Saving?', Abu-Lughod (2002) criticized former First Lady Laura Bush for using women with burqa as a starting point to justify the US military campaign in Afghanistan. The US military attack against the Taliban, Bush said, would 'liberate Afghan women'.

7 The women's mosque movement in Egypt, according to Mahmood (2001, 202), is part of the larger Islamic revival. Women of different socio-economic backgrounds learn Islamic scriptures and social practices in the mosque. The mosque movement, according to Mahmood, represents an unprecedented engagement of women with scholarly materials and theological reasoning that 'had been the purview of learned men'.

8 Muzzafar (2006, 214), for example, observes that 'the holy Qur'an abounds with reference to justice, emphasising a whole variety of human situations that include interpersonal relationships, relations within the family; the community, and in the interaction between communities and nations and between the human being and nature'.

9 The reference that the *Qur'an* indeed promotes gender equality is made in Surah Al-Hujurat (49:13), which says, 'Oh humankind. We have created you from a single pair of a male and female and made you into tribes and nations that you may know each other. The most honoured of you in the sight of God is the most righteous of you' (cited in Badran 2002, 5).

10 Badran (2002, 5) noted that in doing this women activists use feminist hermeneutics, which follow three approaches: first, attempts to revisit the text of the *Qur'an* to correct 'false stories' in common circulation, such as accounts of creation and of events in the Garden of Eden, that have shored up claims of male superiority; second, citing *ayat* or *Qur'anic* verse that unequivocally articulate the equality of women and men; and third, deconstructing *ayat* (*Qur'anic* verse) attentive to male and female difference that have been commonly interpreted in ways that justify male domination.

11 Moghissi (1999, 69) noted that 'Islamic Law is more patriarchal than the Qur'an' so that a reinterpretation will reshape Islamic law. See also Ahmed (1999) on this issue.

12 For further discussion on issues that have been contested between conservative and moderate Muslims, see for example Haddadb and Esposito (1998).

13 The initiative for the need to reread Islamic texts is driven by women's conviction that as believers of Islam, God demands his followers, regardless of their gender, to pursue knowledge to become learned followers of Islam, so that they would be able to read these texts by themselves (Afshar 2008, 123; Anwar 2001, 228). Similarly, Mir-Hosseini (2003, 26) argued that since *Fiqh* knowledge is still under the monopoly of male scholars, women must take part in the production of knowledge and begin to engage in the process.

14 See also Moghadam (2002, 1142) who discusses in detail the discontent of some Iranian women to Islamic feminism. According to her, those who oppose Islamic feminism argue that as long as Islamic Republic is still in place, Islamic feminism will only delegitimize secular trends and 'reinforce and legitimise the Islamic state's gender policy'.

15 Indonesia ratified CEDAW on 13 September 1984. The ratification of this international convention marked the beginning of the state's attempt to introduce women's rights and promote women's equality (Katjasungkana and Wierenga 2003, 66).

16 Malaysia is a constitutional democratic country and has Islam as its official religion. Almost 60 per cent of the Malaysian population profess Islam as their religion. Martinez (2006, 247), however, observes that there has been a growing political discourse among Malaysian conservative Muslims, in particular the All-Malaysia Islamic Party (PAS), to change the constitution and turn Malaysia to become an Islamic state. According to her, the discourse gained its momentum after Prime Minister Mahathir Muhammad declared Malaysia to already be an Islamic state, on 29 September 2001.

17 Morfit (1981, 840) argued that the Indonesian state is not secular in the Western sense due to the fact that the first principle of the state's ideology, 'Pancasila', states 'a belief in one supreme being'. However, Morfit noted that the notion of 'supreme being' encompasses all the official religions recognized by the state: Islam, Christianity (Catholic and Protestant), Hinduism, Buddhism and Confucianism.

18 For more accounts on the dynamic role of Islam in Indonesia, see Effendy (2003), Baswedan (2004) and Hefner (1993).

19 Jayawardena (1986) discussed that in the nineteenth and twentieth centuries, feminism and nationalism were linked during the independence movements. According to her, this is because women and men shared resistance to foreign domination and imperialism.

20 Kartini's day of birth is celebrated on 21 April every year. Kartini (1879–1904) was eventually forced into polygamous marriage and died after childbirth at the age of 25. Kartini herself was born into a polygamous family, and her mother was the unofficial wife of her husband (Cote 2008, 5). A collection of Kartini's letters can be read in Monash Papers on Southeast Asia (2005); see also Tiwon (1996). Kartini's calls for women's liberation were expressed through her letters to her Dutch friends in the Netherlands from 1899 to 1904 (Cote 2008, 4). As a daughter of an aristocrat Javanese, Kartini's awareness of equality was developed as a result of her exposure to Dutch feminist literature that was provided to her by the wife of the local Dutch official (Cote 2008, 5).

21 See also Blackburn (2004, 19), Soewondo (1977, 285) and Suryochondro (2000, 232).

22 For more on the development of polygamy in Indonesia, see Brenner (2007), Blackburn (1999, 2004), and Nurmila (2007).

23 In terms of divorce and polygamy, Law 1/1974 requires the husband to go to the religious court if he wants a divorce. A man is also required to get the permission from a court if he wants to take more than one wife (Katz and Katz 1978, 310–311). Before Law 1/1974 was enacted, a Muslim man was able to take another wife by merely reporting the new marriage to a registrar, and a Muslim man could divorce his wife simply by saying that he is divorcing his wife three times (Katz and Katz 1978, 311). See also Soewondo (1977), Nurmila (2007) and Blackburn (2004).

24 For further discussion on the political situation prior to the passing of the Marriage Law 1/1974, see Hefner (1997, 87) in which he describes the debate among Muslims who support and oppose the law. Hefner argues that the enactment of the new law can be seen as a strategic concession to Muslim communities by the Indonesian government. In addition, Blackburn (2004, 114) explains that those who opposed the law argued that the state must leave matters of polygamy and marriage to the religious or *adat* officials, while others demand state intervention. See also Butt (1999) and Cammack (1989).

25 Saptari and Utrecht (1997, 322) observe how the Indonesian government controlled NGOs activities by enacting a series of regulations. In 1985, the government enacted the Law on Social Organization and in 1990 a ministerial instruction was issued. Both were aimed at controlling and limiting the activities of NGOs by requiring all NGOs to adopt Pancasila as their sole ideological basis.
26 For a more detail account of Dharma Wanita, see Suryakusuma (1996).
27 For more on PKK see for example Marcoes-Natsir (2002).
28 Suara Ibu Peduli (SIP, The Voice of Concerned Mothers) was a women's NGO that played a leading role during the 'reformasi' crisis. It went to the streets before any other civil society organization to voice its concern over the increasing difficult economic situation during the 1997 monetary crisis. Budianta (2002, 36) observes that SIP was the first to initiate street demonstrations to draw public attention to the worsening economy and its impact on women and children.
29 Syafiq Hasyim, a male Muslim feminist, made this comment in an online discussion organized by the Solution Exchange in Banda Aceh. This programme is run by UNFPA as part of its programme to promote women's rights in Islam.
30 P3M was established in 1983 and has been very active in promoting community development programmes through its *pesantren* networks.
31 Nahdlatul Ulama is a traditional mass-based Muslim organization, established in 1926. NU is claimed to be the largest Muslim mass-based organization in Indonesia with over 40 million followers. For more detail on NU see Bush (2009) and Nakamura (1981).
32 Bruinessen (1990, 236) observes that Ibn Umar al-Nawawi al-Jawi was an Indonesian Muslim from Banten. He wrote 22 titles on every aspect of Islamic learning, and his works are mostly commentaries on well-known texts.
33 Kyai Husein is currently one of the more prominent Muslim figures who actively campaigns for issues of justice and women's equality. He serves as the Commissioner on the Indonesian National Commission on Women (KOMNAS Perempuan) and is Deputy Director of Fahmina, an Islamic NGO in Cirebon, West Java.
34 Federspiel (1995, 133) wrote that *Kitab Kuning* are the work of Muslim writers from the middle period. The works cover the subject of jurisprudence (*Fiqh*), nature of God (*Tauhid*), traditions of the prophet (*Hadith*), mystical practice (*tasawuf*) and the Arab language. The *Kitab Kuning* are studied by students at Pesantren and have become standard sources for *pesantren* graduates. Bruinessen (1990b, 227) noted that these texts are called 'kuning' or yellow, because of the tinted paper of books brought from the Middle East in the early twentieth century.
35 See also Kandiyoti (1995, 19–21).

References

Abu-Lughod, Lila 1993, *Writing Women's World: Bedouin Stories*, University of California Press, Berkeley.
Abu-Lughod, Lila 2002, 'Do Muslim Women Really Need Saving? Anthropological Reflections on Cultural Relativism and its Others', *American Anthropologist*, vol. 104, issue 3, pp. 783–790.
Afkhami, Mahnaz 1995, 'Introduction', in Mahnaz Afkhami (ed.), *Faith and Freedom: Women's Human Rights in the Muslim World*, Syracuse University Press, United Kingdom, pp. 1–15.
Afrianty, Dina 2006, 'Transformasi Pendidikan Islam di Sumatera Barat', in Jajat Burhanudin and Dina Afrianty (eds), *Mencetak Muslim Modern: Peta Pendidikan Islam Indonesi*, Raja Grafindo Persada, Indonesia, pp. 23–44.

Afshar, Haleh 2008, 'Can I See Your Hair? Choice, Agency and Attitudes: The Dilemma of Faith and Feminism for Muslim Women Who Cover', *Ethnic and Radical Studies*, vol. 31, no. 2, pp. 411–427.

Ahmed, Leila 1992, *Women and Gender in Islam: Historical Roots of a Modern Debate*, Yale University Press, New Haven.

Ahmed, Leila 1999, *The New Voices of Islam: Rethinking Politics and Modernity*, edited by Mehran Kamrava, University of California Press, Los Angeles.

An-Na'im, Abdullahi 2008a, *Islam and the Secular State: Negotiating the Future of Sharia*, Harvard University Press, Cambridge, MA.

An-Na'im, Abdullahi 2008b, 'Sharia in the Secular State: A Paradox of Separation and Conflation', in Peri Bearman, Wolfhart Heinrichs and Bernard G. Weiss (eds), *The Law Applied: Contextualizing the Islamic Sharia*, I.B. Tauris, London and New York, pp. 321–341.

Anwar, Zainah 2001, 'What Islam, Whose Islam? Sisters in Islam and the Struggle for Women's Rights', in Robert W. Hefner (ed.), *The Politics of Multiculturalism: Pluralism and Citizenship in Malaysia*, University of Hawai'i Press, USA, p. 227.

Arimbi, Diah A. 2009, *Reading Contemporary Indonesian Muslim Women Writers*, Amsterdam University Press, Amsterdam.

Badran, Margot 1995, *Feminist, Islam and Nation*, Princeton University Press, Princeton.

Badran, Margot 2001, 'Understanding Islam, Islamism, and Islamic Feminism', *Journal of Women History*, vol. 13, issue 1, pp. 47–52.

Badran, Margot 2002, 'Islamic Feminism: What's in a Name?', *Al-Ahram Weekly Online*, 17–23 January, issue 569.

Badran, Margot 2005, 'Between Secular and Islamic Feminism/s: Reflections on the Middle East and Beyond', *Journal of Middle East Women's Studies*, vol. 1, issue 1, pp. 6–28.

Badran, Margot 2008, 'Shari'ah Activism in Nigeria under Hudud', in Carolyn M. Elliot (ed.), *Global Empowerment of Women: Responses to Globalization and Politicized Religions*, Routledge, New York and London, pp. 173–190.

Basu, Amrita 1995, 'Introduction', in Amrita Basu and Elizabeth McGregory (eds), *The Challenge of Local Feminisms: Women's Movements in Global Perspective*, Westview Press, Colorado, pp. 1–21.

Baswedan, Anis 2004, 'Political Islam in Indonesia: Present and Future Trajectory', *Asian Survey*, vol. 44, no. 5, pp. 669–690.

BBC 2013, 'Egypt Worst for Women out of 22 Countries in Arab World', BBC News Middle East, 12 November, available at: www.bbc.co.uk/news/world-middle-east-24908109 (accessed 4 February 2014).

BBC News 2009, 'Protests Sudan Woman's Trial', 4 August, available at: http://news.bbc.co.uk/2/hi/8182658.stm (accessed 4 December 2009).

Bernama 2009, 'Model Wants Court to Expedite Whipping Sentence', 22 July, available at: www.bernama.com/bernama/v5/newsindex.php?id=427228 (accessed 10 August 2009).

Bernama 2010, 'Kartika's Caning Sentence Commuted to Community Service', 1 April, available at: www.bernama.com/bernama/v5/newsindex.php?id=487205 (accessed 5 April 2010).

Blackburn, Susan 1999, 'Women and Citizenship in Indonesia', *Australian Journal of Political Science*, vol. 34, issue 2, pp. 189–202.

Blackburn, Susan 2001, 'Women and the Nation', *Inside Indonesia*, April–June.

Blackburn, Susan 2004, *Women and the State in Modern Indonesia*, Cambridge University Press, Cambridge.

Blackburn, Susan 2008, 'Indonesian Women and Political Islam', *Journal of Southeast Asian Studies*, vol. 39, issue 1, pp. 83–105.

Blackburn, Susan and Sharon, B. 1997, 'Marriageable Age: Political Debates on Early Marriage in Twentieth-Century Indonesia', *Indonesia*, Southeast Asia Program Publication, Cornell University, vol. 63, April, pp. 107–141.

Bowen, John R. 1996, 'Religion in the Proper Sense of the Word: Law and Civil Society in Islamicist Discourse', *Anthopology Today*, August, pp. 12–14.

Bowen, John R. 2003, *Islam, Law and Equality in Indonesia: Anthropology of Public Reasoning*, Cambridge University Press, Cambridge.

Bowen, John R. 2007, 'Democracy, Polygamy, and Women in Post-Reformasi Indonesia', in Tony Day (ed.), *Identifying with Freedom: Indonesia After Soeharto*, Berghahn Books, New York and Oxford, pp. 28–38.

Brenner, Suzanne 1996, 'Reconstructing Self and Society: Javanese Muslim Women and the Veil', *American Ethnologist*, vol. 23, issue 4, pp. 673–697.

Brenner, Suzanne 2005, 'Islam and Gender Politics in Late New Order Indonesia', in Andrew C. Wilford and Kenneth M. George (eds), *Spirited Politics: Religion and Public Life in Contemporary Southeast Asia*, Cornell University Southeast Asia Program, Ithaca, NY, pp. 93–118.

Brenner, Suzanne 2007, 'Democracy, Polygamy, and Women in Post-Reformasi Indonesia', in Tony Day (ed.), *Identifying with Freedom: Indonesia After Soeharto*, Berghahn Books, New York and Oxford, pp. 28–38.

Bruinessen, Martin v. 1990a, 'Indonesia's Ulama and Politics: Caught between Legitimising the Status Quo and Searching for Alternatives', *Prisma: The Indonesian Indicator*, no. 49, pp. 52–69.

Bruinessen, Martin v. 1990b, 'Kitab Kuning: Books in Arabic Script Used in the Pesantren Milieu', *Bijdragen tot de Taal Land en Volkenkunde*, no. 2/3, pp. 226–269.

Bruinessen, Martin v. and Wajidi, Farid 2006, 'Syu'un Ijtima'iyah and the Kyai Rakyat: Traditionalist Islam, Civil Society and Social Concerns', Igitur Archief, Utrecht Publishing and Archiving Service, available at: www.temoa.info/node/325519 (accessed 30 November 2014).

Budianta, Melani 2002, 'Plural Identities: Indonesian Women's Redefinition of Democracy in the Post-Reformasi Era', *Review of Indonesian and Malaysian Affairs*, vol. 36, issue 1, pp. 35–50.

Burhanuddin, Jajat and Fathurrahman, Oman. 2004, *Tentang Perempuan Islam: Wacana dan Gerakan*, Gramedia Pustaka Utama, Jakarta.

Bush, Robin 2008, 'Regional Sharia Regulations in Indonesia: Anomaly or Symptom?', in Greg Fealy and Sally White (eds), *Expressing Islam: Religious Life in Politics in Indonesia*, ISEAS, Singapore, pp. 174–191.

Bush, Robin 2009, *Nahdlatul Ulama and the Struggle for Power within Islam and Politics in Indonesia*, Institute of Southeast Asian Studies, Singapore.

Butt, Simon 1999, 'Polygamy and Mixed Marriage in Indonesia: The Application of the Marriage Law in the Courts', in Timothy Lindsey (ed.), *Indonesia: Law and Society*, Federation Press, Sydney, pp. 122–143.

Cammack, Mark 1989, 'Islamic Law in Indonesia's New Order', *International and Comparative Law Quarterly*, vol. 38, no. 1, pp. 53–73.

Chandraningrum, Dewi 2006, 'Perda Sharia and the Indonesian Women's Critical Perspectives', *Conference on New Arbitrary against Women in Indonesia: Perda Sharia and Women's Rights*, 11 November 2006, SOAI, Germany, available at: www.asienhaus.de/public/archiv/PaperPERDASHARIA.pdf (accessed 10 June 2007).

Chudzaifah, Yuniyanti 2007, 'Political-Social Movement: Feminist: Indonesia', *Encyclopaedia of Women and Islamic Cultures*, vol. VI, Brill, Netherlands, pp. 67–70.

Clinton, Hillary R. 2009, '2009 International Women of Courage Award', 11 March, Washington, DC, available at: www.state.gov/secretary/rm/2009a/03/120285.htm (accessed 7 August 2009).

Cooke, Miriam 2000, 'Multiple Critique: Islamic Feminist Rhetorical Strategies', *Nepantia: Views from South*, vol. 1, issue 1, pp. 91–110.

Copnall, James 2009, 'Lubna Hussein, "I'm not afraid of being flogged. It doesn't hurt. But it is insulting"', *Guardian*, 2 August, available at: www.guardian.co.uk/world/2009/aug/02/sudan-women-dress-code (accessed 2 January 2010).

Cote, Joost 2008, *Realizing the Dream of R.A. Kartini, Her Sister's Letters from Colonial Java*, Ohio University Press, Athens.

Crouch, Melissa 2009, 'Religious Regulations in Indonesia: Failing Vulnerable Groups', *Review of Indonesia and Malaysian Affairs*, vol. 43, no. 2, pp. 53–103.

Doorn-Harder, Nelly van 2007, 'Reconsidering Authority: Indonesian Fiqh Texts about Women', in Michael Feener and Mark E. Cammack (eds), *Islamic Law in Contemporary Indonesia*, Islamic Legal Studies Program, Harvard Law School, Cambridge, MA, pp. 27–43.

Effendy, Bahtiar 2003, *Islam and the State in Indonesia*, Institute of Southeast Asian Studies, Singapore.

Eickelman, Dale F. and Piscatori, J. 1996, *Muslim Politics*, Princeton University Press, Princeton.

Federspiel, Howard 1995, *A Dictionary of Indonesian Islam*, Ohio University, Athens.

Feener, Michael 2007, *Muslim Legal Thought in Modern Indonesia*, Cambridge University Press, Cambridge.

Ferree, Myra Marx 2006, 'Globalisation and Feminism: Opportunities and Obstacles for Activism in Glocal Arena', in Myra Marx Ferree and Aili Mari Tripp (eds), *Global Feminism: Transnational Women's Activism, Organizing and Human Rights*, New York University Press, New York and London, pp. 3–23.

Fluer-Lobban, Carolyn 2004, *Islamic Societies in Practice*, Florida University Press, Florida.

Gellner, Ernest 1981, *Muslim Society*, Cambridge University Press, Cambridge.

Haddadb, Yvonne Y. and Esposito, John L. 1998, *Islam, Gender and Social Change*, Oxford University Press, New York and Oxford.

Hasyim, Syafiq 2009, 'Encouraging Men's Participation in Promoting Gender Equality and Women's Rights-Experiences, Advice', *Solution Exchange for the Gender Community*, 25 June.

Hefner, Robert W. 1993, 'Islam, State and Civil Society: ICMI and the Struggle for the Indonesian Middle Class', *Indonesia*, October, vol. 56, pp. 1–35.

Hefner, Robert W. 1997, 'Islamization and Democratization in Indonesia', in Robert W. Hefner and Patricia Horvatich (eds), *Islam in an Era of Nation-States: Politics and Religious Renewal in Muslim Southeast Asia*, University of Hawai'i Press, Hawaii, pp. 75–128.

Hefner, Robert W. (ed.) 2001, *The Politics of Multiculturalism: Pluralism and Citizenship in Malaysia, Singapore and Indonesia*, University of Hawaii Press, Honolulu.

Hesford, Wendy W. and Kozol, Wendy 2005, *Just Advocacy? Women's Human Rights, Transnational Feminisms and the Politics of Representation*, Rutgers University Press, New Brunswick, New Jersey and London.

Hooker, M.B. 2008, *Indonesian Syariah: Defining a National School of Islamic Law*, Institute of Southeast Asian Studies, Singapore.

Hopkins, A. and Patel, Kirit 2006, 'Reflecting on Gender Equality in Muslim Contexts in OXFAM GB', *Gender and Development*, vol. 14, no. 3, pp. 423–435.

Jahroni, Jajang 2005, 'Indonesia', in Suad Joseph (ed.), *Encyclopaedia of Women and Islamic Cultures*, Brill, Netherlands, vol. II, pp. 602–603.

The Jakarta Post 2006, 'Makeup Led to Woman's Branding as Prostitute', 5 April, available at: www.thejakartapost.com/news/2006/05/04/makeup-led-woman039s-branding-prostitute.html (accessed 6 April 2006).

Jamhari and Ropi, Ismatu (eds) 2003, *Citra Perempuan dalam Islam, Pandangan Ormas Keagamanan*, PT Gramedia Pustaka Utama, Jakarta.

Jayawardena, Kumari 1986, *Feminism and Nationalism in the Third World*, Zed Books, United Kingdom.

Kandiyoti, Deniz 1995, 'Reflections on the Politics of Gender in Muslim Societies: From Nairobi to Beijing', in Mahnaz Afkhami (ed.), *Faith and Freedom: Women's Human Rights in the Muslim World*, Syracuse University Press, United Kingdom, pp. 19–32.

Kartowirjono, Sujatin 1977, *Perkembangan Pergerakan Wanita Indonesia*, Yayasan Idayu, Jakarta.

Katjasungkana, N. and Wierenga, Saskia E. 2003, 'Sexual Politics and Reproductive Rights in Indonesia', *Development*, vol. 6, issue 2, pp. 63–67.

Katz, June S. and Katz, R.S. 1978, 'Legislating Social Change in a Developing Country: The New Indonesian Marriage Law Revisited', *The American Journal of Comparative Law*, pp. 309–320.

Lorius, Cassandra 1996, 'Desire and the Gaze: Spectacular Bodies in Cairene Elite Weddings', *Women's Studies International Forum*, vol. 19, no. 5, pp. 513–523.

Mahmood, Saba 2001, 'Feminist Theory, Embodiment, and the Docile Agent: Some Reflections on the Egypt Islamic Revival', *Cultural Anthropology*, vol. 12, no. 2, pp. 202–236.

Mahmood, Saba 2005, *Politics of Piety: The Islamic Revival and the Feminist Subject*, Princeton University Press, Princeton.

The Malaysian Insider 2010, 'Three Women Caned for Syariah Offences', 17 February, available at: www.themalaysianinsider.com/index.php/malaysia/53448-three-women (accessed 20 February 2010).

Marcoes-Natsir, Lies 2002, 'Women's Grassroots Movements in Indonesia: A Case Study of the PKK and Islamic Women's Organizations', in Kathryn Robinson and Sharon Bessell (eds), *Women in Indonesia: Gender, Equity and Development*, Institute of Southeast Asian Studies, Singapore, pp. 187–197.

Marcoes-Natsir, L. and Meuleman, J. (eds) 1993, *Wanita Islam Indonesia Dalam Kajian Tekstual dan Kontekstual*, INIS, Jakarta.

Martinez, Patricia 2006, 'Democracy, the Islamic State, and Embedded Realities in Malaysia', in Tun-Jen Cheng and Deborah A. Brown (eds), *Religious Organizations and Democratization: Case Studies from Contemporary Asia*, ME Sharpe, Armonk, pp. 242–266.

Martyn, Elizabeth 2005, *The Women's Movement in Post-Colonial Indonesia*, RoutledgeCurzon, London and New York.

Mayer, Elizabeth Ann 1995, 'Cultural Particularism as a Bar to Women's Rights: Reflections on the Middle East Experience', in Julie Peters and Andrea Wolper (eds), *Women's Rights Human Rights: International Feminist Perspectives*, Routledge, New York and London, pp. 176–188.

Mernissi, Fatima 1991, *The Veil and the Male Elite: A Feminist Interpretation of Women's Rights in Islam*, Addison-Wesley, Reading, MA.

Mir-Hosseini, Ziba 1996, 'Divorce, Veiling and Feminism in Post-Khomeini Iran', in Haleh Afshar (ed), *Women and Politics in the Third World*, Routledge, London, pp. 142–170.

Mir-Hosseini, Ziba 2003, 'The Construction of Gender in Islamic Legal Thought', *HAWWA*, vol. 1, issue 1, pp. 1–28.

Mir-Hosseini, Ziba 2006, 'Muslim Women's Quest for Equality: Between Islamic Law and Feminism', *Critical Inquiry*, vol. 32, pp. 629–645.

Moghadam, Valentine 1998, '"The Issues at Hand", in Herbert Bodman and Nayereh Tohidi (eds), *Women in Muslim Societies: Diversity within Unity*, Lynne Rienner, Boulder, pp. 277–294.

Moghadam, Valentine M. 2002, 'Islamic Feminism and Its Discontents, Toward a Resolution of the Debate', *Signs*, vol. 27, no. 4, pp. 1135–1171.

Moghadam, Valentine 2009, 'Feminism, Legal Reform and Women's Empowerment in the Middle East and North Africa', *International Social Science Journal*, vol. 59, no. 191, pp. 9–16.

Mojab, Shahrzab 2001, 'Theorizing the Politics of Islamic Feminism', *Feminist Review*, vol. 9, pp. 124–146.

Monash Paper on Southeast Asia 2005, 'On Feminism Nationalism, Kartini's letters to Stella Zeehandelaar 1899–1903', no. 60, Monash Asia Institute.

Morfit, Michael 1981, 'Pancasila: The Indonesian State Ideology According to the New Order Government', *Asian Survey*, vol. 21, no. 8, pp. 838–851.

Morfit, Michael 2007, 'The Road to Helsinki: The Aceh Agreement and Indonesia's Democratic Development', *International Negotiation*, vol. 12, pp. 111–143.

Muzzafar, Chandra 2006, 'Islam, Justice and Politics', in Mehran Kamrava (ed.), *The New Voices of Islam: Reforming Politics and Modernity*, I.B. Tauris, New York, pp. 213–230.

Nakamura, Mitsuo 1981, 'The Radical Traditionalism of the Nahdlatul Ulama in Indonesia: A Personal Account of the 26th National Congress, June 1979, Semarang', *Southeast Asian Studies*, vol. 19, no. 2, pp. 187–204.

Nurmila, Nina 2007, 'Negotiating Polygamy in Indonesia, Between Muslim Discourse and Women's Lived Experiences', PhD Thesis, University of Melbourne.

Ong, Aihwa 1990, 'State versus Islam: Malay Families, Women's Bodies, and the Body Politic in Malaysia', *American Ethnologist*, vol. 17, issue 2, pp. 258–276.

Ong, Aihwa 1995, 'State versus Islam: Malay Families, Women Bodies and the Body Politic in Malaysia', in Aihwa Ong and Michael G. Peletz (eds), *Bewitching Women, Pious Men: Gender and Body Politics in Southeast Asia*, University of California Press, Berkeley, pp. 159–194.

Ong, Aihwa and Peletz, M. (eds) 1995, *Bewitching Women, Pious Men: Gender and Body Politics in Southeast Asia*, University of California Press, Berkeley.

Othman, Norani 2006, 'Muslim Women and the Challenge of Islamic Fundamentalism/ Extremism: An Overview of Southeast Asian Muslim Women's Struggle for Human

Rights and Gender Equality', *Women's Studies International Forum*, vol. 29, pp. 339–353.

Paidar, Parvin 1996, 'Feminism and Islam in Iran', in Deniz Kandiyoti (ed.), *Gendering the Middle East: Emerging Perspectives*, I.B. Tauris, London and New York, pp. 51–67.

Parker, Lynn 2008, 'To Cover the Aurat: Veiling, Sexual Morality and Agency among the Muslim Minangkabau Indonesia', *Intersection*, issue 16, available at: http://intersections.anu.edu.au/issue16/parker.htm (accessed 5 June 2008).

Robinson, Kathryn 2006, 'Islamic Influences on Indonesian Feminism', *Social Analysis*, vol. 50, issue 1, pp. 171–177.

Robinson, Kathryn 2007, 'Islamic Influences on Indonesian Feminism', in Tony Day (ed.), *Identifying with Freedom: Indonesia After Soeharto*, Berghahn Books, New York and Oxford, pp. 39–48.

Robinson, Kathryn 2009, *Gender, Islam and Democracy in Indonesia*, Routledge, United Kingdom.

Robinson, Kathryn and Bessell, Sharon 2002, *Women in Indonesia: Gender, Equity and Development*, Institute of Southeast Asian Studies, Singapore.

Sadli, Saparinah 2002, 'Feminism in Indonesia in an International Context', in Kathryn Robinson and Sharon Bessell (eds), *Women in Indonesia: Gender, Equity and Development*, Institute of Southeast Asian Studies, Singapore, pp. 80–91.

Saeed, Abdullah 2004. 'Apostasy and the Positin of Muslim Thinkers in the Modern Period', in Abdullah Saeed and Hassan Saeed, *Freedom of Religion, Apostasy and Islam*, Ashgate Publishing, England, pp. 89–98.

Saeed, Abdullah and Saeed, Hassan 2004, *Freedom of Religion, Apostasy and Islam*, Ashgate Publishing, England.

Salim, Arskal 2006, 'Islamising Indonesian Laws? Legal and Political Dissonance in Indonesian Sharia 1945–2005', PhD Thesis, University of Melbourne.

Saptari, Ratna and Utrecht, Artien 1997, 'Gender Interests and the Struggle of NGOs Within and Beyond the State: The Experience of Women Organizing in Indonesia', *Journal fur Entwicklungspolitik*, vol. XIII, no. 3, pp. 319–339.

Schacht, Joseph 1964, *An Introduction to Islamic Law*, Clarendon Press, Oxford.

Sen, Krisna 1999, 'Women on the Move: After Three Decades of Patriarchal Conformity under the New Order, Women are Once More a Force for Change', *Inside Indonesia*, April–June, No. 58, available at: www.insideindonesia.org/edit58/women1.htm (accessed 18 December 2008).

Shaheed, Farida 1994, 'Controlled or Autonomous: Identity and the Experience of the Network, Women Living under Muslim Laws', *Signs*, vol. 19, issue 4, pp. 997–1019.

Shaheed, Farida 1995, 'Networking for Change: The Role of Women's Groups in Initiating Dialogue on Women's Issues', in Mahnaz Afkhami (ed.), *Faith and Freedom: Women's Human Rights in the Muslim World*, Syracuse University Press, United Kingdom, pp. 78–103.

Siregar, Hasnil Basri 2008, 'Islamic Law in a National Legal System: A Study on the Implementation of Shari'ah in Aceh, Indonesia', *Asian Journal of Comparative Law*, vol. 3, no. 1, pp. 1–28.

Smith-Hefner, Nancy J. 2007, 'Javanese Women and the Veil in Post-Soeharto Indonesia', *The Journal of Asian Studies*, vol. 66, issue 2, pp. 389–420.

Soetjipto, Ani 2005, *Politik Perempuan Bukan Gerhana: Esai-esai Pilihan*, Kompas, Jakarta.

Soewondo, Nani 1977, 'The Indonesian Marriage Law and its Implementing Regulation', *Archipel*, vol. 13, pp. 283–294.

Sudanese Tribune 2009, 'Sudanese Authorities Bar Female Journalist from Traveling Abroad', 11 August, available at: www.sudantribune.com/spip.php?article32096 (accessed 10 October 2009).

Sumardoni 2009, 'Amnesty International: Cabut Hukuman Rajam dan Cambuk di Aceh', *Berita Musi: Internasional*, 18 September, available at: www.beritamusi.com/berita/2009-09/amnesty-international-cabut-hukuman-rajam-dan-cambuk-di-indonesia/ (accessed 2 February 2010).

Suryakusuma, Julia 1996, 'The State and Sexuality in New Order Indonesia', in Laurie J. Sears (ed.), *Fantasizing the Feminine in Indonesia*, Duke University Press, Durham, NC and London, pp. 93–119.

Suryakusuma, Julia and Tim, L. 2006, 'Porn Bill: Autonomy Means Repression against Women', *Jakarta Post*, 4 January, available at: www.thejakartapost.com (accessed 20 January 2006).

Suryochondro, Sukanti 2000, 'The Development of Women's Movements in Indonesia', in Mayling Oey-Gardiner and Carla Bianpoen (eds), *Indonesian Women: The Journey Continues*, The Research School of Pacific and Asian Studies, the Australian National University, pp. 224–243.

Tiwon, Sylvia 1996, 'Models and Maniacs, Articulating the Female in Indonesia', in Laurie J. Sears (ed.), *Fantasizing the Feminine in Indonesia*, Duke University Press, USA, pp. 47–70.

Tiwon, Sylvia 2000, 'Reconstructing Boundaries and Beyond', in Juliette Koning, Mareen Nolten, Janet Rodenburg and Ratna Saptari (eds), *Women and Households in Indonesia: Cultural Notions and Social Practices*, Curzon Press, Richmond, pp. 68–84.

Tohidi, Nayereh 2003, 'Islamic Feminism: Perils and Promises', *Association for Middle East Women's Studies*, vol. xvi, no.3/4, pp. 135–146.

Tucker, Judith E. 2008, *Women, Family and Gender in Islamic Law*, Cambridge University Press, United Kingdom.

Wadud, Amina 1999, *Rereading the Sacred Text from a Woman's Perspective*, Oxford University Press, New York.

Wierenga, Saskia 2002, *Sexual Politics in Indonesia*, Palgrave, New York.

Wierenga, Saskia 2005, 'Islamization in Indonesia: Women Activists' Discourses', *Signs: Journal of Women in Culture and Society*, vol. 32, issue 1, pp. 1–8.

2 Women and the implementation of Islamic law in Aceh

> Being a woman in Aceh at this time is not easy. Everywhere you go people's
> eyes are on your dress and your head. They look at how you dress and how
> you cover your hair and from there they judge whether you are a good or a
> bad woman.
>
> (Interview, Banda Aceh, 20 December 2007)

In 1999 the central government in Jakarta allowed the Provincial Government
of Aceh to implement precepts of *'syari'at* Islam', that is, Islamic law, in
religious, cultural and educational matters. The granting to Aceh of the rights
to apply *'syari'at* Islam' took place at a time when Indonesia had embarked
on a democratic transition following the fall of Suharto's authoritarian
administration in 1998. In 2001, the local government of Aceh introduced a
number of Islamic legal regulations to enhance the rigorous implementation of
syari'at Islam. It also established local government institutions to oversee the
process of implementation. This marked the beginning of the implementation
of Islamic law in the western-most province of Indonesia.

The implementation of Islamic law in Aceh discriminates against women
and the poor. Many women have been publicly humiliated for failing to cover
their hair with a square fabric called *jilbab* and for wearing trousers instead
of knee-length skirts. The lack of clear legal mechanisms and corrupt public officials resulted in the discriminatory practices against women and the
poor. Acehnese women, civil society activists and a number of reform-minded
Muslims have protested against the way Islamic legal regulations have been
enforced. However, both local and national media tell stories about how
authorities such as sharia police continue to use their power to regulate matters of people's religiosity. In January 2013, Lhokseumawe district mayor
announced a plan to ban women from straddling motorcycles as it is considered un-Islamic (Saragih and Simanjuntak 2013). In North Aceh, starting in
May 2013, the regent banned adult women from participating in traditional
dance performances, claiming that the body movements of adult women are
a form of eroticism (Pasandaran 2013). In another part of North Aceh, the
Dayah community, the traditional Islamic boarding school, was checking
men and women's clothing. They cut men and women's pants considered to

be short and tight. In exchange, the *Dayah* community force them to wear traditional sarongs (*Tribun News* 2014). One shocking news story broke in September 2012, when a 16-year-old girl hanged herself after sharia police accused her of engaging in prostitution as she attended a music concert at night in her village (*The Jakarta Post* 2012).

These stories show that, almost ten years since it was first introduced and despite protests and critiques to the way sharia is formalized and implemented, regional authorities in the province of Aceh are still intent on the project of Islamizing the society. Still, of all the many issues that the Islamic law regulates, women's bodies have become one of the primary targets. Some Acehnese women activists strongly resent the way Islamic law is being enforced and believe that this problem stems from, among other things, the fact that women are neither considered nor included in the process of deliberating *Qanun* on religious matters, which has resulted in the negligence of women's interests.

The focus on women's bodies and clothing is because proponents of sharia believe that much of the problem in the society is derived from the fact that many women no longer observe Islamic tradition. To the many problems that accompany the enforcement of Islamic law, proponents of sharia law, including former Head of Islamic Sharia Office, Professor Alyasa Abu-Bakar, acknowledged that there is still lots of work to be done for Islamic law to be fully implemented (interview, Banda Aceh, 6 March 2007). Thus, Aceh needs to not only learn from practices in different places but also learn lessons from Aceh's past. The continuing debate that still lingers over the implementation of sharia law needs to be understood as a bigger project of future-oriented social transformation of Acehnese society (Feener 2013).

This chapter discusses the political background of the introduction of Islamic law and how sharia law has been enforced through the establishment of a number of institutions. It describes the debate and responses that arise among the Acehnese, in particular women, against the introduction of sharia law as it has affected their lives. This chapter also shows how the enforcement of sharia law has triggered a new conversation, in particular amongst Acehnese women, of the need to understand how Islam guarantees women's rights. Acehnese women have begun to have more interests on issues in Islam, *syari'at*, women's rights and justice, making Islam the subject of 'public scrutiny'.

Politics and the formalization of sharia

Aceh is one of the many provinces in Indonesia that has introduced legal regulations based on Islam. Research shows that, as of 2008, there are more than a hundred districts and provinces throughout the country that have introduced selected precepts of sharia in their bylaws.[1] The moves taken by these districts were made possible by the enactment of Law No. 22/1999 on Local Government, which gave new legislative power to Indonesia's regions.[2] For many Indonesian Muslims this new political development is an opportunity to return to Islam to generate answers to the social, economic and political crises they are facing.[3]

Aceh and West Papua are the two provinces most affected by the enactment of Law No. 22/1999.[4] This law gave Aceh's provincial government the authority to implement Islamic law. Following this, the Special Status of the Province of Aceh was recognized by Law No. 44/1999, which granted the provincial government the power to implement precepts of Islamic law in religious, cultural and educational matters. It also granted *Ulama* (Islamic religious leaders) the right to play a role in the implementation of regional policy (Abubakar 2006, 43). There was also a widespread view among the Acehnese that offering Aceh the right to implement Islamic law was a carefully calculated strategy to win over a number of conservative *Ulama* in Aceh (personal communication, Michael Leigh, 28 April 2010). Likewise, Hefner (2009, 196) observes that giving a concession to the Acehnese on Islamic law was, in fact, the result of influence from officials at Ministry of Religion, who were of the view that Aceh's religious establishment would welcome it. Hefner also says that compared to other national offices, the Ministry of Religion enjoys more respect in Aceh, compared to, for example, other branches of the national bureaucracy or the Indonesian military.

The local government began the application of sharia-based bylaws in the province in 2000 with enactment of PERDA No.5/2000. The enactment of this PERDA on the implementation of Islamic law demonstrated the willingness of the local government to support the implementation of Islamic law. This PERDA regulates issues not only related to Islamic faith and worship but also other matters, such as regulating economic transactions and providing guidance on moral character, including regulation of Islamic dress codes. It also provides guidelines on Islamic education, donations, defence, criminal justice and inheritance. During the course of its implementation, however, it was realized that Law No. 44/1999 did not offer a sufficiently strong or detailed basis for the region to fully implement Islamic law and so the central government replaced it with Law No.18/2001 on 'Special Autonomy for the Special Region of Aceh'.[5]

This new Special Autonomy Law marked the beginning of a more rigorous attempt to implement Islamic law in the province, since it gave the provincial government enhanced legal authority. The adoption of the new law also led to the changing of the name of the province from 'Daerah Istimewa Aceh' to 'Nanggroe Aceh Darussalam' or the 'Abode of Peace' and allowed the provincial government to re-establish sharia courts (*Mahkamah Syari'at*) to strengthen the application of Islamic law. The implementation of Islamic law was later consolidated by the enactment of Presidential Decree number 11/2003, which led to the establishment of the Office of Islamic Sharia (or Kantor Dinas Syari'at Islam). This office is principally responsible for the drafting regional regulations (*Qanun*) based on Islamic Law, which are then enacted by the local parliament. The implementation of Islamic law became even more rigorous with the ratification of Law on Governing Aceh or LOGA on 11 July 2006 (which replaced Law 18/2001).

The Acehnese were divided in their responses to this political development, with some perceiving it as a new beginning that could help bring the ongoing military conflict between the Free Aceh Movement (GAM) and the Indonesian military forces to an end. Many also see the implementation of Islamic law through the *Qanun* as a path to authenticity and the return to Acehnese indigenous values and Islam, in particular. Many hope it will be a path to regain Aceh's glorious past and will distance them from the administration in Jakarta. Other Acehnese, however, resented the implementation of Islamic law, believing it would only create new social problems. There are also many Acehnese who demand reform of the *Qanun*, considering them to be biased and gender-insensitive. Despite their differences, the Acehnese are interested in beginning a conversation on the need for a reinterpretation of the sources of Islamic law. I agree that conversations within society in contemporary Aceh on issues in Islam, *syari'at*, women's rights and justice reflect what Bowen (1993, 27) has described as a form of 'transparent Islam', that is, that Islam becomes subject to 'public scrutiny'. Through these conversations, the Acehnese are developing an 'Acehnese version of *syari'at*'. Or, as Feener (2013) says, the implementation of Islamic law can be read as projects for future-oriented social transformation.

Many Acehnese believe that the decision of the central government in Jakarta to grant the Acehnese the right to implement Islamic law was based on the central government's hope it would help end the conflict between the Acehnese and Indonesian military forces, which had been ongoing since the 1970s. Many Acehnese also believe that Jakarta's decision was based on the understanding that the continuing resentment of the Acehnese towards the central government in Jakarta has been driven by religious sentiments.[6] During the war against the Dutch, for example, Islam was a strong factor that turned the Acehnese fight against Dutch colonial powers into a religious war, a struggle against infidels or unbelievers (Sjamsuddin 1985; Ricklefs 2001; Reid 2006). Islam is again used as the basis for the Acehnese to fight the Indonesian government in the 1950s, when many Acehnese resented the dissolution of the province of Aceh. The *Ulama* leaders in Aceh were also disappointed when the new independent Republic of Indonesia was not based on Islam. Their resentment led the Acehnese to join Indonesia's Darul Islam movement,[7] which aimed to change the secular Republic of Indonesia into an Indonesian Islamic State or *Negara Islam Indonesia* (Sjamsuddin 1985, 83; Sukma 2004, 165; Dijk 1981, 306–320). Daud Beureuh, the *Ulama* who led the rebellion, proclaimed Aceh and its surroundings part of the Islamic State of Indonesia Dijk (1981, 311). Sjamsuddin (1985, 84) wrote that many Acehnese in the Darul Islam movement treated their fight against the central government in Jakarta as another holy war,[8] a fight against non-believers. The Acehnese also saw the rebellion as the continuation of their war against the Dutch. This was reflected in the way the Acehnese called the Indonesian military the *teuntra kaphee* (the non-believers army) (Dijk 1981, 314).

Rightly or wrongly, however, the central government in Jakarta has for some time perceived that the resistance movement in Aceh has been largely driven by Islam.[9] This has been the primary reason for the Indonesian government's belief that to appease the Acehnese they needed to allow the Acehnese to live under Islamic law. In fact, the resistance of some Acehnese who joined the Free Aceh Movement (GAM) in the early 1970s was not driven by so much Islam, but by economic exploitation the province suffered at the hands of Jakarta (Aspinall 2007; Kell 1995; Robinson 1998; Sukma 2004). Siapno (2002, 1) argues that:

> The Indonesian government has framed the struggles for social justice in Aceh as a religious conflict, about '*syari'at* Islam', rather than a structural conflict about the re-organization of the nation-state, economic capital and redress of grievances of human rights violations, among many things.

The expectation that allowing Aceh to apply Islamic law in 1999 would deliver peace fell flat at first. Military conflicts continued and hundreds of civilians were killed during the period 1999 to 2004 (Aspinall 2006; Sulistiyanto 2001; Schulze 2006).[10] Changes to the political regime in Jakarta between 1999 and 2004 affected political developments in Aceh, as transition between four different administrations during the period 1999 to 2004 opened room for peace talks between the Free Aceh Movement and the Indonesian military.[11] In 2000, a temporary halt to the military conflict was achieved as peace talks, facilitated by the Henry Dunant Centre,[12] ended with the signing of the Humanitarian Pause. In 2002, the two conflicting parties agreed to sign another peace agreement, the Cessation of Hostilities or COHA, signed on 9 December 2002.[13] According to Aspinall and Crouch (2003), however, these agreements failed to lead to genuine peace, due to lack of trust and the absence of agreement on whether Aceh should be independent or be part of the unitary Republic of Indonesia.[14]

Following the failure of COHA, and the outbreak of further conflict, the Indonesian government, through Megawati Sukarnoputri's Presidential Decree No. 28/2003, declared Aceh to be under Military Emergency Status on 13 May 2003 and attempted a crackdown on GAM (Aspinall 2005; Aspinall and Crouch 2003; Hedman 2004b).[15] With this development, many Acehnese became convinced that the granting of the right to apply Islamic law was not the same thing as a genuine willingness on the part of the Indonesian government to end the war and to appease Acehnese anger over long-standing massive economic exploitation and centralized administration.[16] It was only the devastating 'Boxing Day tsunami' of 26 December 2004 that finally led Yudhoyono's administration to end the conflict by agreeing to return to peace talks and, finally, sign a peace agreement with the Free Aceh Movement in Helsinki on 14 August 2005.[17] The Helsinki peace agreement was achieved after GAM declared that it set aside its goal of independence for Aceh in

February 2005. GAM then accepted that Aceh would be granted autonomy based on 'self-government', on the proviso that Aceh would remain part of Indonesia (Aspinall 2005, viii).

An interesting development occurred when the Aceh Party (Partai Aceh), which was the transformation of GAM, won the local parliamentarian election in 2009, followed by the election of Irwandi Jusuf, a former GAM leader, as the first Aceh governor elected from in direct local leader election. Since the Aceh Party is publicly known to have no religious platform and that Irwandi Jusuf was understood to have no interest in supporting the implementation of Islamic law, the conservative *Ulama* fear the administration will not support the total implementation of Islamic law (*pelaksanaan syariat Islam secara kaffah*) (Salim 2009). However, many women activists have, in fact, had different views as they are concerned that the local parliament would create policies that lack gender sensitivity. This is because, as one activist said, the majority of the newly elected local parliament is very conservative and many of them have strong views against women's equality and women's rights issues (interview, Banda Aceh, 2 May 2009). The fear of women activists materialized when the provincial parliament passed the bill on Islamic Criminal Code or Qanun Jinayah in 2009. The bill regulates among other things, criminalization of homosexuality and a penalty of death by stoning for convicted adulterers. The bill has only been taken into law in 2014 after the governor, Zaini Abdullah, who was elected in April 2012, passed the bill into law. The previous governor, Irwandi Jusuf, refused to sign the bill (Burhanuddin 2012).

The debate

In contemporary Aceh, the term 'sharia' is popularly rendered '*syari'at*'. The common understanding among Muslims is that *syari'at* comprises the rules and regulations derive from the *Qur'an* (Islamic Holy book believed to be the literal word of God) and the *Hadith* (documented sayings of the Prophet Muhammad) for all believers to look at and to live with (Keddie 2007; Hefner 2011). To be a true follower of Islam, many believe they have to live according to *syari'at*. From my conversations with the people of Aceh it is clear that they believe that their ancestors have lived under *syari'at* continuously since the Acehnese Islamic kingdom of the fourteenth century. Some of them expressed their understanding of *syari'at* as religious obligations, such as praying five times a day, performing fasting during the holy month of *Ramadan*, paying religious alms, and conducting pilgrimage to Mecca. Performing all these religious rituals will, they believe, prevent Muslims from perpetrating unlawful acts. The spirit to live by the *syari'at* led many Acehnese to consider that *Qur'an* and *Hadith* must be the only normative sources to regulate Muslim lives and thus need to be formalized into a living law.

Many Acehnese also see *syari'at* as a set of regulations issued by the rulers and religious leaders, based on the sources of Islamic teaching. Many Acehnese argue that it was during the period when Aceh was an Islamic kingdom that it became so powerful and managed to expand its territory in Southeast Asia (see also Riddell 2006, 38–51). Historical accounts suggest that under the leadership of Sultan Iskandar Muda, certain elements of Islamic law were introduced, including stoning for adulterers and the amputating of the hands of thieves (Riddell 2006, 43).[18] Proponents of the implementation of Islamic law in Aceh continue to refer to this period and stories to support their argument that if Aceh was under Islamic law the Acehnese could regain their economic prosperity.[19]

It is interesting to note that although the majority of Acehnese have a positive view of *syari'at*,[20] Acehnese society is divided in its response to the formalization of Islamic law. I categorize these different views in two groups. The first believes that Islamic legal regulations that derive from sharia principles need to be formalized in the form of public legislations, while the other argues that formalization of sharia will only result in the politicization of religion.[21] Those who are of the second view argue that the implementation of Islamic law is part of an attempt by the central government in Jakarta to pacify the Acehnese over socio-economic and political grievances. They argue that Islamic law in Aceh is not a divine law that comes from God, so it is open to criticism. They believe that the current sets of Islamic legal regulations are merely political decisions that can be amended. There is also a view amongst activists that the granting of Islamic law in Aceh is the result of a top-down evaluation made by the authorities in Jakarta. This is because there was never any formal consultation made with the Acehnese as to whether or not they wanted to live under Islamic law.[22] This group therefore believes that the granting of Islamic law was a political compromise aimed at blocking demands for a legal solution to past human rights abuses.

At an international conference organized by the BRR (the Agency for Rehabilitation and Reconstruction) and the Asia Research Institute of National University of Singapore (NUS) in Aceh on February 2007, a female activist, who was aligned with the Free Aceh Movement, Maryati, bluntly said that the implementation of Islamic law was just another political strategy adopted by Jakarta to appease the anger of Acehnese without addressing the real problem of 'unjust economic distribution'.[23] She went further, saying that the implementation of Islamic law should be seen as a new episode in Jakarta's occupation of Aceh because, to her, the new law that is being introduced is not based on Acehnese understandings of Islam. That is, it is mainly based on the interpretations of people in Jakarta and so is not in line with the expectations of many Acehnese. Another leading women's activist, Suraiya Kamaruzzaman (2004), has similarly argued that 'Islamic law is not the answer to the war in Aceh'. She contends that although the implementation was linked to government efforts to resolve the problem in Aceh, it does not actually address the root cause of the conflict, Aceh's socio-economic grievances and Aceh's political relationship with the central government.

Despite the perspectives of some activists, there is a growing perception among Acehnese that Islamic law might be a possible source of better social, economic and political policies that could help end social and economic problems.[24] The belief is that once the system of governance is based on Islam, there will be no more injustices, as Islam teaches only about justice. This confirms what Lindsey and Hooker (2007, 217) state, that the resurgence of sharia and the support of proponents of sharia to the implementation of Islamic law should be seen in the context of Aceh being economically, socially and politically marginalized within Indonesia's national development. This argument has it that Islam 'is seen not only as an assertion of Acehnese identity, but also as a mean of re-emphasising perceived traditional Acehnese values and, thereby, it is hoped that Aceh will regain its past prosperity' (Lindsey and Hooker 2007, 217).

In 2006, a local NGO, Yayasan Insan Cita Madani (YICM) conducted a survey to discover the response of the Acehnese to the implementation of Islamic law using short message service (SMS) polling to generate public responses. In-depth interviews were also carried out. YICM also wanted to know how society assessed the contribution of *Qanun* or the provincial regulations to the creation of good governance in the province. The result of the SMS-polling showed that only 9 per cent of the 804 respondents agreed that the current implementation of Islamic law has fulfilled the expectations of Acehnese, and 81 per cent said that they do not think the current implementation has met their expectations. The in-depth interview showed that less than 25 per cent of 354 respondents were happy with the current implementation, more than 30 per cent were disappointed, and the rest remain 'unsure' (YICM Report 2006, unpublished document). Another survey was carried out in the same year by Yayasan Keumala, which revealed that the implementation has generated discrimination, for example, because the sharia police or Wilayatul Hisbah (WH) checks women's clothing but not men's. It recorded that most women respondents also resented practices that targeted women and, in particular, women who rode motorbikes, while ignoring women who are driving cars. Of 1,800 respondents, 572 agreed that the implementation of Islamic law has only focused on certain groups, such as women and the poor. The other 488 respondents said that they were satisfied with the results of enforcement, and about 395 said that *Qanun* should be reinterpreted based on the current situation (*Serambi Indonesia* 2006a).

The results of these two surveys were resented by local authorities and critiqued the work of local NGOs. The results of the survey soon became headlines in the local newspapers and the head of MPU (Majelis Permusyawaratan *Ulama* or Aceh's *Ulama* Consultative Council), Professor Tgk Muslim Ibrahim, made a strong statement that the surveys were only meant to disturb the process of sharia implementation (*Serambi Indonesia* 2006b). Despite this, the survey made it clear that the Acehnese are not satisfied with the implementation of Islamic law in general, regardless of the argument that it allows Acehnese to express their cultural and religious identity.

A local intellectual, Bustamam-Ahmad (2007, 159), argues that the Acehnese are divided into two groups in terms of how they respond to the implementation of Islamic law. The first supports the formalization of Islamic law and the way it has been implemented. The other group is critical of the way Islamic law has been formalized and implemented. The first group views Islamic law as a healer of rampant socio-economic, moral and political illnesses, such as corruption, collusion and nepotism that have severely damaged the province and its society. The other group perceives that the process of the implementation of Islamic law is merely focused on formalizing and symbolizing Islamic teachings, without paying enough attention to the process. As a result, the issues of veiling, Muslim dress and the use of Arabic writing have become important. To the second group, Islamic law will neither be able to act as an effective tool to solve conflict, nor be useful as a panacea to solve moral ills in society.

Many Acehnese women have voiced concern over discriminatory practices in the implementation of Islamic law, through activities in local women's groups and women's NGOs. Some Acehnese women activists see the implementation of Islamic law as only giving attention to the regulation of women's religiosity, including women's dress and women's sexual mores.

Despite this debate, the local government continues its efforts to maintain Aceh as the sole province in a secular Republic of Indonesia that lives under Islamic law. The local authorities rely on Islam not only to mark their ideological difference from the Republic of Indonesia but also to symbolize their cultural identity and integrity.[25] This is in line with Benda-Beckman (2009, 219), who argues that 'the population and its leaders use Islam to distinguish themselves from the central government and other regions'.

Institutionalization of sharia law

Critiques often depict the poor performance of institutions established to support the implementation of Islamic law as leading to the discriminatory practices and the poor implementation of Islamic law. The local government established new local government institutions and strengthened the existing ones, the Majelis Permusyawaratan Ulama (MPU) or the *Ulama* Consultative Assembly and the Sharia Court or *Mahkamah Syari'at*. The new institutions are Dinas Syari'at Islam (or Office of Islamic Sharia) and the Wilayatul Hisbah (the sharia police). Of these institutions, Wilayatul Hisbah is the most criticized and notorious. There were cases where sharia police officers abused their authority. For example, in 2010, sharia police detained and raped a woman in their own office (*Tempo interaktif* 2010). I discuss each of these abuses in turn below, where it is shown that the complexities in the implementation of sharia law derive from the lack of government support to the institutions responsible for this.

The Ulama *Consultative Assembly or Majelis Permusyawaratan Ulama (MPU)*

The autonomy law in 1999 granted the Acehnese *Ulama* (Islamic religious leaders) the right to take a role in the process of Aceh's socio-economic and political development. They were given the authority to help form regional regulations or *Qanun*, and participate in the policy-making process.[26] This was part of an attempt to return to the traditional role that Acehnese *Ulama* had in the past. The *Ulama* understand their authority as granted in paragraph 8 Chapter I (1) of the Law No. 44/1999, which provides that 'The special status (*keistimewaan*) is the special authority to regulate religious, cultural, education and the role of the *Ulama* in making regional regulations'. Salim (2006, 195) argues that granting the *Ulama* wider authority in Aceh's regional development was part of the central government strategy to cure the declining position of the technocrats and *Ulama* in the local politics and an attempt at countering the increasing popularity of GAM.

The authority of *Ulama* at the MPU was later strengthened by PERDA No. 3/2000, enacted on 22 June 2000, which officially established MPU and guaranteed it equal political authority with the provincial parliament and the government of Aceh, as stated in Article 3 (2) of the *Qanun*.[27] In 2009, the legislature passed *Qanun* No. 2/2009, which strengthened the influential position of the MPU in the local governance, with Article 5 of that *Qanun* providing, for example, that the MPU can issue *fatwa* (religious rulings) on the issues of governance, development, economy, social and culture.

Prior to 2000, MPU was effectively the provincial branch of the Council of Indonesian *Ulama* or MUI[28] (Majelis Ulama Indonesia) (Salim 2006, 195–196; Kell 1995, 50). The transformation of MUI to MPU took place when hundreds of *Ulama*, consisting of leaders of *Dayah* (traditional Islamic boarding schools) and other Islamic institutions, met at the 'Musyawarah Silaturahmi *Ulama* se-Daerah Istimewa Aceh' or the Acehnese *Ulama* of Congress in June 2001 (Salim 2006, 196).

Scholarly works have elaborated the high position of *Ulama* in Acehnese society (Hurgronje 1906; Siegel 2000; Reid 1979; Sjamsuddin 1985; Morris 1985). The *Ulama* took a major role in the fight against foreign powers in the seventeenth and eighteenth centuries. Both Snouck Hurgronje (1906) and Siegel (2000) emphasized the strategic position of *Ulama* within Acehnese society, with Siegel (2000, 58) finding that villagers regarded the *Ulama* very highly as they believe they have certain powers such as having 'the ability to command a blessing or a curse, and causing sickness or ensuring a recovery'.

In the late eighteenth century, with the establishment of Islamic schools, a new generation of *Ulama* began to assert authority not just as religious leaders of society but also as initiators of practical projects in the community. Siegel (2000, 63) describes *Ulama*, including Daud Beureuh, initiating the building of irrigation, roads and bridges, gaining more respect with the villagers than the local government. Similarly, Kell (1995, 51) has noted that the *Ulama* played a role in public works projects. In addition, Kell noted that during the New Order the Acehnese *Ulama* always protected Aceh's status as a 'special region' or *Daerah Istimewa*[29] by safeguarding society from moral pollution. This can be seen, for example, from the objection of *Ulama* in Aceh to the New Order policy of banning the veil (*jilbab*) in schools (Kell 1995, 51).

On 5 May 1939 the Acehnese *Ulama* agreed to create the All-Aceh Association of *Ulama* or Persatuan *Ulama* Aceh (PUSA) (Alfian 1977, 214; Morris 1985, 86; Sjamsuddin 1985). PUSA operated not only at the local level but also at the national level by becoming part of the Majelis Islam Ala Indonesia (MIAI), which also took part in the fight against colonial powers. Aspinall (2007, 250–251) wrote that the network that PUSA had with these national Islamic institutions made an important contribution to Indonesian nationalism and helped make Acehnese politically integrated with the Indonesian Muslim community. In addition, Morris (1985, 86) notes that PUSA acted as proponents of the reformist movements that spread throughout the Islamic world in the early twentieth century.

Office of Islamic Sharia and Wilayatul Hisbah or sharia police

The Office of Islamic Sharia was established under the enactment of the Provincial Regulation or PERDA No. 33/2001 on the Formation, Structure of Organization and Function (*Tata Kerja*) of the Office of Islamic Sharia of the Special Province of Aceh. The creation of this institution followed the Special Autonomy Law No. 18/2001. Chapter 2 of Provincial Regulation No. 33/2001 stated that the office consists of several authorities and serves as a tool for implementing the institution of sharia Islam, led by an office head who is responsible to the governor through the provincial secretary (Abubakar 2006, 149–160).

Professor Alyasa Abubakar was the first chairman of this institution, appointed by Aceh's governor, Abdullah Puteh, in 2002. Professor Abubakar is also the Chairman of the Muhammadiyah provincial branch in Aceh and a professor at the Islamic Law faculty of IAIN Ar-Raniry. The main responsibility of the office is to draft the *Qanun* and oversee its implementation, and to make sure that the implementation of Islamic law is thoroughly applied at all levels of society. The office is established at both the provincial and district level and the leaders are appointed respectively by the governor and the district mayor (ICG Report 2006).

At its early establishment, this office was supported by Wilayatul Hisbah (WH), a form of 'morality police' who enforce Islamic law, established pursuant to *Qanun* No. 5/2000. The WH has the authority to monitor and enforce Islamic law (ICG Report 2006). In Gubernatorial Decree No. 1/2004 on the creation of Organization and Work Arrangement of the Wilayatul Hisbah, the WH is defined as an institution that has the authority to control, instruct (*membina*) and advocate the implementation of Islamic law in order to actualize the spirit of *amar makruf nahi munkar*, or good deeds in the name of God. The range of authority of the WH is outlined in more detail in Chapter 4 of Gubernatorial Decree No. 1/2004 and includes monitoring the application of regulations in the field of Islamic law. They are also responsible for giving instructions and providing religious counselling to those who are found in violation of Islamic law. The *Muhtasib*, or the officers of the WH, are required to inform the *Keuchik* or village leader and the family of the violators of cases detected.[30]

Of all the public institutions, the WH has received the most criticism. A research paper released by the Aceh Institute (Danial 2007) explores the impact of the current implementation of Islamic law and discusses how the activities of the WH have contributed to the creation of new forms of violence, including psychological and verbal violence. For some Acehnese and non-Acehnese who reside in the province, the WH officers are perceived as 'monsters' ready to publicly humiliate people or even make accusations that can lead to caning. Part of the concern is that while the WH is mandated to monitor sharia compliance, they have often overstepped their jurisdiction and treated the population in a manner that could potentially violate constutional law and human rights principles. The WH has become increasingly 'arrogant and overzealous', said one activist (Soraya Devy, interview, Banda Aceh, 2 February 2007), reflecting the views of many Acehnese.

Professor Abubakar, however, has argued that while some Acehnese blame the WH for taking the implementation of *Qanun* too far, many others expect it to protect the morality of the people and to be more vigilant in overseeing the implementation of *Qanun* (interview, 20 March 2008). He explained that many villagers, for example, bring burglars or other criminals to the WH office instead of taking them to the police. This, according to Abubakar, is because many Acehnese have lost trust in the police. He believed problems occur because the number of WH is very small compared to the number of population in the district. For example, in the district Banda Aceh of the total population of 177,881 there were only 45 WH employed by the local government in 2007. In Pidie district, in the northern part of Aceh, only 30 WH were employed for the population of 474,359 (Danial 2007). Similar trend also appeared in other districts across the province.

Lack of professionalism on the part of its personnel due to the low level of education of the officials and a poor recruitment process are some of the major causes of WH poor performance. WH officials are not adequately trained in criminal procedure or human rights principles (UNDP Report 2006, 92). Professor Abubakar replies, however, that these are among the challenges of a new institution. He pointed out the fact that the authority above his institution, the governor, has not clearly outlined the extent of the authority of Dinas Syariat Islam and the small budget the local administration allocated to his office (interview, Banda Aceh, 20 March 2008).

Muhibuthibri, the head of WH, has concerns that the provincial government has been ambivalent towards his institution (interview, Banda Aceh, 24 January 2008). The WH is expected to guard the implementation of Islamic law but is not supplied with adequate facilities. One of the crucial problems for the WH is that only 30 percent of the total officials at WH have been promoted to be civil servants (Pegawai Negeri Sipil or PNS). Having the status of PNS officials would give them job security and a salary based on the national remuneration standard. Seventy per cent of them are, however, still employed casually, which means lower pay and job insecurity. Those who are employed casually receive only IDR 500,000 (AUD$ 58) per month, while civil servants receive about IDR 1,500 (AUD$ 176). With these limitations, Muhibuthibri said, 'It is difficult for WH to recruit qualified resources as suggested by the ICG or expected by the society'.

Information gathered from the Office of Islamic Sharia shows that, in 2007, there were only 32 WH officers with a university degree out of 214 officers in five districts. About half of the officers have graduated from high school. This is interesting, because, as mentioned earlier, the WH is tasked to provide religious counselling for those in violation of Islamic law. The head of the Women's Studies Center at the IAIN Ar-Raniry has said, 'How can we expect WH to understand what Islam says about women's clothing and behavior if they have only completed high school, where religious knowledge is limited?' (interview, Banda Aceh, 4 March 2007). Data from the Office of Islamic Sharia Law listed that in the district of Lhoksemawe, only six officials held an undergraduate degree, seven had a diploma, and about 27 had only a high school background.

In addition, representation of women at the WH office is very low. Out of five districts throughout the province, there are only 92 female WH officers among a total of 259. Muhibuthibri said that 'Becoming a WH officer is simply not what Acehnese men and women dream of'. The percentage of female officials in five districts, including Aceh Tamiang, Aceh Utara, Lhoksemawe, Bieureun, Banda Aceh, is ranged between 25 and 28 per cent of the total number of officials. The very small number of women representation in WH is in the district of Lhoksemauwe with only three women compare to 37 male WH officers. In Banda Aceh, there were 13 female and 32 male officers working at the office.

With all of the institutional problems that surround the implementation of Islamic law, it is hard to see how Islamic law can fulfil the expectations of the Acehnese people. The process of the implementation of Islamic law will thus inevitably continue to generate resentment from some sections of the Acehnese community.

Sharia court or Mahkamah Syari'at

Aceh's sharia court or *Mahkamah Syari'at* was created based on the special status of Aceh as stipulated in the Special Autonomy Law No. 18/2001. Lindsey and Hooker (2007, 235) noted that the sharia court or *Mahkamah Syari'at* in Aceh was, in fact, a new name given to the pre-existing religious courts found throughout Indonesia. With a majority Muslim population, Indonesia has long had religious courts that handle issues of marriage, divorce, child custody and inheritance (Lindsey and Hooker 2007, 235).[31] In Aceh itself, there are 20 religious courts in various districts across the province. The newly established sharia court takes the structure of the religious courts but has a wider jurisdiction (Salim 2006, 207). It can also hear cases involving criminal offences such as gambling, consumption of liquor and *khalwat*, or close proximity between people of the opposite sex who are not clearly related. Only a small number of cases on breaching these *Qanun* on *khalwat*, gambling and consumption of alcohol are filed at the sharia court (Feener 2012, 278).

The enactment of Law No. 11/2006 on the Law of Governing Aceh (LOGA) re-emphasized the jurisdiction of the court to examine, try, decide and settle matters pertaining to *ahwal al-syakhshiyah* or family law, *mu'amalah* (civil law) and *jinayah* (criminal law), as stipulated in Chapter XVIII Article 128 (3) of LOGA. The sharia court exists at the district or municipal level and the Aceh sharia court acts as the court of appeal. Article 131 of LOGA stipulates that a ruling issued by the Aceh's sharia court can be appealed to the Supreme Court, including rulings on Islamic divorce/separation, marriage and reconciliation cases.

The establishment of the sharia court in Aceh has historical precedence from the time when Sultan Iskandar Muda (1607–1636) ruled the kingdom of Aceh under Islamic law (Riddell 2006, 40–42). According to Riddell (2006, 42), during his first three years in power, Sultan Iskandar Muda strengthened the legal system by establishing four separate courts, which included the civil court, criminal court, the court at the custom house and a religious court. In post-independence Indonesia, a sharia court was established in Aceh in 1947 when Aceh was part of the North Sumatra province but was not recognized by Jakarta until 1957 (Siregar 2008, 6).[32] This court had authority over domestic issues, including marriage and inheritance. Given this limited authority, the Acehnese *Ulama* demanded that Aceh be allowed to have a court with a more extensive mandate that includes regulating religious piety.

Abdullah Puteh, one of Aceh's former governors, said that the establishment of a sharia court in Aceh to support the implementation of Islamic law was part of an attempt to make sure that the implementation of Islamic law would not infringe human rights and, in particular, women's rights (BBC News 2003a). While people from outside Aceh see the establishment as a move towards Aceh becoming more conservative, many Acehnese support the establishment of the sharia court (BBC News 2003b). This is because, unlike the religious courts, sharia courts handle criminal cases and have the authority to convict those who violate Islamic law and they expect that this will curb criminal activities.

Discriminatory *Qanun*

The word *Qanun* has become a catchphrase in contemporary Aceh. *Qanun* is an Arabic term for Provincial Regulation or PERDA (Peraturan Daerah). While PERDA is used by other provinces for their provincial regulations, the term *Qanun* is used in Aceh to refer to the 'special status of Aceh' and to emphasize the Islamic character of the province, as recognized by Law No. 18 of 2001 on the Special Autonomy for the Special Province of Aceh. Chapter I

Article 1 (8) of the Law No. 18/2001 on the Special Autonomy for the Special Province of Aceh stipulates:

> The *Qanun* of Nanggroe Aceh Darussalam are provincial regulations in the province of Aceh Darussalam under the framework of the implementation of special autonomy.

Article 232 of the Law on Governing Aceh (LOGA) stipulates that all provincial *Qanun* need to be ratified by the governor of Aceh after being passed by the provincial parliament, while district or municipal *Qanun* shall be ratified by regents or mayor after being agreed by the local district parliament. Before ratifying the *Qanun*, the local government must consider whether the *Qanun* contravenes public interests, contradicts another *Qanun* or supersedes laws or regulations as stipulated in Article 235. If a *Qanun* encroaches any of the three criteria, the Indonesian Supreme Court can review the *Qanun* (Article 235 of LOGA). This is because the *Qanun* of Aceh is part of the hierarchy of laws within the Indonesian legal system, including the Constitution (Undang Undang Dasar RI 1945), Laws (Undang-Undang), Government Regulations (Peraturan Pemerintah), Presidential Regulations (Perpres) and Regional Regulations (PERDA) (Crouch 2009).

The power of the local government of Aceh to create *Qanun* was originally granted by the Autonomy Law No. 44/1999, which stipulates that the implementation of Islamic law in the province of Aceh is regulated under the provincial regulations (PERDA) or *Qanun*. During the period between 1999, when the Autonomy Law was granted, and until 2008, 58 *Qanun* were enacted. The governor's office website reported that in 2002 there were about 16 *Qanun* enacted and 13 *Qanun* enacted in 2003. Of the 16 *Qanun* passed in 2002, one relates to the implementation of Islamic law. There were three *Qanun* enacted in 2003 and two *Qanun* enacted in 2004 that directly regulate Muslim everyday activities. These include *Qanun* No. 11/2002 on the implementation of Islamic law in the areas of faith (*aqidah*), worship (*ibadah*) and dissemination of Islamic teachings (*syi'ar* Islam). It is this *Qanun* that requires all Muslims to wear Muslim dress which cover the *aurat* (those parts of bodies which should not be seen by others) and requires Muslim men to perform Friday prayer. The three *Qanun* in 2003 are *Qanun* number 12 on *Khamar* (the consumption of alcoholic beverages), number 13 on *Maisir* (gambling), and number 14 of 2003 on *Khalwat* or close proximity.[33] The last was *Qanun* No. 7/2004 on the management of *Zakat* (alms-giving). Of all these *Qanun*, the first four *Qanun* (No. 11/2001 on Muslim dress, No.12/2003 on *Khamar*, No. 13/2003 *Maisir* and No. 14/2003 on *Khalwat*) have continued to create controversy.

In 2004, the local government of Aceh enacted 11 *Qanun*. In 2005 and 2008, two *Qanun* were enacted. Six *Qanun* were enacted in 2006, and in 2007, there were eight *Qanun* enacted. Of the total 58 *Qanun* enacted from 2002 to 2008, there were five that closely relate to, and support, the implementation of

Islamic law. In 2009, the local government enacted six *Qanun*, including *Qanun* No. 6 on the Empowerment and the Protection for Women, which marked a new beginning for the issue of women's empowerment in Aceh. The local government also enacted *Qanun* No. 2/2009 on the Majelis Permusyawaratan *Ulama* or Consultative Council of *Ulama*. On 14 September 2009, the provincial parliament of Aceh passed two *Qanun* bills on *Jinayah* (Islamic criminal legal code): a bill on Islamic penal rules (*Rancangan Qanun Hukum Jinayah*) and a bill on Islamic penal procedures (*Rancangan Qanun Hukum Acara Jinayah*).[34]

From my observation, the resentment of some Acehnese towards the implementation of Islamic law is mainly related to how *Qanun* are drafted, how they are deliberated in the parliament, and how they are implemented. They mainly target *Qanun* that regulate issues pertaining to the religiosity of Acehnese. In an interview with Otto Syamsudin Ishak, a leading human rights activist in Banda Aceh on 17 March 2007, he argued, for example, that *Qanun* [on religiosity] reflect the interests of the government and the interpretations of local religious leaders to regulate people's religiosity. In his opinion, Islamic law has been corrupted and has failed to create a more 'Islamic' Acehnese society. Despite this criticism, he does not reject the idea that Aceh be based on *syari'at*. He said, 'that is what Acehnese want'. In an interview, Otto Syamsuddin Ishak, a human rights activist, told me:

> If it is already institutionalised, sharia becomes political. Just look at the *Qanun* and you can see what it is all about, it is no longer a religious invention, but something that is created by politicians in the parliament by those who either have a beard or not.[35] For this reason, we can see that in the process of making the *Qanun*, starting from the early discussions until *Qanun* is ratified, everything is political.
> (Otto Sjamsudin Ishak, interview, Banda Aceh, 20 March 2007)

Imposition of caning

There are two *Qanun* regulating people's religiosities, which have created major resentment, according to some Acehnese (especially activists): *Qanun* No. 11/2002 on the implementation of Islamic law that regulates Muslim clothing and Friday prayer for men, and No. 14/2003 on *Khalwat* or close proximity. This resentment derives from perceptions that the process of implementing these two *Qanun* has been discriminatory, especially as regards women and the poor. Article 1 (20) of *Qanun* No. 14/2003 on *Khalwat*, defined it as:

> Any activity carried out by two or more individuals of opposite sex who are not bound as a family nor legally bound under marriage.

Since this *Qanun* was enacted, there have been many stories of couples caught by the Wilayatul Hisbah for being in close proximity or for having sexual relations outside marriage. These stories have become major headlines in the local newspaper in Aceh (Heryanto 2008). This happens not only in the city area but also in many villages across the Aceh province. In the local tabloid *Modus Aceh*, Heryanto (2008), for example, reported that many different actors, including villagers, students, government officials to local MPs, have been caught allegedly committing *khalwat*. Some of the violators have been tried and prosecuted by caning, but there are cases where the violators managed to negotiate their cases with the authorities. Among them are the cases of local MPs in Lhoksemauwe and in Aceh Tamiang (*Serambi Indonesia* 2006g).[36] The local MPs managed to escape the rattan cane because of their power, while others with no power would most likely be being whipped for breaching the law. This indicates that in the process of implementing this *Qanun* discrimination occurs.

Another story I heard is the fact that an Acehnese man and woman riding a motorbike together could become an easy target of the WH, while a man and woman who sit in the car probably would not be harassed. I asked the head of the WH field office about this. He accepted the accusation, but explained that, when a man and a woman ride together motorbike, and the woman is sitting on the back of the bike with her arms around his waist, they could easily commit *zina*[37] (engage in illicit sexual activities outside of marriage) (interview, Banda Aceh, 9 July 2009). He further said, 'They will be tempted by *Syaitan* (Satan), on the other hand, those who sit in the car are not in position of closely holding each other, and thus they will not be tempted by *Syaitan*'.

Another controversial *Qanun* that has become the target of criticism for some Acehnese women is *Qanun* No. 11/2002 on sharia implementation, which regulates, among other things, Muslim clothing and Friday prayer for men. Article 13 (1) provides that 'All Muslims are oblige to wear Islamic dress' and article 21 (1) stipulates an obligation for men to perform Friday prayer. In 2006, the Wilayatul Hisbah found 593 cases of infringement of *Qanun* 11/2002 and 2,034 in 2007 in the district of Banda Aceh alone.[38] Although no women have been reportedly caned for failing to comply with *Qanun* No. 11/2002 on Muslim dress, activists consider this *Qanun* to be the most unpopular.

The mainstream interpretation by officials at the Wilayatul Hisbah and the Office of Islamic Sharia is that women must cover all their hair by wearing a certain kind of veiling popularly known as *jilbab*.[39] Muslim clothing for women, according to WH officials that I talked with, consists of a skirt, a loose dress or a type of *baju kurung* that will not show women's 'body shape' and *jilbab* that covers the women's chest. Hence, they consider women who wear tight pants, jeans and tight t-shirts as not in line with what is required by the *Qanun*.

According to some Acehnese women, the form of *jilbab* that has become popular in Aceh has no history in Aceh. As one of my informants said, '"*Jilbab*" is an "Arabic way" of covering the hair of women, it is not "Acehnese"'.[40] In relation to clothing, women found it unusual not to be allowed to wear pants because, in the past, Acehnese women wore traditional black pants known as '*luweu tham asee*' or 'dog chasing trousers' with a traditional loose type of '*baju kurung*', a long-sleeved top that goes to the knees (Siapno 2002, 26). The tradition of Acehnese women wearing trousers can also be seen from brides wearing trousers as part of their traditional wedding costumes. Reference is also made to the fact that Acehnese women have always been involved in economic activities by working in their paddy fields with their husbands, or performing other jobs that require them to move easily. In the current context of Aceh where women have increasingly enjoyed higher mobility, women found it ineffective if they wear the sort of clothing the WH requires, because it will limit their movement. They argue that, as long as riding a motorbike is the main form of transport for women, it will always be difficult to force them to wear skirts. One informant said, 'It is not only ineffective but most of all it is not safe for women who ride bikes to wear long and big skirts', as they could get caught in the bike's machinery (interview, Banda Aceh, 20 March 2007). The recent initiative of Lhokseumawe's mayor to ban women from straddling motorbikes is, according to women's activist Suraiya Kamaruzzaman, another kind of discrimination against the poor, because the motorbike is the main form of transport used by poor women (Natahadibrata 2013).

The controversy that surrounds the implementation of Islamic law is the fact that *Qanun* on sharia imposes caning as punishment for some offences. Caning was first implemented as a penalty on the first day of *Ramadan* or fasting month in October 2002, by the *Ulama* Consultative Assembly (MPU). Those who were not fasting during the month of *Ramadhan* were liable to be punished in this way. However, at that time, it was not clear how many lashes a violator would receive.

Qanun No. 11/2002 on sharia implementation and *Qanun* No.12/2003 on *Khamar* (the consumption of alcoholic beverages), *Qanun* No.13/2003 on *Maisir* (gambling) and *Qanun* No.14/2003 on *Khalwat* (illicit relations outside marriage) also imposed caning on offenders. The amount of caning that an offender can receive varies. Article 26 of *Qanun* No.12/2003 on *Khamar* provides that those in violation of *Qanun* could receive up to 40 lashes and violators of *Qanun* No. 14/2003 on *Khalwat* could receive three to nine lashes. Those who breach *Qanun* No. 13/2003 on *Maisir* (drinking alcoholic beverages) can receive between six and 12 lashes, as stipulated in Article 23. Men who are found not performing Friday prayers three times in a row are also subject to three lashes, as stipulated in *Qanun* No. 11/2002, article 21 (1).

The MPU has argued that it is much better to apply caning than to fine the violators, as fines only encourage more crime and are too easy on rich people. While some Acehnese women activists condemn the regulation on caning, a lecturer at Faculty of Sharia Law of IAIN Ar-Raniry, Muhammad Yasir Yusuf, argues that caning should be considered financially effective for the government because it does not have to spend more money on prisons. He added that for violators, caning is also better because they will receive their punishment straight away, without having to stay in prison for a period of time. He said, 'Once the caning is carried out, they can go back to their jobs and return to their family' (interview, Banda Aceh, 1 March 2007).[41] A member of the Provincial Legislature (DPRA) from the Prosperous Justice Party (Partai Keadilan Sejahtera or PKS), Raihan Iskandar, argued that the application of caning is the result of the implementation of Law No. 18/2001 on the Special Autonomy of Aceh and Law No. 11/2006 on the Governing of Aceh (*Rakyat Aceh Online* 2007). Based on these two laws, he argued there should be no more criticism of the implementation of caning in Aceh. According to him, criticizing the imposition of caning as a violation of human rights is a broader attack on the implementation of Islamic law in Aceh, which is something that has been legally authorized by Indonesia's national government.

The first caning took place on Friday, 24 June 2005 in Biereun district. Eighteen violators of *Qanun* No. 13/2003 on *Maisir* received six to eight lashes in front of the grand mosque of Biereun (Suryadi 2009). Hundreds of local Acehnese gathered around the mosque to witness the first ever caning to take place in their region.[42] This event marked the beginning of a new episode in the implementation of Islamic law in the province. In August 2005, four women were caned for the first time, along with several other men, for alleged gambling activities in Biereun district. The caning again took place in front of the Biereun grand mosque in the north of Aceh. These women received six to ten blows on their backs. All wore white tunic dresses along with their white *jilbab*. They knelt and their backs were lashed with a rattan cane.

Following this event in Biereun, other districts also witnessed canings. In the district of Banda Aceh there were 16 cases of caning in 2005, mostly relating to infringements of *Qanun* No. 13/2003 on *Maisir*. Data from the Office of Islamic Sharia of Banda Aceh district reported that in 2006 one person was caned for *Maisir* (gambling), one for being found in the possession of drugs, and a couple (man and woman) were caned for *khalwat* offences. In 2007, there was only one case of caning, which involved a couple who infringed *Qanun* No. 14/2003 on *Khalwat*. However, caning has still occurred in Banda Aceh until recently.

Infringement cases during 2006 and 2007 were, however, quite high. However, the number of canings gradually decreased from when they were first carried out. In the district of Banda Aceh it was reported that in 2006 the Wilayatul Hisbah caught 211 couples who infringed *Qanun* No. 14/2003 on *Khalwat*. In 2007, the number increased to 366 couples. *Qanun* No. 11/2002 on the implementation of sharia, which regulates Muslim dress and Friday prayers for men, caused the highest number of infringements, with 2,034 people reported for infringing this *Qanun* in 2007, a significant increase from only 593 people in 2006. There is no clear data on how many of the violators were women. It was clear only that two women were caned for *khalwat* violations.

Recent developments show that the authorities do not always follow legal procedures in dealing with *Qanun* infringements. The legal process for those who violate *Qanun* No. 14/2003 on *Khalwat* should be for the WH to report the case to the police before they report to the prosecutor and the court.

Instead of doing so, the WH and Office of Islamic Sharia usually ask couples they find committing *khalwat* offences to get married, calling their parents to come to WH office and for the parents to agree to marry their children (interview with the field commander WH Banda Aceh, Banda Aceh, 8 June 2009). There is, however, a tendency for villagers who catch a couple in adultery not to hand the violators either to the WH or to the Office of Islamic Sharia. Rather, villagers will bring them to the mosque and parade them around the village as a form of punishment. In the mosque, the local *Ulama* will marry them with the consent of their parents. Another case worthy of note relates to how violations of *Qanun* are handled. It was reported in the local newspaper that when villagers found the director of the local electricity office in Sabang with a woman who was not his wife, the villagers took them to the local Office of Islamic Sharia. Immediately after that, the village head came to the Office of Islamic Sharia and picked him and the woman up, telling the officials at the Office of Islamic Sharia that the village would deal with the problem. The village leaders then held a meeting and decided that the couple would be punished by paying five million rupiahs to the village office. On the next day, the director of the local electricity office paid the money and both were released (*Serambi Indonesia* 2008).

Some women activists argue that the way women are treated in the context of the implementation of Islamic law is driven by the lack of understanding of what is written in the *Qanun*, and the teachings of Islam more broadly. One woman activist argued, for example, that *Qanun* No. 11/2002 on Muslim clothing is not only vague but also problematic in other ways (Soraya Devy, interview, Banda Aceh, 5 March 2007). Article 13 (1) of the *Qanun* says that 'All Muslims are obliged to wear Islamic dress'. In its explanation section, the *Qanun* provides that 'Islamic dress consists of clothing that covers *aurat* or *awra*, which is not transparent, and does not show the body shape'. According to Devy, the way this *Qanun* defines Islamic dress can create confusion. How, for example, can women make sure that their body shapes will not be seen?

Acehnese women have a different understanding of what constitutes 'Islamic dress'. Some Acehnese women have long understood that what Acehnese women wore in the past should be considered Islamic dress, because Aceh was once under Islamic law. Thus, wearing a traditional *selendang* or scarf or thin veil to cover women's hair and wearing trousers should be considered appropriate Islamic dress, as can be seen from the images of Acehnese woman heroines such as Tjut Nyak Dhien and Cut Mutia and women leaders who ruled Aceh when it was an Islamic kingdom.[43]

According to women activists, *Qanun* No. 11/2002 on Muslim dress has also been used by conservative Acehnese men to justify their control of women's clothing. Students from traditional *pesantren* or *Dayah* (Islamic traditional boarding school), for example, believe that they have the right to check on women's clothing, and to approve or condemn it.

In addition, authorities such as security guards at mosques also perceive that they have the right to judge a woman's religiosity from her dress. One incident I experienced myself shows how the security guard of the Grand Baiturrahman Mosque enforced his interpretation of 'appropriate' Muslim clothing for women.

On Sunday morning, 26 January 2008, my last day in Banda Aceh, I planned to perform afternoon prayer at the Grand Baiturrahman Mosque with an Acehnese friend. However I was prevented from doing so. A young man wearing a white uniform matched with a green hat and holding a metre-long rattan cane stopped me from entering the mosque complex. He pointed his rattan cane to my legs, then waved it in front of me and asked me to leave the mosque. He said that women who wear pants are not allowed to enter the mosque. I was, in fact, wearing loose cotton pants, not jeans. I was also wearing a loose, long-sleeved top that hung halfway to my knees and, of course, a *jilbab*. I tried to confront him by saying that I was not wearing jeans or a tight dress and I needed to perform my *dzuhur* prayer, but he just shook his head. I was bewildered as it was, in fact, not my first time entering and performing prayer in the Grand Baiturrahman Mosque wearing pants. This experience shows how rigidly conservative Acehnese interpret *syari'at* or *Qanun* on Muslim dress and how some men consider that they have absolute authority to judge women's religiosity.

Women activists argue that the religious *Qanun* and their implementation provide opportunities for the patriarchal society and the conservative religious community to return society, and women in particular, to patriarchal interpretations of Islam. The way *Qanun* have been implemented has also given men the opportunity to control what women should wear, how women should behave, and how women should observe their religion.

Qanun or *Fiqh* of Aceh

Dr Nurjannah Ismail,[44] a leading woman intellectual who is a lecturer at IAIN Ar-Raniry, often warns her audiences in many of her speeches that it is important for people to understand the difference between sharia and *Qanun*. She said:

> If '*syari'at*' is criticised for causing discrimination against women and violation of human rights, this criticism has come from someone who does not understand the different between sharia and *Qanun*.

She contends that what many Acehnese have been arguing about and criticising in Aceh is not *syari'at*. She argued that while sharia is a divine law based on the *Qur'an* and *Hadith*, the *Qanun* are the '*Fiqh* of Aceh',[45] a product of Acehnese *Ulama*'s interpretation of Islamic scriptures that is then used by politicians. She contends that if there has been a negative impact of the implementation of Islamic law, it should not be seen to be because of sharia or Islam, but because something may have gone wrong in the process of interpreting sharia. Since it is a product of human interpretation it is possible that these *Qanun* still do not meet the needs of the Acehnese. She added that the *Qanun* are formed after a series of processes involving various individuals and institutions, who have different religious understandings and political concerns.

During my conversation with her,[46] Dr Ismail said that she has become increasingly worried by the fact that public discourse has moved towards criticizing sharia and Islam, which according to her is 'sacred'. She was afraid that this kind of accusation against sharia or Islam will lead to unfair assessments, as people will judge and blame Islam as the cause of the problem, or say that it is sharia that has caused women's oppression and discrimination. She pointed out to the fact that foreigners often 'jump in easily' to conclude that sharia is indeed the source of women's subjugation and oppression. In fact, she contends that people should understand that the problem in Aceh is in the implementation of the *Qanun*, a product of human beings and implemented by human beings. She further noted that Aceh's political context might also cause some issues in the implementation of the Islamic regulations. This is in line with Hooker (1983, 161), who argues that there is a need to distinguish between the religion of Islam and its law. He wrote that:

> While Islam is a revealed religion its laws, while an integral part of religion and indeed fundamental to its expression, are also concerned with the humanly practical and the strictly temporal.

Professor Alyasa Abubakar, the former Chairman of the Office of Islamic Sharia, argued that much of both the criticism and support that has been given to the implementation of Islamic law derives from people's own understandings of sharia, and the critiques may thus appear because people lack common understanding on this issue. He agrees with the point that people need to differentiate between sharia, *Fiqh* and *Qanun*. He said what people have been criticizing is *Fiqh*, in this case, the *Qanun*. He argued that this lack of knowledge has led to further misunderstanding of sharia, and the ruining of the name of Islam as a religion.

These two Acehnese intellectuals, affiliated with IAIN Ar-Raniry, the State Institute of Islamic Studies, argue that Islamic law cannot merely be associated with forms of punishment, seen as violating international norms of human rights. Rather, Islamic law is a set of regulations that includes aspects of education, economics, social issues and various other things introduced in the *Qur'an* and *Hadith*. Since the *Qanun* is a product of current interpretations made by the *Ulama*, Professor Abubakar contends that there are possibilities for the *Qanun* to be reformed, based on new interpretations, if that is what the people of Aceh want. *Qanun* in Aceh is created neither on the basis of experience of Saudi Arabia, Sudan or Iran, nor following the Anglo-Saxon legal system but is implemented under the framework of Indonesia's legal system (Abubakar 2006, 196). Professor Abubakar expects that in the future the *Qanun* Aceh will later become the '*Fiqh* of Aceh' or Aceh's 'contemporary Fiqh' (Abubakar 2006, 197).

Professor Abubakar may be the only individual in Aceh aside from the officials of the WH who has been the victim of regular attack and criticism, and who is confronted by Acehnese and non-Acehnese with different views on the implementation of Islamic law. During my interview in his office, he said, people who still doubt the implementation of Islamic law in Aceh need to understand the history of Aceh (interview, Banda Aceh, 30 January 2008). According to him, ever since Aceh became part of Indonesia, various social organizations in Aceh have been calling on Jakarta to allow Aceh to implement Islamic law.[47]

Professor Abubakar accepts the fact that during the course of the implementation of the *Qanun*, there have been weaknesses and mistakes. He admits that there are problems in the way *Qanun* are being drafted, enacted and implemented. He also understands that there have been cases where the WH has treated the Acehnese inappropriately. He argues, however, that these incidents should be seen as part of the bigger process of Aceh's transition from conflict, and its post-tsunami reconstruction as well. He acknowledges that his institution faced serious problems that directly affect the process of implementation. He points to a lack of both the financial and human resources necessary to support his institution to promote a just and non-discriminatory implementation of Islamic law. As long as issues faced by the institution are not adequately addressed, he is worried that the implementation will create problems in society. Thus, he contends that the institutional capacity of all the government institutions that are directly responsible for the implementation of Islamic law need to be improved.

What has happened in the recent years following the implementation of Islamic law in Aceh mirrors what Bowen (1993, 27) has demonstrated in his anthropological work in Gayo, in the central part of Aceh. From the period of 1928 to 1942, Islam, according to Bowen, emerged as a 'scholarly and universalistic' topic, as it became 'transparent' and 'subject to public scrutiny'. He observes that the community from lay people to scholars began to discuss Islam, debating it in public sermons in the mosques, or during coffee time in the local village shops. He also notes that women began to take part in informal discussions in women's study groups. Following Bowen's argument, I see similar developments occurring more broadly in Aceh since the introduction of Islamic law in 1999. Islam has become subject to wider public discussion among Acehnese. Many Acehnese begin to learn the teachings of Islam in more detail and debate them to better understand their religion.

Conclusion

The discussion above demonstrates that the implementation of Islamic law has progressed alongside Aceh's transition to special autonomy. It has also developed under the particular socio-economic circumstances of Aceh as it undergoes transition from conflict and is reconstructed following the tsunami. The presence of democratic mechanisms has allowed civil society to participate in developing the faces of *syari'at*, as many Acehnese have openly expressed their views on the implementation of Islamic law. The Acehnese have continued to engage in public discussion on matters related to sharia and Islamic teachings and Acehnese civil society has demonstrated that their conversations on Islam and *syari'at* may end with the creation of a new and different '*Fiqh* Aceh'. In my view, this is an important point to note, since Acehnese civil society is often erroneously said to have been sidelined by the broader process of the formalization of Islamic law. Take for example Johnson (2007), who argued that within the debate on Islamic law, Acehnese perspectives have been marginalized.

Social disruption in Aceh has not been as significant as in some other places where precepts of sharia has been introduced, since the Acehnese have long since internalized many of the norms underpinning the province's *Qanun* (Suryakusuma and Lindsey 2006). Thus, the resentment of some Acehnese towards the application of Islamic law should not necessarily be interpreted as a rejection of the idea of implementing Islamic law. Although to a certain degree women's voices and experiences are often disenfranchised within the implementation of Islamic law, in the case of Aceh this does not necessarily mean that they demand the abolition of Islamic law. On the other hand, women's criticisms of the current practice of Islamic law have increasingly gained leverage within the wider public discussion. There has been also growing acceptance from the authorities of the need to include women's voices in the process of deliberating *Qanun*.

Notes

1 See for example, Crouch (2009), who observes that to date there have been 170 PERDA Syariah applied throughout Indonesia. See also Lindsey (2008, 206) who observes that there are 160 Islamic regional regulations or PERDA Syariat that have been introduced in 24 of Indonesia's 33 provinces. On the tendency of districts and provinces to adopt sharia-based bylaws, see Azra (2004, 133–147), in which he argued that those who dream of applying sharia into law failed to fight their cause at the national level through the parliament, and so have taken advantage of decentralization to adopt sharia-based bylaws (Azra 2004, 147).

2 This law was enacted with the objectives of promoting better delivery of government's services and raising the level of government accountability and also as a response to the pressures of dissatisfaction of communities in the outer islands beyond Java, who had experienced massive political and economic exploitation (Suwondo 2002; Usman 2001). In an INFID Background Paper, Suwondo (2002) discusses the political background of the enactment of this regulation during the Habibie presidency, which lasted only a year, from 1998 to 1999. Article 1(3) of Law No. 22/1999 provides that decentralization is the transfer of authority of the government by the central government to autonomous regions, within the framework of the Unitary State of the Republic of Indonesia. In addition, Article 1(h) of the Law defines Regional Autonomy as the authority of an autonomous region to regulate and govern the interests of the local people according to their own initiative, based on the aspirations of the people in accordance with rules and regulations.

3 See, for example, Hefner (2001), in which he discusses how Muslims in Indonesia continue to look to their religion for principles of public order as well as for spirituality. Despite arguments that Islam will not be compatible with democracy, the case of Indonesia suggests the contrary is possible. Debates among Muslims as to whether or not Indonesia should be based on Islam have so far not hampered Indonesia's path towards democracy. This has been shown by the increased number of religious organizations that continue to play a part in the process of Indonesia's democratization.

4 For more accounts of this see, for example, McGibbon (2004, ii–viii) who explains that although the Special Autonomy Law is designed as the Indonesian government's broadest response to secessionist struggles in places such as West Papua and Aceh, it does not represent a solution to separatist conflict. He argues that it acts as part of a broad process of bargaining and negotiation. In his words, 'special autonomy represented a unilateral concession on the part of Jakarta that lacked any links to the main political forces advocating independence'.

5 See for example Miller (2004). The Law on Special Autonomy for the Special Province of Aceh was passed by President Megawati Sukarnoputri on 9 August 2001. Miller (2004, 334) argued that the law aimed to offer a solution to secessionist demands by granting Acehnese 'wide-ranging powers of self-governance'. Aside from regulating aspects of Islamic law, it also addressed economic grievances, such as the return of Aceh's resources revenue, and allowed the Acehnese to hold direct local elections.

6 On the roots of rebellion, scholars working on Aceh are divided on what has been the driving factor for Acehnese resistance to Jakarta. Smith (2002, 69), for example, has identified two views on this issue. The first sees the roots of resistance as primarily religious, while a second group view it as mainly a result of nationalist or separatist sentiments. According to Smith, scholars like Sukma (2002), Robinson (1998), Kell (1995), Aspinall (2007) and Siapno (2002) are among those who believe that the conflict was mainly driven by separatist sentiments.

7 The Darul Islam movement was first established in West Java in 1948, led by Kartosuwiryo, followed by Kahar Muzakkar in South Sulawesi in 1950 and lastly by the Acehnese, led by Acehnese Ulama, Daud Beureuh, in 1953. Laffan (2003, 407) explains that the Darul Islam movement emerged as the result of some Indonesian Muslims' disappointment at the state's decision not to choose Islam as the state's ideology. For more on the Darul Islam movement, see Dijk (1981).

8 Morris (1985, 84) argues that in leading the fight against the Dutch, the *Ulama* used the powerful weapon of an 'epic poem', the 'Hikayat Perang Sabil' (The Epic of the Holy War) and told the Acehnese that they will gain 'fantastic rewards' in paradise should they fall in the holy war against the infidels. See also Sjamsuddin (1985).

9 Many Indonesians see the Acehnese as pious Muslims and strict followers of Islam. This is in line with Federspiel (1998, 104) who observed that 'feeling about Islamic obligation is high among the Acehnese'.

10 Sulistiyanto (2001, 449) for example, noted that from August to October 2000 about one hundred people from both the Indonesian military and Acehnese were killed. In addition, Aspinall (2006, 163) showed that after 1999, several massacres took place, including the Simpang KKA massacres in Aceh Utara, and the killing of the respected Acehnese Ulama Tgk Bantaqiah and his 56 followers in Central Aceh (known as 'Beutong Ateuh' Massacre). See also Robinson (1998) and Schulze (2006), who discuss the increasing violence and tactics employed by the Indonesian military to crackdown on GAM.

11 Between the period after the fall of Suharto in 1998 to 2004, Indonesia witnessed four changes of governments; from President Habibie, 1998–1999, President Abdurrahman Wahid, 1999–2001, President Megawati, 2001–2004, to the current president, Susilo Bambang Yudhoyono, from 2004.

12 For more accounts on the role of Henry Dunant Centre on the peace negotiation, see Huber (2004).
13 See Sukma (2004) and Aspinall and Crouch (2003) on the security operation and situation in Aceh after the signing of the Humanitarian Pause.
14 For details of the failure of these negotiations see Aspinall (2005).
15 Aspinall and Crouch (2003) offer a rigorous explanation of the development of peace negotiations between the two parties since the fall of the New Order regime.
16 In the debate about the implementation of Islamic law, some activists in Aceh argue that the decision of the Indonesian government to grant Aceh the right to apply Islamic law is a political strategy to curb independence aspirations that were looming throughout the province following the independence of East Timor in 1999. In 1999, thousands of Acehnese marched to the city of Banda Aceh, demanding a referendum. Aspinall and Crouch (2003, 8) argue that to most Acehnese, 'referendum' was, in fact, a code for 'independence'. For more accounts of the political situation and the referendum movement, see Reid (2003) and Aspinall (2009).
17 See, for example, Aspinall (2005), Sukma (2002) and Schulze (2006).
18 See also Ricklefs (2001), Riddell (2006), Siapno (2002) and Reid (2006).
19 See Lindsey *et al.* (2007).
20 A survey carried out by the Indonesian Survey Foundation (Lembaga Survey Indonesia, LSI) in 2006 showed that about 76.7 per cent of the Acehnese population 'strongly agree' with the imposition of Islamic law in the province while 19.2 per cent agree and only 1.2 per cent disagree (Antara 2006).
21 An-Na'im (2008a) discusses how in the current context of the modern nation-state, sharia can be understood as part of a state's political expression.
22 For another discussion on the political background to Jakarta's decision, see ICG Report (2006).
23 Maryati is affiliated with a women's group that supports the Free Aceh Movement. Among women activists, she is considered as wanting to see Aceh separate from Indonesia.
24 Historical accounts suggest that when Aceh was an Islamic kingdom it was economically strong. For example in the sixteenth and seventeenth centuries it supplied almost half of the world's pepper and it was part of the Indian ocean 'Islamic oecumene' (Reid 2003, 1).
25 This notion of Islam as a sole ideological course and as a symbol of cultural identity and integrity is used by Kandiyoti (1989, 5, cited in Shaheed 1994, 998) to describe the tendency of Muslim countries that look to Islam in coping with social change. In the case of Aceh, Islam has been continuously used to signify Aceh's cultural differences to the rest of the region. See Sjamsuddin (1985).
26 For details on the legal drafting process in Aceh see UNDP Report (no year of publication).
27 See Salim (2006, 196–197), and IDLO Report (no year of publication).
28 According to Bruinessen (1990, 64), the creation of MUI by the New Order in 1975 is to 'translate the government policy into a language that the ummah (the Muslim communities) understands'. For more accounts on the development of *Ulama* Council in Aceh see Kell (1995, 50–52).
29 The Special Region status was granted to Aceh in 1962 as a political compromise following Aceh's Darul Islam rebellion which was launched in 1953 (Sukma 2002, 165; Sjamsuddin 1985). The Special Region status or Daerah Istimewa granted Aceh a broad autonomy in the fields of religion, *adat* (customary law) and education (Sukma 2002, 166).
30 Chapter 5 of Gubernatorial Decree No. 1/2004 explains that Muhtasib are officers at Wilayatul Hisbah who have the authority to receive reports from the people.
31 Benda-Beckman (2009, 219) wrote that the religious courts do not refer directly to the *Qur'an* but rather apply the Compilation of Religious Law, an adapted version

84 *Women and Islamic law in Aceh*

of Islamic law produced by the Indonesian government in 1991. For more on the history of religious courts in Indonesia, see Cammack (1989).

32 For more discussion on background to the sharia courts in Aceh see Bowen (1993), and Morris (1985).

33 Federspiel (1995, 128) defines *khalwat* as engaging in unauthorized contact with the opposite sex. It is usually used in a negative sense as a prohibition on non-married males and females undertaking sexual activity with one another. I found it hard to find an English translation for this term. In many writings, the translation varied from adultery to sexual relations between unmarried parties. The reality is that *khalwat* also means anything from sexual activities outside marriage to a situation where man and woman who do not have kinship relations are in close proximity both in public and private areas. It is considered *khalwat* if, for example, a school boy and girl spend time in a soccer field talking by themselves. It can also be considered *khalwat* if a couple have drink or food at a food stall by themselves. Another interesting interpretation, as some of my informants told me, is that those men and women who ride together on a bike can be considered to be *khalwat*, because they sit close to each other. However, men and women who drive in the car might not be considered *khalwat*, as they are not 'physically close' to each other. Othman (2006, 345) argues that in the Malaysian context, *khalwat* is defined as a sexual offence of being in close proximity between a male and female who are not *muhrim* (a relative or kin whom one cannot marry).

34 Although the provincial parliament has passed this bill, the Governor of Aceh had not signed the bill at the time of writing, as is discussed in the Postscript.

35 From my observation, it has become more popular now in Indonesia for men to have beards as they believe they will be considered more pious and as having more religious knowledge. The beard has thus become part of the religious identity for many Indonesian Muslim men, although others perceive this trend as merely a sign of the 'Arabization' of Islam in Indonesia.

36 It was reported that a local legislator of Lhoksemauwe was charged in violation of *Qanun* No.o 14/2003 on Khalwat, but his case has never been brought to the sharia court. Another member of local parliament of Aceh Tamiang was also in violation of this *Qanun* but he was able to make a deal with the local authorities and so escaped trial (Heryanto 2008).

37 Federspiel (1995, 296) defines *zina* as fornication or any sexual intercourse between persons who are not in a state of legal matrimony or concubinage.

38 Kantor Dinas Syariat Islam Banda Aceh (2008).

39 I interviewed at least three officials at the Wilayatul Hisbah, and all of them agreed that women must wear loose dress and veiling. They felt that the proper form of veiling is for women to cover all their hair, not versions that leave some hair uncovered.

40 Interview, Suraiya Kamaruzzaman, Banda Aceh, 24 December 2007.

41 Interview with Muhammad Yasir, Pagar Air, Aceh Besar, 1 March 2007.

42 Article 28 of *Qanun* No. 14/2003 on Khalwat provides that caning must be carried out in places where people can watch, and must be attended by the public prosecutor and a medical team.

43 Siapno (2002, 26) observes that the popular representation of Tjut Nyak Dhien, the Acehnese women heroine, depicts her 'wearing a "selendang"' (a thin veil) half-covering her head. Other pictures in the Museum of Aceh in Banda Aceh of prominent Acehnese women of former Islamic kingdoms also capture the women wearing only selendang or shawl draped loosely over the head and shoulders.

44 Dr Nurjanah Ismail is a leading academic at the IAIN Ar-Raniry who is also member of MPU. She has become a regular commentator on the implementation of Islamic law and frequently gives speeches in various forums in Aceh.

45 Bowen (2003, 9) defined *Fiqh* as a human effort to resolve disputes by drawing on scripture, logic, the public interest, local custom and the consensus of the community. See Chapter 2 for a discussion of *Fiqh* and sharia.
46 Personal communications when Dr Nurjannah Ismail visited Melbourne in April 2008.
47 See for example Sjamsuddin (1985) and Dijk (1981).

References

Abubakar, Alyasa 2006, *Syariat Islam di Provinsi Nanggroe Aceh Darussalam: Paradigma, Kebijakan dan Kegiatan*, Dinas Syariat Islam Provinsi Nanggroe Aceh Darussalam, Banda Aceh.

Abubakar, Alyasa 2008, *Penerapan syariat Islam di Aceh: Upaya Penyusunan Fiqih dalam Negara Bangsa*, Dinas Syariat Islam Provinsi Nanggroe Aceh Darussalam, Banda Aceh.

Alfian (ed.) 1977, *Segi-segi Sosial Budaya Masyarakat Aceh: Hasil-hasil Penelitian dengan Metode Grounded Research*, LP3ES, Jakarta.

Alfian, Teuku Ibrahim 2005, *Wajah Aceh dalam Lintasan Sejarah*, Gajah Mada University Press, Yogyakarta.

Alfian, Teuku Ibrahim 2006, 'Aceh and the Holy War (Prang Sabil)', in Anthony Reid (ed.), *Verandah of Violence: The Background to the Aceh Problem*, Singapore University Press, Singapore.

An-Na'im, Abdullahi 2008a, *Islam and the Secular State: Negotiating the Future of Sharia*, Harvard University Press, Cambridge, MA.

An-Na'im, Abdullahi 2008b, 'Sharia in the Secular State: A Paradox of Separation and Conflation', in Peri Bearman, Wolfhart Heinrichs and Bernard G. Weiss (eds), *The Law Applied: Contextualizing the Islamic Sharia*, I.B. Tauris, London and New York, pp. 321–341.

Antara 2006, 'Majority of Acehnese People Agree with Plan to Impose Sharia Law', 17 August, viewed September 5, 2006.

Aspinall, Edward 2003, 'Modernity, History and Ethnicity: Indonesian and Acehnese Nationalism in Conflict', in Damien Kingsbury and Harry Aveling (eds), *Autonomy and Disintegration in Indonesia*, RoutledgeCurzon, London and New York, pp. 128–147.

Aspinall, Edward 2004, 'Indonesia: Transformation of Civil Society and Democratic Breakthrough', in Muthiah Alagappa (ed.), *Civil Society and Political Change in Asia*, Stanford University Press, California, pp. 61–96.

Aspinall, Edward 2005, *Opposing Soeharto: Compromise, Resistance and Regime Change in Indonesia*, Stanford University Press, California.

Aspinall, Edward 2006, 'Violence and Identity Formation in Aceh under Indonesian Rule', in Anthony Reid (ed.), *Verandah of Violence*, ISEAS, Singapore, pp. 149–176.

Aspinall, Edward 2007, 'Peace without Justice? The Helsinki Peace Process in Aceh', A report published by Center for Humanitarian Dialogue, Switzerland, Geneva.

Aspinall, Edward 2009, *Islam and Nation: Separatist Rebellion in Aceh, Indonesia*, Stanford University Press, California.

Aspinall, Edward and Crouch, Harold 2003, 'The Aceh Peace Process: Why it Failed', *Policy Studies*, East West Center Washington, Washington, DC.

Azra, Azyumari 2004, 'Political Islam in Post-Suharto Indonesia', in Virginia Matheson Hooker and Amin Saikal (eds), *Islamic Perspectives on the New Millennium*, Institute of Southeast Asian Studies, Singapore, pp. 133–149.

BBC News 2003a, 'Aceh Sharia Court Opens', 4 March, available at: http://news.bbc.co.uk/go/pr/fr/-/2/hi/asia-pacific/2816785.stm (accessed 20 November 2007).

BBC News 2003b, 'First Sharia Court for Aceh', 26 February, available at: http://news.bbc.co.uk/2/low/asia-pacific/2801537.html (accessed 25 November 2009).

Benda-Beckman, Keebet von 2009, 'Balancing Islam, Adat and the State: Comparing Islamic and Civil Courts in Indonesia', in Franz von Benda-Beckman, Keebet von Benda-Beckman and Anne Griffiths (eds), *The Power of Law in a Transnational World*, Berghahn Books, United States, pp. 216–235.

Bowen, John R. 1993, *Muslims through Discourse*, Princeton University Press, Princeton.

Bowen, John R. 1996, 'Religion in the Proper Sense of the Word: Law and Civil Society in Islamicist Discourse', *Anthopology Today*, August, pp. 12–14.

Bowen, John R. 2003, *Islam, Law and Equality in Indonesia: Anthropology of Public Reasoning*, Cambridge University Press, Cambridge.

Bruinessen, Martin van 1990, 'Indonesia's Ulama and Politics: Caught between Legitimising the Status Quo and Searching for Alternatives', *Prisma: The Indonesian Indicator*, Jakarta, no. 49, pp. 52–69.

Bungong 2007, 'Farida Handayani: Tidak Ada Guna Uang Selama Hati Terluka', no. XI I December.

Burhanuddin, Mohamad. 2012. *Inilah wawancara dengan Zaini Abdullah*, 22 April, available at: http://nasional.kompas.com/read/2012/04/22/19392764/Inilah.Wawancara.Kompas.dengan.Zaini.Abdullah (accessed 10 October 2013).

Bustamam-Ahmad, Kamaruzzaman 2007, 'The Application of Islamic Law in Indonesia: The Case Study of Aceh', *Journal of Indonesian Islam*, vol. 1, no. 1, pp. 135–180.

Cammack, Mark 1989, 'Islamic Law in Indonesia's New Order', *International and Comparative Law Quarterly*, vol. 38, no. 1, pp. 53–73.

Crouch, Melissa 2009, 'Religious Regulations in Indonesia: Failing Vulnerable Groups', *Review of Indonesia and Malaysian Affairs*, vol. 43, no. 2, pp. 53–103.

Danial 2007, 'Pelaksanaan Syari'at Islam dan Kekerasan di Nanggroe Aceh Darussalam', *The Aceh Institute*, Banda Aceh.

Dijk, C. van 1981, *Rebellion under the Banner of Islam: The Darul Islam in Indonesia*, Nijhof, The Hague.

Federspiel, Howard 1995, *A Dictionary of Indonesian Islam*, Ohio University, Athens, OH.

Federspiel, Howard 1998, 'Islamic Values, Law and Expectations in Contemporary Indonesia', *Islamic Law and Society*, vol. 5, no. 1, pp. 90–116.

Feener, Michael R. 2012, 'Social Engineering through Sharia: Islamic Law and State-Directed Da'wa in Contemporary Aceh', *Islamic Law and Society*, pp. 275–311.

Feener, Michael 2013, 'Social Engineering through Sharia: Islamic Law and State-Directed Da'wa in Contemporary Aceh', *Islamic Law and Society*, vol. 19, pp. 275–311.

Hedman, Eva-Lotta 2004a, 'Aceh Under Martial Law: Conflict, Violence and Displacement, a Day of Analysis, Refugee Studies Center', Working Paper, vol. 24, University of Oxford.

Hedman, Eva-Lotta 2004b, 'Resumption of Martial Law in Aceh', *Forced Migration Review*, issue 19, p. 54, available at: www.fmreview.org/FMRpdfs/FMR19/FMR19full.pdf (accessed 20 August 2006).

Hefner, Robert W. (ed.) 2001, *The Politics of Multiculturalism: Pluralism and Citizenship in Malaysia, Singapore and Indonesia*, University of Hawaii Press, Honolulu.

Hefner, Robert W. 2009, 'Aceh: Indonesia: Securing the Insecure State', by Elizabeth F. Drexler, reviewed in *American Ethnologist*, vol. 36, no. 1, pp. 195–196.

Hefner, Robert 2011. *Shari'a Politics: Islamic Law and Society in the Modern World*, Indiana University Press, Bloomington.

Heryanto, Dadang 2008, 'Sekali lagi, Cerita Khalwat di Negeri Syariat', *Modus Aceh*, no. 6, available at: www.modusaceh-news.com (accessed 24 June 2008).

Hooker, M.B. 1983, 'Muhammadan Law and Islamic Law', in M.B. Hooker (ed.), *Islam in South-East Asia*, E.J. Brill, Leiden, pp. 160–182.

Hooker, M.B. 2008, *Indonesian Syariah: Defining a National School of Islamic Law*, Institute of Southeast Asian Studies, Singapore.

Hooker, M.B. and Lindsey, Tim 2002, 'Public Faces of Syariah in Contemporary Indonesia: Towards a National Mazhab?', *Australian Journal of Asian Law*, vol. 4, issue 3, pp. 259–293.

Huber, Konrad 2004, 'The HDC in Aceh: Promises and Pitfalls of NGO Mediation and Implementation', *Policy Studies*, no. 9, East West Center, Washington, DC.

Hurgronje, Snouck C. 1906, *The Acehnese*, trans. A.W.S. O'Sullivan, vol. I, E.J. Brill, Leiden.

ICG Report 2001, 'Aceh: Can Autonomy Stem the Conflict', *Asia Report*, no. 18, available at: www.crisisgroupd.org (accessed 20 February 2006).

ICG Report 2006, 'Islamic Law and Criminal Justice in Aceh', *Asia Report*, July, no. 117, available at: www.crisisgroup.org (accessed 25 August 2006).

IDLO Report n.d., 'Guardianship, Inheritance and Land Law in Post-Tsunami Aceh', available at: www.idlo.int/publications/19.pdf (accessed 2 January 2010).

The Jakarta Post 2012, 'Aceh Teen's Suicide Linked to Sharia Practice', 14 September, available at: www.thejakartapost.com/news/2012/09/14/aceh-teen-s-suicide-linked-sharia-practice.html (accessed 20 April 2013).

Johnson, Troy 2007, 'Voices from Aceh: Perspectives on Syariat Law', *SEARC Working Papers Series*, The University of Hong Kong.

Kamaruzzaman, Suraiaya 1999, *Hak Asasi Manusia dan Kekerasan Terhadap Perempuan di Aceh*, Ureca, Banda Aceh.

Kamaruzzaman, Suraiaya 2000, 'Women and the War in Aceh: Those Women Want to Silence All the Guns, Whether Indonesian or Acehnese', *Inside Indonesia*, vol. 64, available at: www.insideindonesia.org/content/view/521/29 (accessed 2 April 2009).

Kamaruzzaman, Suraiya 2004, 'Women and Syariah in Aceh: Aceh's Women find themselves between an Armed Conflict and Islamic Law', *Inside Indonesia*, no. 79, available at: www.insideindonesia.org/feature-editions/women-and-syariah-in-aceh (accessed 10 January 2008).

Kamaruzzaman, Suraiaya 2006, 'Violence, Internal Displacement and its Impact on the Women of Aceh', in Charles A. Coppel (ed.), *Violent Conflicts in Indonesia: Analysis, Representation, Resolution*, Routledge, London and New York, pp. 258–268.

Keddie, Nikki 2007, *Women in the Middle East: Past and Present*, Princeton University Press, Princeton.

Kell, Tim 1995, *The Roots of Acehnese Rebellion 1989–1992*, Cornell Modern Indonesia Project, Southeast Asia Program, Cornell University, Ithaca, New York.

Laffan, Michael 2003, 'The Tangled Roots of Islamist Activism in Southeast Asia', *Cambridge Review of International Affairs*, vol. 16, no. 3, pp. 397–414.

Lindsey, Tim 2008, 'When Words Fail: Syariah Law in Indonesia: Revival, Reform or Transplantation?', in Penelope Nicholson and Sarah Biddulph (eds), *Examining*

Practice, Interrogating Theory: Comparative Legal Studies in Asia, Martinus Nijhoff Publisher, Leiden, pp. 195–222.

Lindsey, Tim, and Hooker, M.B. 2007, 'Sharia Revival in Aceh', in R. Michael Feener and Mark E. Cammack (eds), *Islamic Law in Contemporary Indonesia: Ideas and Institutions*, Islamic Legal Studies Program, Harvard Law School, Cambridge, MA, pp. 216–254.

Lindsey, Tim and Kingsley, J. 2008, 'Talking in Code: Legal Islamisation in Indonesia and the MMI Sharia Criminal Code', in Peri Bearman, Wolfhart Heinrichs and Bernard G. Weiss (eds), *The Law Applied: Contextualizing the Islamic Sharia: A Vol. in Honor of Frank E. Voge*, I.B. Tauris and Company, London, pp. 295–320.

McGibbon, Rodd 2004, 'Secessionist Challenge in Aceh and Papua: Is Special Autonomy the Solution?', *Policy Studies*, no. 10, East-West Center Washington, Washington, DC.

Miller, Michelle Ann 2004, 'The Nanggroe Aceh Darussalam Law: A Serious Response to Acehnese Separatism?', *Asian Ethnicity*, vol. 5, no. 3, pp. 333–351.

Miller, Michelle Ann 2009, *Rebellion and Reform in Indonesia: Jakarta's Security and Autonomy Policies in Aceh*, Routledge, New York.

Morris, Eric, 1985, 'Aceh: Social Revolution and the Islamic Vision', in Audrey R. Kahin (ed.), *Regional Dynamics of the Indonesian Revolution: Unity from Diversity*, University of Hawaii Press, Honolulu, pp. 83–110.

Natahadibrata, Nadya 2013, 'Domestic Violence on the Rise in Aceh', *The Jakarta Post*, 5 June, available at: www.thejakartapost.com/news/2013/06/05/domestic-violence-rise-aceh.html (accessed February 2014).

Othman, Norani 2006, 'Muslim Women and the Challenge of Islamic Fundamentalism/ Extremism: An Overview of Southeast Asian Muslim Women's Struggle for Human Rights and Gender Equality', *Women's Studies International Forum*, vol. 29, pp. 339–353.

Pasandaran, Camelia 2013, 'North Aceh Head Bans Women from Dancing in Public', *The Jakarta Globe*, 26 May, available at: www.thejakartaglobe.com/news/north-aceh-head-bans-women-from-dancing-in-public-2/ (accessed 20 April 2014).

Rakyat Aceh Online 2007, 'Raihan: Apa Maunya Komnas Perempuan? Soal Hukum Cambuk', 27 January, available at: www.rakyataceh.com/print.php?newsid=1416 (accessed 5 July 2007).

Reid, Anthony 1979, *The Blood of the People: Revolution and the End of Traditional Rule in Northern Sumatra*, Oxford University Press, Kuala Lumpur and New York.

Reid, Anthony 2003, 'War, Peace and the Burden of History in Aceh', *Asia Research Institute Working Paper Series*, ARI, Singapore.

Reid, Anthony (ed.) 2006, *Verandah of Violence: The Background to the Aceh Problem*, Institute of Southeast Asian Studies, Singapore.

Ricklefs, M.C. 2001, *A History of Modern Indonesia since c.1200*, Palgrave, Basingstoke.

Riddell, Peter G. 2006, 'Aceh in the Sixteenth and Seventeenth Centuries: "Serambi Mekkah and Identity"', in Anthony Reid (ed.), *Verandah of Violence: The Background to the Aceh Problem*, National University Press, Singapore, pp. 38–51.

Robinson, Geoffrey 1998, 'Rawan is as Rawan Does: The Origins of Disorder in New Order Aceh', *Indonesia*, vol. 66, pp. 127–157.

Salim, Arskal 2006, 'Islamising Indonesian Laws? Legal and Political Dissonance in Indonesian Sharia 1945–2005', PhD Thesis, University of Melbourne, Melbourne.

Salim, Arskal 2009, 'Islam and Modernity: Syariah, Terrorism and Governance in Southeast Asia', *ARC Federation Fellowship*. Melbourne: Melbourne Law School.

Salim, Arskal and Nurlaelawati, Euis 2009, *Demi Keadilan dan Kesetaraan: Dokumentasi Program Sensitivitas Jender Hakim Agama di Indonesia*, PUSKUMHAM, Jakarta.

Saragih, B.T. and Simanjuntak, Hotli 2013, 'Aceh City to Ban Women from Straddling Motorbikes', *The Jakarta Post*, 30 January, available at: www.thejakartapost.com/news/2013/01/03/aceh-city-ban-women-straddling-motorbikes.html (accessed 8 May 2013).

Schulze, Kirsten E. 2004, 'The Free Aceh Movement (GAM): Anatomy of a Separatist Organization', *Policy Studies*, vol. 2, East-West Center, Washington, DC.

Schulze, Kirsten E. 2006, 'Insurgency and Counter-Insurgency: Strategy and the Aceh Conflict, October 1976–May 2004', in Anthony Reid (ed.), *Verandah of Violence: The Background to the Aceh Problem*, National University Press, Singapore, pp. 225–271.

Schulze, Kirsten E. 2007, 'From the Battlefield to the Negotiating Table: GAM and the Indonesian Government 1999–2005', *Asian Security*, vol. 3, no. 2, p. 80.

Serambi Indonesia 2005, 'Tim Terpadu Masuk Salon dan Lancarkan Razia Jilbab', 20 May, available at: www.serambinews.com (accessed 9 January 2006).

Serambi Indonesia 2006a, 'Hasil Polling Yayasan Keumala. Syaria Islam hanya untuk Masyarakat Kecil', 27 July, available at: www.serambinews.com/old/index.php?aksi =bacaberita&rubrik=5&topik=48&beritaid=19183 (accessed 30 July 2006).

Serambi Indonesia 2006b, 'Imbauan KPU: Umat Islam Diimbau tak ikuti Polling YICM', 28 December, available at: www.serambinews.com/old/cetak.php/ (accessed 25 January 2007).

Serambi Indonesia 2006c, 'Mengawal RUU-PA sampai ke Ibukota', 25 January, available at: www. (accessed 26 January 2006).

Serambi Indonesia 2006d, 'Operasi Jilbab di Dewantara: Puluhan Perempuan Terjaring', *Serambi Pase*, 6 September.

Serambi Indonesia 2006e, 'Qanun Khalwat, Maisir dan Khamar perlu direvisi', *Serambi Pase*, 20 December, available at: http://serambinews.com/cetak. php?aksi=cetak&beritaid=23331 (accessed 10 January 2007).

Serambi Indonesia 2006f, 'Umat Islam Diimbau tak Ikuti Polling YICM', *Serambi*, 28 December, available at: www.serambinews.com (accessed 20 January 2007).

Serambi Indonesia 2006g, 'Warga Petanyakan Vonis Khalwat Anggota Dewan', *Serambi Pase*, 4 August, available at: www.serambinews.com (accessed 10 August 2006).

Serambi Indonesia 2007, 'Konferensi Internasional berakhir: Lembaga Riset disepakati', 28 February, available at: www.serambinews.com (accessed 29 February 2007).

Serambi Indonesia 2008, 'Kasus Mesum Kepala PLN Calang: Pelaku di Kenai Denda Adat Rp. 5 Juta', 3 June, available at: www.serambinews.com (accessed 3 June 2008).

Serambi Indonesia 2009a, 'Api Sekam Qanun Jinayah', *Anjong*, 29 October, available at: http://serambinews.com/news/view/16616/api-sekam-qanun-jinayah (accessed 30 October 2009).

Serambi Indonesia 2009b, 'Bupati Aceh Barat Larang Perempuan Bercelana Panjang: Celana Ketat akan Digunting', 27 October, available at: www.serambinews. com/news/view/16482/bupati-aceh-barat-larang-perempuan-bercelana-panjang (accessed 27 October 2009).

Serambi Indonesia 2009c, 'Penduduk Aceh Capai 4.67 Juta Jiwa', *Utama*, 16 April, available at: http://serambinews.com/news/view/2711/penduduk-aceh-capai-4-67-juta-jiwa (accessed 20 June 2009).

Serambi Indonesia 2009d. 'Pasca Tsunami, kendaraan di Aceh tambah 100, 932 unit', 13 May, available at: http.//serambinews.com/news/pascatsunami-kendaraan-di-aceh-tambah-100-932-unit (accessed 13 May 2009).

Serambi Indonesia 2010a, 'Gubernur: Cukup Aceh Barat Saja yang Bikin Qanun soal Rok', *Utama*, 9 March, available at: www.serambinews.com/news/view/25804/cukup-aceh-barat-saja-yang-bikin-qanun-soal-rok (accessed 10 March 2010).

Serambi Indonesia 2010b, 'Gugat Cerai Tinggi Karena Emosional tak Terkendali', 18 January, available at: www.serambinews.com/news/view/22049/gugat-cerai-tinggi-karena-emosional-tak-terkendali (accessed 23 March 2010).

Serambi Indonesia 2010c, 'Peringati Hari Perempuan Seduina: Aktivis Minta Pemerintah Peduli Gender', *Kutaraja*, 9 March, available at: www.serambinews.com/news/view/25794/aktivis-minta-pemerintah-peduli-gender (accessed 23 March 2010).

Serambi Indonesia 2010d, 'Tiga Oknum WH diduga Perkosa Tahanan', *Utama*, 10 January, available at: http://m.serambinews.com/news/view/21459/tiga-oknum-wh-diduga-perkosa-tahanan (accessed 11 January 2010).

Shafira 2004, *Ketika GAM Merenggut Segalanya*, Pena, Jakarta.

Shaheed, Farida 1994, 'Controlled or Autonomous: Identity and the Experience of the Network, Women Living under Muslim Laws', *Signs*, vol. 19, issue 4, pp. 997–1019.

Siapno, Jacqueline 2002, *Gender, Islam, Nationalism and the State in Aceh: The Paradox of Power, Co-optation and Resistance*, Routledge, London.

Siegel, James T. 2000, *The Rope of God*, The University of Michigan Press, Ann Arbor.

Siegel, James T. 2005, 'Peduli Aceh', *Indonesia*, April, no. 79, pp. 165–167.

Siregar, Hasnil Basri 2008, 'Islamic Law in a National Legal System: A Study on the Implementation of Shari'ah in Aceh, Indonesia', *Asian Journal of Comparative Law*, The Berkeley Electronic Press, pp. 1–28.

Sjamsuddin, Nazaruddin 1985, *Republican Revolt: A Study of the Acehnese Rebellion*, Institute of Southeast Asian Studies, Singapore.

Smith, Anthony L. 2002, 'Aceh: Democratic Times, Authoritarian Solutions', *New Zealand Journal of Asian Studies*, vol. 4, issue 2, pp. 68–89.

Sukma, Rizal 2002, 'Seccesionist Challenge in Aceh: Problems and Prospects', in Hadi Soesastro, Anthony L. Smith and Mui Ling Han (eds), *Governance in Indonesia: Challenges Facing Megawati Presidency*, Institute of Southeast Asian Studies, Singapore, pp. 165–181.

Sukma, Rizal 2004, 'Security Operations in Aceh: Goals, Consequences and Lessons', *Policy Studies*, no. 3, East West Center, Washington, DC.

Sulistiyanto, Priyambudi 2001, 'Wither Aceh?', *Third World Quarterly*, vol. 22, no. 3, pp. 437–452.

Suryadi 2009, 'Cambuk Hilang, Togel Kambuh Lagi', *Tabloid Berita Mingguan Modus Aceh: Kriminal*, November, no. 28/2009, available at: www.modusaceh.com/html/read/kriminal/2056/cambuk_hilang_togel_kambuh_lagi.html/ (accessed 2 March 2010).

Suryakusuma, Julia and Lindsey, T. 2006, 'Porn Bill: Autonomy means Repression against Women', *Jakarta Post*, 4 January, available at: www.thejakartapost.com (accessed 20 January 2006).

Suwondo, K. 2002, 'Decentralization in Indonesia', *International Non-Government Organization Forum on Indonesian Development (INFID) Annual Advocacy 2002*, available at: www.infid.be/INFID%20Background%102002%20pdf (accessed 25 March 2007).

Syafputri, Ella 2013, 'Tahun ini DPR Aceh loloskan 18 Qanun', *Antara News*, 28 December, available at: www.antaranews.com/berita/411490/tahun-ini-dpr-aceh-loloskan-18-qanun (accessed 2 February 2014).

Tempo interaktif 2010, 'Polisi Syariah yang Memperkosa Kabur', 19 January, available at: www.tempo.co/read/news/2010/01/19/063219947/Polisi-Syariah-yang-Memperkosa-Kabur (accessed 20 August 2011).

Tribun News 2014, 'Warga relat celana ketatnya disemprot cat diganti sarung', 23 January, available at: www.tribunnews.com/regional/2014/01/23/warga-rela-celana-ketatnya-disemprot-cat (accessed 25 January 2014).

UNDP Report 2006, *Access to Justice in Aceh: Making the Transition to Sustainable Peace and Development in Aceh, Indonesia*.

Usman, Syaiku 2001, 'Indonesia's Decentralization Policy: Initial Experiences and Emerging Problems', *EUROSEAS Conference*, September, London.

3 Gender and women's movements in Aceh

Introduction

Women organize into women's movements on the basis of their gender identity and gender interests (Beckwith 2007, 313). Identity signifies the notion of otherness while it creates shared norms, values and ways of thinking within particular individuals and communities (Cooke 2007, 140). Identity is not static: it constantly changes and is shaped by different causes from religion, nationality, ethnicity, race, age, profession and gender (Cooke 2007, 140).

The identity of Acehnese women and gender relations in Acehnese society are important aspects to understand women's movements in Aceh. The identity of Acehnese women is shaped by Aceh's history, the three decades of conflict with the Indonesian military, the recent application of Islamic law, and the devastation caused by the tsunami, which all contribute to the emergence and development of women's NGOs, women's organizations and women's movements. Women's movements in Aceh have tried to advance women's status and women's gender interests by referring, in many cases, to Aceh's 'glorious past', in which Islam played an important role in the lives of the Acehnese. The social and political developments in Aceh have shifted the focus of women's movements from the struggles on economic, social and cultural rights to those that touch issues on equality, non-discrimination, civil and political rights. The discourse on equality, non-discrimination and rights has risen as local women's activists engage with the broader women's movements at the national level.

The signing of the Helsinki peace agreement in 2005 paved the way for a freer political environment, providing Acehnese women more opportunity to engage in wider civil society movements. Women are increasingly organized themselves into women's organizations, developing women's movements and participating in democratic reform. The development of women's movements in Aceh has progressed in part because of the availability of the support from, and access to the networks of, both national and international women's movements.

Women's identity and gender relations in Aceh

Aceh has a long history of war against colonial powers. It launched its war against the Dutch in 1873 (Reid 2005, 267; Ricklefs 1993, 145–146; Ricklefs

2001, 185–188). In the 1950s, Aceh embarked on a new military conflict against the newly-independent Republic of Indonesia (Sjamsuddin 1985). The 1950s rebellion was ignited by the dissolution of Aceh as a province in January 1951 and its incorporation into North Sumatra province (Sjamsuddin 1985, 47). In addition, the fact that the independent Indonesia had adopted a secular ideology instead of Islam as the basis of the state strengthened the cause of rebellion. Although the rebellion was inspired by a demand that Indonesia be ruled by Islamic law, the rebels did not seek the separation of Aceh from Indonesia (Aspinall 2007; Sukma 2004; Dijk 1981). This conflict finally ended when the Indonesian government granted Aceh 'Special Region' status in 1957, which gave the Acehnese the authority to regulate education, religion and customary law based on Islam (Sjamsuddin 1985; Reid 1979; Morris 1985).

Throughout the history of Aceh, Islam has played a major role in shaping the character of Aceh's identity. The Acehnese identify themselves as Muslims and that it is 'not possible' for an Acehnese not to be a Muslim (Aspinall 2007, 247–248). The strong identification of Acehnese with Islam is due to several reasons, including the fact that Aceh was an important power in the Malacca Straits in the sixteenth century, and became a centre of Islamic learning and trade in the archipelago (Aspinall 2007, 247). Islam is also believed to be part of the spirit that united both the Acehnese and the rest of Indonesia in their fight against the Dutch (1873–1903).

Various accounts suggest that throughout the pre-colonial history of Aceh, women had high social status, in both public and private spaces. Aceh's cultural tradition places women in respected positions in the family structure and in the public domain. Reid (1988, 635), for example, reported several seventeenth-century accounts of Acehnese women (including those who occupied the throne during the period of the Islamic kingdom) being involved in trade and commercial activities. Sultan Iskandar Muda, likewise, employed about 3,000 women to work in his palace, with some undertaking the role of bodyguard. It is also suggested that the autocratic ruler, Sultan al-Mukammil (1584–1604) elected a woman, Laksamana Kamalahayati, to be the commander of the navy (Davis 1600, 50, cited in Reid 1988, 638). Moreover, it has been claimed that some 16 women in the history of Aceh made significant contributions to public decision-making, both before and after Aceh began its wars against the Dutch in 1873 (Noerdin 2007). This story of the role of women in Aceh's past is well understood and circulated widely, giving Acehnese women young and old some sense of pride of their place in the society.

The first woman to lead Aceh was Sultana Taj al-'Alam al-Din Shah (1641–1675), the daughter of Sultan Iskandar Muda. After her, three female leaders ruled Aceh: Sri Sultan Nur al-'alam Nakiyat al-Din Shah, from 1675 to 1678; Sultana Inayat Shah Zakiyat al-Din Shah from 1678 to 1688; and Sultana Kamalat Shah from 1688 to 1699 (Riddell 2006, 41–42; Siapno 2002, 51; Ricklefs 2001, 40). Female leadership only became impossible in the kingdom after a *fatwa*[1] was issued by the 'Sheriff of Mecca' in Saudi Arabia, which stated that a woman could not become a sultan or a leader, as that would be un-Islamic (Riddell 2006, 42). This *fatwa* ended Sultana Kamalat Shah's leadership in 1699. Later, when Aceh started its fight against the Dutch colonial government,[2] at least four Acehnese women took part in the war in leadership roles: Tjut Nyak Dhien, Cut Mutia, Teuku Fakinah and Pocut Bahren (Siapno 2002, 59). All these historical accounts have, according to Amir (2002, 46), created images that Acehnese women are 'heroic'. The images of Acehnese women as heroic in fighting against colonial power are also depicted in the history books at Indonesian schools.

The high status of women in Southeast Asia has been well covered by scholars in the field (Andaya 1995; Reid 1988; Boserup 1970). Reid (1988, 146) for example, has suggested that 'the comparatively high status of women in the social system is distinctively Southeast Asian'. The high status of women in the pre-modern history of Southeast Asia was also due to women's control over economic resources, because society highly valued the work of women and the influence of indigenous religious beliefs, which emphasized women's participation (Andaya 1995, 166–167). Although women in Southeast Asia have been historically recognized as having high status, in the case of Indonesia it is not easy for women to enter the public political arena and articulate their needs and concerns to the state (Blackburn 2004, 6).[3] This is because gender relations between men and women in Indonesia are constructed by beliefs and practices based on the 'appropriate' behaviour and treatment of men and women (Blackburn 2004, 3).

As regards women's status in Aceh, local Acehnese believe that throughout history Acehnese women enjoyed high status and respected positions in society. According to him, this was because Islamic teaching recognizes gender equality between men and women. A noted Acehnese historian, Hasbi Amiruddin, confirmed this depiction by saying that it is indeed Islam that lays the basic foundation for gender relations in Aceh, guaranteeing Acehnese women equal opportunities with men in exercising their public and private roles (Amiruddin 2004).

Exploring the complexity of gender representation in rural Aceh by looking at Aceh's oral traditions, Siapno explained that gender roles are plural in the everyday lives of rural Acehnese society (Siapno 2002, 91). For example, she discussed an oral story, 'Pak Pande', which describes how Acehnese females perform all the men's jobs, including being heads of households and guardians of Islamic identity, as men are incapable of doing these jobs. According to Siapno (2002, 91), this story shows that in the everyday lives of rural Acehnese, there are complex representations of gender roles that to a certain extent contradict Islamic norms regarding men and women's roles in domestic relations as one interpretation of Islam is that women cannot be leaders in domestic relations.

In reporting anthropological work he conducted during the 1960s, Siegel (2000, 139–140) has described the position of women in the family structure in Aceh. He described how Acehnese women enjoyed certain privileges in their households. According to him, Acehnese women had authority to rule their household, and the right to make decisions in the family. Women's positions in their households, according to Siegel, relate to traditional practices by which the houses where women and their husbands live were the gift of the women's parents (Reid 1988; Siegel 2000; Siapno 2002; Jayawardena 1977). Thus, the house was considered to be the property of the woman. According to tradition, Acehnese parents gave their daughter a house at the time of their daughter's marriage and the house later legally became the full property of the daughter. Other than ownership of the house, a married woman also has ownership over the rice field that she and her husband work. This is due to the spatial mobility of men who often travel outside their villages for trade.[4] While their husbands are away, women are responsible for managing their fields. To help with the harvest, the wife usually hires labourers to work the rice fields. The wives also controlled the money earned from selling the harvest (Siegel 2000, 143–145). In short, Siegel (2000, 145) wrote that 'regardless of ownership of land, control of it is given to women'.

The fact that women spent most of their time in the village, Jayawardena (1977, 159) argues, made women the 'fixed point of reference' in the social organization of village life in Aceh. According to Siapno (2000, 279), this relative power and the autonomy that women have in terms of ownership of land, control of the household, family and local village affairs have given women (be they mothers, grandmothers or older sisters) the privilege of dominant power in all important family decisions. It is this tradition that, according to Siapno, has meant Acehnese women do not suffer the same anxieties as women elsewhere in Indonesia.

In terms of marriage, Acehnese women also had freedom to choose their spouses. Siegel says that although parents often arrange marriages in Aceh,[5] an Acehnese woman had a veto if she did not like the man they chose, and could refuse to go through with the marriage (Siegel 2000, 165). In Acehnese tradition, both men and women have their own ideas about the kind of person they want to be their husband or wife. In married life, women were the ones with the authority and decision-making power for the whole family. The husband who often left the house to travel and trade did not have the right to participate in making decisions (Siegel 2000, 178). This is because, as Siegel (2000, 178) noted:

> From the women's point of view, the family consists of the people who occupy the house compound – themselves, their sisters, mothers and children – and their husbands have no place and hence no right to make decisions.

According to Siapno (2002), what Siegel described above is Aceh's matrifocal *adat*, whereby women's places are at the centre of the family, a culture that contradicts Islamic values that emphasize men's position as head of the household, performing the role of a father and husband. This matrifocal *adat,* according to Siapno, has been increasingly challenged, in particular by attempts to revive Islam and strengthen *adat* based on Islamic teachings. Siapno (2002, 37) wrote:

> Islam and Islamic culture achieved hegemonic status in Aceh, but within this hegemony there are opposing forms of Islam; on the one hand is the traditionalist Islam practiced syncretically with matrifocal (mother-centred and woman-centered) *adat.* On the other hand is modernist Islam with strong attempts at purification – the removal of practices such as matrifocal *adat* (e.g. women as head of the family) which supposedly conflict with 'pure' Islam.

The role and high status of Acehnese women can also be seen in the colonial period. During the fight against the colonial occupation, Tjut Nyak Dien became a symbol of women's resistance (Reid 2006, 101). She heroically led the fighting after the death of her husband, Teuku Uma. Tjut Nyak Dien was not the only woman involved in the fight for Aceh's liberation. Based on archival accounts from 1905 to 1930, she found that many Acehnese women were involved in the fighting against the Dutch and a significant number were killed (Siapno 2002, 25–27). Unfortunately, their names were not recorded in reports, as most of these women were not recognized as individuals but were listed under the name of their husband or fathers or brothers. This happened because women at that time wore the same clothing as men, a pair of black trousers and a traditional *baju kurung,* which made it difficult for the Dutch police to identify them (Siapno 2002, 26).

It can therefore be understood why many Acehnese that I talked with during my research (including Acehnese women) rejected the portrayal of Acehnese women as oppressed and discriminated against, both in public and family structures. Even Acehnese women activists were adamant that Aceh's past was not one of oppression or discrimination against women. Many of them also referred to their experiences with their own families, which were not gender-biased, they said.

The International Development Law Organization (IDLO), one of the internationally based NGOs that came to Aceh after the tsunami, praised the role of women in Acehnese society in their regular posts on the local media (*Serambi Indonesia,* 19 April 2008). One IDLO article (2008) even argued explicitly that the portrayal of Acehnese women as subordinated and discriminated against is misleading. The article contends that in reality Acehnese women are not less powerful than men. The article went on to emphasize the fact that from both an Islamic and an Acehnese legal perspective, women are not typically subordinated and have usually shared equal rights and responsibilities with men. To support its argument the article quoted a statement made by the leader of the Consultative Council of *Ulama* (Majelis Permusyawaratan *Ulama* or MPU), Professor Tgk Muslim Ibrahim, who argued that 'Islam perceives men and women equal', quoting a *Hadith* which says that 'heaven is under your mother's feet'. For him, IDLO argues, this *Hadith* clearly demonstrates how Islam respects and reveres women, and that Islam does not allow women to be the subject of discrimination. Given what he said, in reality Ibrahim is not pro-woman, in particular when it comes to women's clothing. He is of the view that women must ensure that their clothing does not show their body shape (*Serambi Indonesia*, 4 November 2009). The attitude of the MPU towards women in Aceh is described in more detail in Chapter 2.

The Deputy Governor of Aceh, Muhammad Nazar, has similarly argued that women have always been given respected positions in decision-making. In front of hundreds of women from different districts in the province who attended a conference organized by the Australian NGO, LOGICA-AIPRD, in collaboration with BRR and local women's NGO Beungung Jeumpa on 8 March 2007, the Deputy Governor used Aceh's history to show that Acehnese women enjoyed equal opportunities with men, as some women gloriously led the wars against the colonial powers. He argued that women's high status in Acehnese society is due to Islam, which he said has become 'the Acehnese way of life'. By saying this, he denied allegations that Islam causes women's subordination. He contended that Acehnese women only encountered discrimination and subordination after Aceh joined the Indonesian Republic and that this only became worse when the New Order was in power and women became targets of exploitation and state violence.

Despite this historical background and the defensive narrative pertaining to the status of women and the gender relations in the society described above, the reality is that representation of women in the public domain remains minimal in contemporary Aceh. Safril (2008), for example, observes that in 2008 there were only two women serving as policy-makers in the government offices, out of a total of 74 high-ranking officials. Of about 6,000 villages across the province, only six were led by women. In legal matters, there were only four women judges in the provincial *Syari'at* court and none at the *Mahkamah Syari'at* or the sharia court. There were only 15 Islamic women judges in the *Mahkamah Syari'at* of a total of 138 Islamic judges. At the administrative level, there were only 145 women working at the BRR, the Bureau for Reconstruction and Rehabilitation, of 1,219 employees. Safril (2008) also noted that the commitment of the local government to make women's issues a priority is questionable, as the allocated budget for women's welfare and children was only about 0.82 per cent of the total reconstruction budget in the first year of the reconstruction period following the tsunami, and reduced to 0.045 per cent in the second year. Arabiyani Abubakar, the manager of the Women and Children unit at BRR, mentioned that her unit was allocated IDR 55 million in 2005, IDR 65 million in 2006, IDR 45 million in 2007 and IDR 6 million in 2007 (interview, Banda Aceh, 15 December 2007). In the area of education, no women have ever reached the highest position (that of Rector) at the two public higher educational institutions in Aceh, the Syiah Kuala University and IAIN Ar-Raniry (Inayatillah 2009).

In 2007, a local women's NGO, RPUK (Relawan Perempuan Untuk Kemanusiaan or Women Volunteers for Humanity) conducted research aiming to look at gender equality in the agriculture, irrigation and fisheries sectors. The research found that women's earning capacity is destroyed when machines take various agricultural jobs, because development projects force mass production. During conflict, women's roles in the public economic sphere were also much diminished, due to the absence of a supportive security system to protect women, which prevented women from travelling from home to their fields and to sell their harvest in markets. Agriculture has historically been one of the main forms of women's economic activities in Aceh.

In her research on gender representations of male and female lecturers at the State Institute for Islamic Studies, IAIN Ar-Raniry, Inayatillah (2009, 5) found a lower involvement of women. Inayatillah argues this happens because of the bias of institutional regulations, women's 'double burden' (to contribute to the family income and to take care of the children), and the patriarchal culture of the society. To become a lecturer at IAIN, the regulation requires a postgraduate degree, but the opportunities for men and women to access higher education are not equal. In the 1950s and 1960s, she says, many Acehnese had to travel to other areas (in particular Java or West Sumatra) to access higher education due to the absence of good educational institutions in the province and the fear caused by frequent military conflict. In this situation, many parents did not allow their daughters to pursue higher education, because it was too far away, and because many believed that women did not need it. Many Acehnese at that time still believed that if a woman gets higher education, she might not get a husband. As a result of this, in 2006 IAIN Ar-Raniry had only 57 female lecturers, compared to about 208 male lecturers. Of the five faculties at IAIN – *Adab* (history), *Dakwah* (Islamic preaching), *Syariah* (Islamic law), *Tarbiyah* (Islamic education) and *Ushuluddin* (Islamic theology) – the *Syariah* and *Ushuluddin* faculties have the smallest number of female lecturers, with just six female lecturers.

From these two studies, it is clear that the gender problem in Aceh emerged not only because of tradition, but also as a result of economic development and state gender policies, as Nazar claimed. Gender roles in Aceh were indeed subjected to Indonesia's New Order gender policy, with its expectations of how women and men should behave according to their ascribed sex (Blackburn 2008, 8). In addition, however, the Aceh religious community also continues to use Islam to justify the confinement of women's roles to domestic affairs. Both of these issues are explained further in Chapter 4.

Women's movements and women's NGOs in Aceh

There has been a continuing debate on the definition of women's movements within the disciplines of political science, sociology and women's studies (Beckwith 2005, 2007). To classify a movement as a women's movements we can define it based on three initial questions (Beckwith 2007, 313).

These include 'Who are the actors?', 'Who are the leaders?' and 'What are the gendered identity claims by women in the movement?'. Thus, Beckwith makes the point that 'women's movements encompass both feminist and non-feminist organising and activism, focusing specifically on women and gender identity'. This definition helps me to categorize women's activisms in Aceh as women's movements regardless of, as the next chapter will show, Acehnese women activists' reluctance to be associated with feminism. Still based on Beckwith, Acehnese women's activisms are women's movements because women become the major actors and leaders, mobilize women, and place women at the centre of the movement. In their activisms, it can be seen how Acehnese women politicize their identities as women, how they organize around those identities, what organizational forms advance women's issues, and what strategies women employ to meet their ends (Beckwith 2005, 588).

Three factors facilitate the establishment of a social movement, including the presence of group consciousness, the availability of resources and the sense of efficacy (Chafetz 1990, 167). Apart from this, the structural and historical are two preconditions that help understand the establishment of women's movements (Ray and Korteg 1999, 52). On the relations of women's NGOs and women's movements, Alvarez (1999, 185–186) argues that women's movements can consist of women's collectives, women's groups and women's NGOs. She defines NGOs as forms of organizations that have a specialized agenda, are run by professional staff and have collaborative networks with foreign and national agencies to develop reports or projects. In most cases, NGOs activists, according to Alvarez (1999, 187), build horizontal linkages with a wide variety of other organizations or individuals who have the same agenda of claiming women's rights and gender justice. It is the linkages between women's NGOs and other forms of women's organizations, Alvarez says, that make women's movements.

Some Acehnese women have become increasingly aware of their rights as a result of seeing the suffering of many Acehnese women at the hands of both the Indonesian military and the Free Aceh Movement. Women worked voluntarily both individually and organized into local women's NGOs. They relied on limited resources. Later, women's NGOs in Aceh developed into professional NGOs, and their staff began to receive honoraria. This happened as women's NGOs begin collaborating with foreign NGOs, international donors and national-based NGOs. However, in 2000 the Indonesian government increased pressure on both local and foreign NGOs by, for example, breaking into NGO offices or intimidating NGO activists (Schulze 2006, 253–254). In 2003, the Indonesian government passed a Presidential Decree No. 43/2003 to regulate the activities of foreigners, NGOs and journalists in Aceh.

The next section aims to discuss the emergence and development of women's movements in Aceh along with the social and political circumstances of each period. In general, it is argued that the development of women's movements in Aceh has been shaped by decades of military conflict, the authoritarian and centralist New Order administration and patriarchal interpretations of religious doctrines. As argued earlier in this chapter, many people that I spoke with contend that subordination or discrimination against women is not something that is inherently embedded in Acehnese society and culture. Rather, they see it as a product of more recent socio-political development of Aceh, including Dutch colonization and Indonesia's nation-building project (see for example, Siapno 2002; Aspinall 2006; Noerdin 2007). More recently, women's movements in Aceh have also been influenced by the outcome of peace rehabilitation and reconstruction after the signing of peace agreement in Helsinki.

To understand local women's NGOs and women's movements in Aceh, the sections below examine two different political environments that have shaped the character of local women's NGOs and women's movements in Aceh: the military conflict and the signing of the peace agreement in 2005.

Military conflict

Three political conflicts have emerged between the Indonesian government and Acehnese since Indonesia's independence in 1945 (Sukma 2004). The first emerged in the early 1950s, when a group of Acehnese joined the Darul Islam struggle to change Indonesia into an Islamic state. It was finally curbed when Aceh was granted 'special status', as discussed in Chapter 2. The second resurgence emerged in the 1970s, after a group of Acehnese, this time led by Teuku Hasan di Tiro, demanded a complete separation of Aceh from Indonesia. With the support of small groups of Acehnese, who were mostly peasants, Teuku Hasan di Tiro declared Aceh's independence and established 'Acheh Merdeka' or 'Independent Acheh' in 1976 (Siegel 2000, 336). The nineteenth-century English spelling of 'Acheh' was intended by Hasan di Tiro to show his rejection of any association with Indonesia, including the Indonesian language (Siegel 2000, 336). The third and the last struggle of the Acehnese against the Indonesian government emerged in 1989 and, according to Sukma (2004), was more of a continuation of the 1970s uprising, as it also sought an Aceh separate from Indonesia.

Scholars have argued that these two latest insurgencies were driven by massive economic exploitation, centralistic administration, unjust industrialization and development projects, and military repression (Robinson 1998; Kamaruzzaman 2006; Kell 1995; Sukma 2004; Schulze 2006). Robinson (1998, 135) made a point that the resentments of Acehnese towards the central government were largely driven by the economic activities of the Indonesian government and foreign companies including Mobil Oil in extracting Aceh's rich natural resources, such as oil, gas and pulp, found in the northern part of Aceh. It was reported that the revenue from these economic activities made Aceh the largest contributor to the national income (Robinson 1998, 135; Sukma 2004, 3). Kell (1995, 14), for example, noted that at the end of the 1980s economic activities from exporting Aceh's oil and gas contributed almost 30 per cent of Indonesia's national income and made Indonesia the world's largest gas exporter. Yet, these huge economic benefits were not evenly distributed to the Acehnese, so that the promise of a 'trickle down' economic effect was seen only as rhetoric (Robinson 1998, 135). Local residents that lived around the industrial complex in North Aceh were disappointed, as they were not given jobs (Robinson 1998, 136). The nature of capital-intensive industries and the lack of required skills of the Acehnese were used as excuses by the companies for not employing the local population (Kell 1995, 16). Instead, the companies hired labour from outside the area, creating what Kell (1995, 17) describes as 'ghettos of migrants'. Even further, the arrival of migrants creates social and cultural disparities between those employed by the industry and the local population surrounding the industrial complex. The demand for Acehnese independence was also a response of some displaced Acehnese, because their land was taken to build the plant (Siegel 2000, 336). Robinson (1998, 136) also reveals other undesirable side effects of the industrialization projects, ranging from 'environmental degradation, to encouraging practices found offensive to Islam and local customs, such as gambling, drinking and prostitution'.[6]

It was these resentments that fuelled Acehnese attacks on Indonesian police and military compounds posted around big oil company installations, such as those on Exxon Mobil Oil in the northern part of Aceh (Amnesty International 1993; ICTJ 2008).[7] Given the intensity of the continuing attacks, the Indonesia military launched the Red Net operation or *Operasi Jaring Merah* and declared Aceh a Military Operation Zone (*Daerah Operasi Militer* or DOM) in 1989 (Kamaruzzaman 2006; Robinson 1998; Sukma 2004; Schulze 2006). This military conflict continued to escalate in the 1990s, and by the mid-1990s, the administration in Jakarta refused to negotiate with GAM and began to orchestrate a 'total military strategy' (Robinson 1998, 140–141). Some of the tactics used by the Indonesian military to crackdown on GAM supporters included burning villages, houses, schools, carrying out armed night raids, house-to-house searches, arbitrary arrests, routine torture of detainees and sexual harassment of women (Robinson 1998; Al-Chaidar 1999; Schulze 2006).[8] A recent survey conducted in 2006 by the International Organization for Migration (IOM), Harvard Medical School and Syiah Kuala University on the psychological assessment of Acehnese communities in three different sub-districts highly affected by the conflict found that it has had profound psychological effects on many Acehnese. Both men and women from the survey experienced extraordinary levels of violence, and many experienced different types of trauma due to many years of repeated experiences of violence and insecurity.

Women were targeted by both the Indonesian military and by GAM (Kamaruzzaman 2006, 261). Women often had to deal with the military who came to their houses, searching for men they suspected of being GAM followers. At the same time, women also had to deal with GAM personnel who came to their houses to extract money. As the conflict intensified, many Acehnese women and children decided to flee their houses and villages, and became displaced. The regular fights between GAM and the military, and burning of houses and schools also forced villagers to leave their houses and property for safety reasons. According to Kamaruzzaman, women who became internally displaced experienced both physical and psychological impacts, while their children missed schooling, as families left their villages. During displacement, women felt unwanted and lost the space they had in their own houses. They found they were forced to 'leave the kitchen', because in the shelters, cooking became a public task and they were not needed (Kamaruzzaman 2006, 263).

Women were not only displaced, but many became objects of violence. Various reports indicate, for example, that women were killed, tortured, sexually harassed and raped by the Indonesian military (Kamaruzzaman 1999, 61–63). From the period of 1989 to 1998 about 600 women were raped by the military (Eye on Aceh 2004). Overall, the *Operasi Jaring Merah* or the Red Net Operations from 1989 to 1998 had caused 625 cases of rape and torture against women (Schulze 2007, 85). Other sources reveal that from 1989 to 1998 about 16,375 children became orphaned and 3,000 women became widowed (Sulistiyanto 2001, 442).

Neither the local or national authorities protected women who were casualties of the conflict (Kamaruzzaman 2006). This may be because women, including women's right activists, were reluctant to report incidents to the authorities, fearing that reporting the case could trigger new problems. Other troubling effects of the conflict include how it limited women's access to education. With many schools burned down[9] and a widespread absence of security, many Acehnese parents chose not to send their children (especially young girls) to school. Parents also prohibited their daughters from going to the mosque to learn reading the *Qur'an* in the evenings for safety reasons. As a result, Aceh's educational level is low compared to other provinces in Indonesia. A report from Poverty Assessment in 2008, for example, revealed that the graduation rate of elementary school students in 2004/2005 was only 96.8 per cent, which is below the national rate of 99.6 per cent. The pass rate of high school students in Aceh was also lower than that at the national level: only 89.5 per cent, compared to 98 per cent nationally. The impact of conflict on Aceh's education is also currently reflected in the small number of Acehnese who are able to recite the *Qur'an*, despite the claim that Acehnese are 'pious Muslims'.[10] As one civil society activist has said, the conflict has indeed cost Aceh one of its generations (Fajran Zein, interview, Banda Aceh, 3 February 2008). This fact later served as background for Islamists to make it compulsory for Acehnese women and men to be able to read the *Qur'an*.

Women not only had to suffer from physical and physiological violence (as already elaborated above), but they also became victims in the economic sphere. Kamaruzzaman (1999), for example, narrates a story in which women in one area around Pidie district, in North Aceh, had to give up their small business activities of producing sleeping mats made from green *pandan* leaves. Before the conflict, these women were able to get the raw materials they needed from their own villages, for free. When the military came in, they began destroying the plantation. For women, this meant that they had to find the raw materials from other villages, and had to pay for it. As a result, the cost of producing their *pandan* mats increased. In addition to the increased production cost, women also had to spend more time travelling to neighbouring villages, when it was also not safe for them to do so. All these circumstances caused many women to give up their business, as it no longer offered economic benefits for their families.

One male activist, Fajran Zein, told me of another consequence of the military operations for Acehnese women (interview, Banda Aceh, 11 February 2008). He described how during the military operations many among the Indonesian military developed friendships with Acehnese female teenagers, which in most cases included sexual relations. These relationships were usually short-lived, because military personnel have to move from one place to another. According to him, in many cases these relationships ended with the female teenagers becoming pregnant, by which time their military partners had already moved on. According to him, the parents were aware that their daughters' friendships with the military men could have negative consequences, but, at the same time they were scared to ask the military men to end their friendships with their daughters. According to this activist, what the military soldiers did to Acehnese women normalized sexual relationships outside marriage. It also explains, he says, why now there are many cases of Acehnese women and men having sexual relations outside marriage. In a seminar organized by Aceh Institute on 13 December 2007 in Banda Aceh, Ita F. Nadia, a woman activist from Jakarta, argued that what the soldiers had done to Acehnese women was part of the systematic approach of the Indonesian military to 'destroy the wombs of Acehnese women', with the aim of destroying the whole Acehnese population.

It was these contextual figures that triggered Acehnese women to form solidarity movements to offer protection to other Acehnese women. Under military suppression women have the necessary basis to organize into women's movements, because women cannot participate in formal political parties, typically considered a male sphere by authoritarian regimes (Waylen 1993[f], 573). Kumar (2001, 8) observes that a military conflict could have an impact on women and gender relations because it changes the demographic composition and social relations of the society. Acehnese women were moved by not only the suffering of their fellow Acehnese women but also because little attention has been given by either national or international human rights organizations to the need to address the horrendous suffering of Acehnese women during the conflict (Kamaruzzaman 1999, 57). In regards to this, Basu (2000, 76) made an interesting analysis saying that transnational women's groups in fact would be enthusiastic in supporting campaigns against sexual violence where the state is repressive. However, the Indonesian military government's policy of closing Aceh to international or foreign links had prevented local women activists from getting the support. Acehnese women did not stop there and they in fact initiated the establishment of women's organizations in Aceh. The latter development of local women's NGOs in Aceh was then, to an extent, influenced by the emergence of women's activism at the national level, as I will now seek to show.[11]

The first women's organization that emerged in Aceh was Flower Aceh, which was established in 1989 by Soraya Kamaruzzaman,[12] a student of the Faculty of Chemistry at Syiah Kuala University. Kamaruzzaman chose the name Flower Aceh (FA) because she and her colleagues believed that picking a foreign word such as 'Flower' would minimize suspicion by the Indonesian military. Siapno (2000, 281) argued that the decision to use the word 'flower', a very 'feminine', unthreatening name, was to disguise the organization's real political objectives. In its early days, Flower Aceh focused its activities on helping women who became victims of violence perpetrated both by GAM and the Indonesian military. During the military operation from 1989 to 1998, Flower Aceh actively tried to raise people's awareness of the sufferings of Acehnese women. They campaigned both at national and international levels. Kamaruzzaman spoke relentlessly about the gross human rights violations, which caused the suffering of women who became the target of torture, mass rape, disappearances and killings (Kamaruzzaman 1999, 54). She resented the fact that almost no attention was paid to women's suffering during the conflict. She argued that academics, politicians and legal practitioners in Aceh, as well as those at the national level, were just not interested in the plight of Acehnese women and their need for justice (Kamaruzzaman 1999).

The other women's organization established during this period was Yayasan Pengembangan Wanita (YPW, or Women's Development Organization). This NGO focused its activities on providing economic assistance to women at the village level. Women who lived in conflict-prone areas were among the primary targets of this organization. Given the widespread nature of the conflict, YPW concentrated its work in Aceh Tengah (Central Aceh) and still operates only in Takengon. Samsidar is the founder of this organization.[13] In an interview I had with her on 1 January 2008, she explained that the idea to establish YPW came after she and her friends carried out their undergraduate fieldwork research (or Kuliah Kerja Nyata/KKN) in the area under the Plant Protection Project of the Agriculture Department at Syiah Kuala University. During this fieldwork, she discovered how women in the villages were discriminated against and how their lives had been badly affected under the Military Operation Status (DOM). Many women were left alone with their children, while their husbands escaped to the mountains to avoid becoming the target of either the military or GAM. As a result, women had to assume the jobs of their husbands in order to maintain their children's health, welfare and education. However, it was not easy for the women to do this, since they had limited access to the economy by reason of continuous attacks from both GAM and the military.

YPW therefore initiated a programme to empower women in the village so that they could have better access to the economy. In Samsidar's view, improving the economic capacity of women was crucial not only for them to be able to support their children, but also to empower them to escape from future discrimination. She added that the other reason why her organization decided to work on economic issues was because it was the only possible topic that would not invite potential suspicion from both of the warring parties. She said that the situation in Aceh at that time did not allow them to use the same language as women activists used in Jakarta, such as demanding 'rights' or 'justice'.

YPW initiated a programme to help women generate income from agricultural activities. They taught women, for example, how to grow good quality coffee. However, it was through the training on agricultural matters that she conducted in villages that she delivered the message on the need for daughters to get education and for parents to treat their children equally, regardless of their sex. She also tried to make these village women understand their citizen rights, and that they have equal rights with men. She said that at that point she just wanted to develop awareness among the village women of their rights, both in the family and in the public sphere. In running the programme, YPW conducted its work on a voluntary basis and never received any funding from outside sources. YPW has continued to grow and by 2008 it had about 1,125 women members in the Aceh Tengah district.

Apart from Flower Aceh and YPW, there were also individual women activists who tried to assist their fellow Acehnese women during this period. One such activist is Farida, who lives in Pidie district. She worked to uncover the various forms of violence that Acehnese women experienced in her surrounding district. In carrying out her mission, she worked through a network of women's *Qur'anic* reading groups that existed in the village. More recently, she set up a women's organization named PASKA to continue her work in helping the victims of conflict.[14] These activist movements, both at the organizational and individual level, were the foundation for modern women's movements in Aceh.

Reform era

The political democratization that began in Indonesia in 1998 following the end of Suharto's authoritarianism paved the way for a new beginning in the history of women's movements in Aceh. Important political developments took place in Aceh when, on 7 August 1998, General Wiranto publicly apologized to the Acehnese on behalf of the Indonesian government for the brutal war that it had waged with the Free Aceh Movement during the Military Operation Status from 1989 to 1998. This historic event ended the Military Operation Status in Aceh (Sulistiyanto 2001, 444).[15] One of the biggest developments following this political transformation was the development of freedom of the press, which prompted the media and Acehnese to report stories of violence they witnessed and endured (Reid 2003).[16] As human rights abuses perpetrated by the Indonesian military were revealed, the Acehnese demanded the trial of human rights violators and asked the government to provide justice to all the victims. Along with this movement, a number of civil society organizations also began to emerge, including women's organizations. Acehnese began to witness a proliferation of NGOs working on gender during this political transformation (Siapno 2001, 279–280).

More importantly, this political reform prompted the two parties to resort to peace talks that resulted in the Humanitarian Pause in 2000 and Cessation of Hostilities in 2002 (Aspinall 2003; Schulze 2006; Sulistiyanto 2001). A Swiss-based international organization, the Henry Dunant Center, mediated the peace talks. Despite the peace agreements, however, tension between the Indonesian military and GAM continued, resulting in the breakdown of the accords. The attack by GAM on the Exxon Mobil Oil production facilities and pipelines in North Aceh in March 2001 forced the Indonesian President Abdurrahman Wahid to pass Presidential Decree No. 4/2001 on Security Recovery Operations (Schulze 2006, 234). However, this failed to stop the regular counter-insurgency and guerrilla war perpetrated by GAM. The intensifying military conflict reignited new military action with Indonesian President Megawati Soekarnoputri declaring Aceh under military emergency and martial law was again imposed on 19 May 2003.

The result of these ongoing military contacts was that thousands of Acehnese women became internally displaced.[17] Many were stranded in mosques or other temporary shelters as their houses were burned down. This development prompted some Acehnese women to form new women's NGOs, including RPUK (Relawan Perempuan Untuk Kemanusiaan or Women's Volunteers for Humanity), MISPI (Mitra Sejati Perempuan Indonesia or True Partner of Indonesian Women), KKTGA (Kelompok Kerja Transformasi Gender Aceh or the Working Group for Gender Transformation in Aceh), Yayasan Pulih, and Duek Pakat Inong Aceh or Aceh Women's Congress, LBH Apik, and ORPAD (Organisasi Perempuan Aceh Demokratik or Aceh Women's Democratic Organization).

RPUK was established in 1999. RPUK focused its activities on providing basic needs for women such as clothing, medicine and foods.[18] Khairani, the current leader of RPUK, said that many women were trapped in shelters and mosques across the province with no public facilities. These women who were displaced could not go out to get food for themselves and for their children. Many became ill, as there was no sanitation or access to health services. Khairani said RPUK's women activists collected sanitation materials to be distributed to women in the shelters, because RPUK did not yet have any donors (interview, Banda Aceh, 22 February 2008).

In 2000, an All-Acehnese Women's Congress (*Duek Pakat Inong Aceh* or DPIA) was established, and held its first regional meeting in Banda Aceh from 20–22 February 2000. Many women activists remember this event as the beginning of a new era for Aceh's women's movements. More than 400 women from different parts of Aceh attended. The congress can be seen as a benchmark, because women attending declared their first political position in regards to the ongoing conflict, demanding that all parties involved end the conflict (Djohar 2003). They also demanded the withdrawal of troops and requested that women be guaranteed 30 per cent of seats in the parliament. They signed a 22-point resolution, and put peace and justice as their main demands. With Islamic law in place, the congress acknowledged Islamic law as the governing legal basis of Aceh. Yet, these activists insisted that the sources of sharia need to be reinterpreted so that Islamic law in Aceh would treat men and women fairly. They also called for the creation of *Qanun Ureung Inong Aceh* (Aceh's Women's Legal Forum) to focus on discovering egalitarian Islamic interpretations to enhance women's position in public life. They also called for women to have equal rights in *adat* (traditional customary law), and demanded greater inclusion of women in economic life (Bianpoen 2000, 364).

Duek Pakat Inong met again just few months after the devastating tsunami. This time the congress, which was attended by at least 400 women from about 21 districts around the province, recommended that women must be included in the process of reconstruction in Aceh. They expressed resentment that women have been excluded from the reconstruction process and called for both the Indonesian government and GAM to give women access to participate in the peace process through non-violent and democratic means (UNIFEM 2005; Crisis Management Initiative 2006).

Another local women's NGO established was *Yayasan Putroe Kandee*. It was established in 1990. The name of *Putroe Kandee* literally means 'women as the illumining light'. Roosmawardani, a respected woman judge at the *Mahkamah Syari'at* or sharia courts, currently leads this NGO. During my interview with her on 14 January 2008, she said that the idea of establishing this NGO came from her concern about the suffering of women and children forced to stay in refugee camps. Her organization aims to promote justice for women and their families, based on the rule of law and sharia, because the current situation still discriminates against women and other vulnerable groups.

In its response to the implementation of Islamic law, *Putroe Kandee* designed programs to empower judges of the Islamic courts. In 2006, with support received from the Asia Foundation, *Putroe Kandee* conducted a programme to improve gender sensitivity for judges and officers at the Office of Religious Courts (KUA) and the Sharia Courts (Salim *et al.* 2009, xxi). The programme was designed to disseminate ideas of gender sensitivity to judges at the sharia courts on issues such as marriage, divorce, domestic violence, *mut'ah* or alimony, provision of marital property, inheritance and polygamy. Judges were also introduced to a new methodology for reading and reinterpreting Islamic texts from a gender perspective (Salim *et al.* 2009, 16). According to one activist from RPUK who often deals with legal cases at the sharia court, these programmes have been successful, because judges of the sharia courts are now more gender-sensitive, by comparison with judges of the (secular) district court or Provincial High Court (interview, Banda Aceh, 9 June 2009).

As demonstrated above, the work of women's NGOs in this period focused more on searching for justice for women victims of conflict. However, despite activism to protect women in conflict areas, women's NGOs and activists were still excluded from the peace negotiation process.

Post-tsunami and post-MOU Helsinki

A report released by Gender Working Group (GWG) in 2007 identified a number of challenges confronting Acehnese women in post-tsunami and post-conflict Aceh. They include problems arising from women's limited access to economy, housing, cases of inheritance and land ownership,[19] child custody, women's health, education and the reintegration of women ex-combatants into society (GWG unpublished report 2007). In regards to violation against women, the National Commission of Women's Rights reported that there were at least 191 violations of women's rights during the period of October 2005 to 2006. These include 38 cases of discrimination, seven cases of eviction and 146 cases of physical and sexual violence (Almubarok 2006).

Various reports on the impact of the tsunami suggest that the number of women killed by the tsunami was higher than men (UNFPA 2006; Oxfam Briefing Note 2005; Fitzpatrick 2008).[20] Some Acehnese used this to argue that the tsunami was God's will, His way of punishing Acehnese women who had betrayed Islamic values and local *adat*. A report released by Oxfam (2005, 2) and UNFPA (2005, 8) argued that more women were killed compared to men because the tsunami happened on a Sunday morning, when most Acehnese women were home with their children. Women were also less likely to be able to swim or climb to higher places, such as trees, when the tsunami struck. In coastal areas, such as in the northern part of Aceh, men were already at sea fishing, so they were able to survive.

Women survivors who stayed in temporary shelters also became prone to violence due to a lack of security and absence of privacy. Women became the targets of sexual harassment, including rape, and other forms of intimidation while in shelters (UNIFEM 2005). This is in part due to the fact that most of the temporary shelters were not equipped with proper infrastructure, such as separate toilets for men and women. Women activists criticized both the government and the international agencies for failing to consider gender interests in building temporary shelters.

The tsunami worsened Aceh's economy, at first, at least, and it badly hit women. The World Bank (2008, 12) reported that the poverty levels in post-tsunami Aceh increased to 32.6 per cent from 28.4 per cent in 2004. In fact, in 2004 Aceh's poverty level was already higher than the national poverty level of 16.7 per cent. While women have to support their families as many of their husbands were killed, women's participation in the public economic sector remains difficult. Data released in 2005 by the Statistical Bureau of Banda Aceh as cited by Vianen (2006, 4–5) reveals a low participation rate of women in the labour force. According to Vianen (2006, 1), women's low participation in labour is due to several factors, including: discriminatory employment practices, low access to information, lack of skills, low access to finance and social discourse (that women must take care of their families, for example) that continues to discourage women from participating in productive work. In addition, statistics also showed that of a total population of Aceh in 2005, of 4,031,589 there were about 2,025,826 women compared to 2,005,763 men. This showed that although more women should participate in building Aceh's economy, their lack of access and skills impede them from contributing.

Another significant development to Acehnese women in post-tsunami Aceh is the increasing number of divorces. In an interview with the head of Women and Children Agency of Banda Aceh, Raihan Putri revealed that many women are now seeking to divorce to their husbands (Banda Aceh, 7 June 2009). Although her office did not yet have the exact data on what lies behind this trend, she predicts that the economic difficulties that Acehnese families are facing have contributed to the increase in divorce rates. On activist from KKTGA says divorce in post-tsunami Aceh occurs because many couple got married only to replace their lost husband and wife immediately after the tsunami, without knowing each other first (interview, Banda Aceh, 9 June 2009).

KKTGA, a local women's NGO that focuses its work on providing legal advocacy for women, reveals that there has been a significant increase in the number of women seeking legal assistance to file for divorce. In the period of March 2008 to March 2009, KKTGA received a total of 107 legal cases, with about 81 per cent of them being divorce cases. Women were filing for divorce for different reasons. Many had experienced various forms of domestic violence. Others wanted a divorce because their husband had taken a second wife. In the Aceh Besar district, the sharia court dealt with 154 divorce cases from 2008 to October 2009 (*The Globe Journal* 2009). Of this number, 112 cases were filed by the wives. Similarly, *Serambi Indonesia* (18 January 2010) also reported that in 2009, the divorce rate reached 1,678 cases throughout Aceh. One official at the sharia court in Aceh Besar district as cited in *The Globe Journal* (2009) claimed that most of the divorce cases were driven by economic reasons. The director of KKTGA argues, however, that this increase in the number of women filing for divorce is largely because Acehnese women are become increasingly aware of their rights so, for example, they no longer accept their husband taking a second wife or physically assaulting them.[21] She found that only a small number of women who filed for divorce did so purely for economic reasons.

Women former combatants

In the context of the post-conflict rehabilitation, some Acehnese women were also confronted by their reintegration into society. During conflict, many Acehnese women joined the Free Aceh Movement and became part of *Teuntra* National Aceh (TNA; Aceh National Army).[22] The women fighters were called *Inong Balee*, which literally means 'women widows'. *Inong Balee* was created by GAM in 1999 with the function of administering logistics, communications and intelligence matters (Schulze 2006, 228). Many of them were widows, as their husbands had been killed by the Indonesian military and they joined TNA for vengeance. This fits an historical pattern. Siapno (2002, 28) says that during the war against the Dutch the widows of male nationalist leaders such as Tjut Nyak Dhien, Tjoet Meutia, Pocut Bahren and Teungku Fakinah held powerful political positions after replacing their husbands who had been killed for their anti-colonial resistance. However, many other Acehnese women joined GAM purely because they want to fight the Indonesian military and supported Aceh's independence (*Aceh Magazine* 2007).

During the conflict, the presence of women fighters was acknowledged by GAM, however, there are indications that they were ignored in the process of reintegration of former combatants. *Aceh Magazine* (2007), for example, reported that none of the *Inong Balee* were listed in the 3,000 names of people entitled to get war compensation.[23] This compensation was mentioned in the Helsinki MOU and outlined in its Chapter on Amnesty and Reintegration into Society, which says:

> GOI [Government of Indonesia] and authorities of Aceh will take measures to assist persons who participated in GAM activities to facilitate their reintegration into the civil society. These measures include economic facilitation to former combatants ... A reintegration fund under the administration of Aceh will be established.[24]

GWG reported that it was only in 2007 that the Rehabilitation Commission of Aceh (KPA) proposed an additional 6,200 names to receive the compensation, and about 30 per cent of them were *Inong Balee*, that is, 1,680 women. This number remains low, however, when compared to the initial number of women ex-combatants.

As argued above, Acehnese women are clearly confronted by complex and growing challenges. Some Acehnese women have responded to this situation by organizing and establishing new women's NGOs. These NGOs pursue new agendas to meet the various challenges facing Acehnese women, ranging from providing economic assistance, health services (including providing trauma healing to those who have become victims of conflict), legal advocacy and assisting women ex-combatants to reintegrate into society.[25] One woman's NGO that has a direct link with the former combatants is Liga Inong Aceh (LINA, or the Aceh Women's League).

LINA was first launched on 12 June 2006. LINA was established with the objective of accommodating the aspirations of women who were involved directly in the Free Aceh Movement, as combatants. LINA was established by women activists including Shadia Marhaban, Maryati, Dewi Mutia (who is the wife of the current Deputy Governor of Aceh, Muhammad Nazar) and

Cut Fatma. The establishment of LINA was supported by a Swedish-based NGO, the Old Polopment National Swedia. Shadia Marhaban, a former nego- tiator for GAM during the peace process, was the leader of LINA. LINA sets out its programme as being to assist women to reintegrate into the society and believes that in empowering these women, it must equip them with political education. It organized computer and English training for women. Shadia insists that her organization is not interested in working on issues related to sharia law as she does not see sharia implementation as problematic for women (interview, Banda Aceh, 14 March 2007). Shadia was, in fact, quite critical of the activities of other women's NGOs in Aceh, especially those who provide advocacy on sharia and women. In her view, the best way to empower Acehnese women is to provide them with access to participate in local politics. One way to achieve this is to equip women with political skills like negotiation or lobbying. For her, Acehnese women can only get wider public recognition if women understand politics, so that they can achieve their goals.

New women's NGOs

There were several new women's organizations established in the 2000s. They include Bungeong Jeumpa, An-Nisa, Sri Ratu and Patima Dora. There are also branches of national women's organizations that work in Aceh and have established offices there, such as Solidaritas Perempuan (SP, Women's Solidarity) and Kapal Perempuan (Women's Ship). International NGOs are also present and carry out some of their programmes on women's empowerment, including IDLO (International Development for Law and Organization), HIVOS, GTZ, UNIFEM, UNFPA and many others. The establishment of the new local NGOs was prompted in part by the arrival of these international and national NGOs

Beujroh is another newly-established women's NGO in Aceh, established in January 2005, with the idea of providing Acehnese women with better access to the economy. Its website states that the word 'Beujroh' is taken from the Acehnese language and literally means 'hopefully all we do will succeed and receive the blessing from God'. It has three main objectives to improve the lives of Acehnese women, which include empowering women's economic capacity, providing women with good education, and promoting public cam- paigns and education to promote women's agenda. When I visited Beujroh's office in 2008, it displayed various handicrafts made by women in Meulaboh. This handicraft activity, according to Beujroh, has given women the ability to generate income.

Beujroh is the only local women's NGO in Aceh that publishes a monthly women's magazine, called *Bungong*. The magazine focuses on reporting various issues related to women. It also gives women a forum to write about their experiences and how they deal with the various challenges they face. Beujroh hopes that *Bungong* will be an alternative media for Acehnese women. Beujroh's office is also equipped with a library with a collection of books on women, politics and Islam. Raihan Diani is the current leader of Beujroh, and was one of the female student activists involved in the 1998/1999 student movements. Diani was the former leader of a student organization, ORPAD (Organisasi Perempuan Aceh Demokratik, or Aceh's Women's Democratic Organization). The Indonesian police detained her in June 2002 when her organization held a demonstration demanding that the Indonesian President Megawati Sukarnoputri and her Vice President Hamzah Haz step down, and she was sentenced to six months in jail in 2002. Diani did not stop her activism when released, instead establishing Beujroh in 2005. In 2009, Raihan nominated herself as a legislative candidate for Partai Rakyat Aceh (PRA; Aceh People Party), but was not elected (interview, Banda Aceh, 15 January 2008).

Local government institutions

The chapter has discussed how many Acehnese women have responded to the social and political circumstances by organizing into NGOs and women's movements to provide protection, support and help for other Acehnese women. Acehnese women's activism has become an alternative axis of power for Acehnese women (Siapno 2002, 4). This section now aims to discuss how the local government protects the rights of women and advancing women's status in this context.

Molyneux and Razavi (2002, 20) argued that 'the central instrument for the protection of women's rights has been, and must remain in the hand of the state'. In the case of Aceh it is obvious that the state has failed to protect women. While Acehnese women suffered in the conflict, little was done by the local and national authorities to protect women (Kamaruzzaman 2006). The government failed to provide protection to women and fulfil women's gender needs during conflict, which eventually prompted Acehnese women to form solidarity movements to take on the role that should be played by government.

As regards the role of the state in promoting women's rights and fulfilling women's gender interests, the United Nations acknowledges the need of the presence of state institution to promote women's needs and status. During the UN First World Conference on the Status of Women in Mexico City in 1975, the Conference mandated all governments to engage in the promotion of gender equality by creating an agenda for women's equal participation in education, employment, politics, health services, nutrition and family planning. Two other UN events followed the 1975 Mexico conference: the 1980 Copenhagen conference and 1985 Nairobi conference. These endorsed the need for the creation of government institutions in every country to promote women's status. At this stage, the discussion focused on the role of government institutions in advancing women's issues. During the Beijing World Conference on Women in 1995 the focus shifted to problems related to gender equality (Rai 2003, 2).

Following the Beijing Declaration, the Indonesian government adopted a series of policies to enhance the role and status of women in what is called a National Action Plan. One of its five major goals is to encourage government organizations, private agencies, socio-political organizations and community organizations to provide more opportunities for women to take public roles (The State Ministry for the Role of Women 1996, cited in Davies 2005, 236). A major step taken by the Indonesian government was the enactment of the Presidential Instruction No. 9/2000 for the State Minister for Women's Empowerment to launch a Manual of Implementation Guidelines on Gender Mainstreaming in National Development. This instrument provides that all heads of government institutions at the national and sub-national levels are responsible for applying the gender mainstreaming strategy within the scope of their respective tasks, functions, levels of authority, monitoring and evaluation. In the case of Aceh, Presidential Instruction No. 9/2000 also became the basis for the local government of Aceh to implement a Gender Mainstreaming Strategy.

As a follow-up, the local government of Aceh established the Women's Empowerment Bureau (Biro PP), based on the Governor of Aceh Special Region Decree No. 58 of 1999. It is established under the governor's office and was specifically designed to address problems related to women's issues and children. This institution began its work on 20 January 2000 and coordinated the development of governmental policies pertaining to women's empowerment in Aceh. It had the objective of promoting gender equality and justice, prosperity and protection of children within the family, society and state. It also sought to increase the quality of women's education, health and economy, and to increase women's involvement in politics and other public roles.[26] The authority of this bureau was later strengthened by enactment of the regional regulation (PERDA) No. 3/2001, which assigned Biro PP to be under the organizational structure of the Provincial Secretariat.

Another important government institution for women's empowerment in Aceh that was created following the tsunami was a special division under the Agency for the Rehabilitation and Reconstruction of Aceh and Nias (BRR). In its policy paper, the Deputy Director of Education, Health and Women Empowerment acknowledged the need to address problems that confront women post-tsunami. They identified problems such as violence against women; the practice of marrying girls underage; the decline in quality of women's health and limited access of women to economic sources; and issues of ownership, including inheritance. BRR has also outlined its principles on gender policy, based on equality and good governance. This means active participation and representation of women and men is perceived as a precondition for the success of the process of rehabilitation and reconstruction and social transformation. Second, equality and economic development, that is, equal access and opportunities for women and men to economic resources, is also fundamental for achieving sustainable development in Aceh.

However, both government institutions that have been given mandates to provide protection to women and to fulfil women's gender interests have been criticized by women activists. Local women activists perceive that government institutions have failed to protect women. One activist said that government institutions have only been successful in returning women back to their houses, and many of their programmes have, in fact, strengthened gender segregation based on sex. For example, the Bureau of Women's Empowerment, she said, has provided women only with programmes focused on domestic skills such as cooking, baking cakes and sewing.

Similarly, GWG has also criticized the BRR for its failure to create a sustainable strategy to empower Acehnese women as part of the post-tsunami reconstruction. This failure is due to the absence of thorough assessment of what should be done for Acehnese women. In reconstructing infrastructure, BRR has also failed to integrate gender sensitivity in building shelters or various public facilities. GWG also found that BRR has failed to include gender mainstreaming in its programme generally, because BRR did not use gender analysis in carrying out the assessment, planning and implementing of its programme. Another disturbing aspect of BRR's activities is the fact that women's representation was very small, as mentioned earlier. According to GWG, the poor representation of women within government institutions that directly deal with women's issues has contributed to the fact that many of BRR's policies and agenda are not gender-sensitive.

Conclusion

As shown above, Acehnese women have organized into women's NGOs and mobilized as a women's movement as a response to the complex challenges that Acehnese women face. Conflict and the state's repressive gender policies during the New Order authoritarian administration have created serious gender problems in Aceh. Post-tsunami the situation has become even worse, due to the various social and economic difficulties discussed above.

It is these challenges that have driven women to mobilize and organize themselves into voluntary organizations aimed at supporting other Acehnese women. During conflict, local women's NGOs activities have centred on providing protection, shelters and other basic needs for many Acehnese women and children. They have also started to engage with the promotion of women's rights within the available political space.

The character of women's movements in Aceh has also changed following Aceh's transition to democracy in the late 1990s. As discussed, political democratization has become an important part of the political background to the proliferation of local women's organizations in Aceh. It has also shifted the agenda of local women's NGOs from focusing on economic, social and cultural rights to equality and civil and political rights. This shift has been possible with the arrival of national and international NGOs and foreign institutions in Aceh after the tsunami, which then boosts the development of local women's NGOs. Women's organizations have not just become part of women's movements but developed as part of transnational global women's movements.

While this chapter has highlighted the social and political circumstances surrounding the emergence of local women's NGOs and women's movements in Aceh, the next chapter will discuss how women's NGOs and activists have responded to the implementation of Islamic law, and how their networks with international institutions and foreign NGOs have introduced them to a wider discussion on gender equality and women's rights in international norms that has proved relevant to Acehnese responses to legal Islamization.

Notes

1 Bowen (2003) defines *fatwa* as legal opinions provided by Islamic scholars or jurists. For more accounts of *fatwa* in Indonesia, see for example Kaptein (2004) and Feener (2002, 2007).

2 For more on the political development in the lead up to Aceh's war against the Dutch see for example Ricklefs (2001, 185–187).

3 See Chapter 1 for a discussion of Indonesia's gender policies.

4 See also Jayawardena (1977, 159) in which she observed that men were not permanent residents in the village and they often left home. Men travelled for short or long periods for various economic activities, including to collect jungle products, to trade, or to attend centres of religious teaching. She calls it 'sojourn away from the village'.

5 For more accounts of marriage in Aceh see Jayawardena (1977). Jayawardena (1977, 159–160) also comments on the role of parents in arranging marriage for their children. She has argued that in the past the practice of kin-marriage was common, the objective being to preserve property within the family, and the status of the family's honour.

6 See also Robinson (1998), in which he elaborates the economic and political setting of the rise of Gerakan Aceh Merdeka (GAM). According to Robinson, the oil and gas exploration activities at PT Arun and Mobil Oil were viewed by the leader of Gerakan Aceh Merdeka (GAM), Hasan di Tiro, as 'symbol of what was wrong in Aceh'. Robinson (1998, 139) argued that it was the state-capital link and the extreme centralization of economic decision-making that has stimulated a consciousness of shared fate among Acehnese and reinforced existing ideas of Acehnese identity and increased the credibility of Gerakan Aceh Merdeka. See also Siegel (2001) on villagers' support for Gerakan Aceh Merdeka.

7 In a briefing paper released by ICTJ *et al.* (2008, 4), it was revealed that in 2000, the Exxon Mobil Oil paid the Indonesian military about US$500,000 per month for protecting the complex from attack by GAM. In addition, the Exxon Mobil Oil also provided military equipment and training for the Indonesian military personnel.

8 For further accounts on various forms of tortures and military tactics orchestrated by the military, see Al-Chaidar (1999), Robinson (1998) and Schulze (2006).

9 It was reported, for example, that on the first day of the imposition of Martial Law on 13 May 2003 dozens of schools around the province were burnt to the ground (BBC News 2003). See also Schulze (2006, 232) who discusses the strategy of both sides, GAM and TNI, to burn schools.

10 At the time of my fieldwork, all university students were required to take *Qur'an* lessons. These new students were tested at the time of their enrolment to the

university. The result of the test was used to identify the class level they should be in. One of my informants, a fourth-year student at the Syiah Kuala University, was one of the volunteers who teach these new students. She said that she was some-times frustrated to see that there are lots of Acehnese who cannot read the *Qur'an* at all. Some of them do not even recognize the Arabic alphabet, which means these students have to learn from a very basic level.

11 Ita F. Nadia, interview, 23 February 2008.

12 Soraya Kamaruzzaman is currently a lecturer at Syiah Kuala University. Kamaruzzaman's parents were both teachers. Many of her siblings become teach-ers and lecturers. She is one of the few activists with aristocratic blood, as she is the niece of Abu Lam U, one of the most famous *Ulama* leaders who owned a respected *Dayah*/Islamic traditional boarding school. In an interview she told me that the idea to create a women's organization was driven by the increasing vio-lence that Acehnese women had suffered.

13 Samsidar has been nominated to win the Nobel Prize and is a special rappor-teur on violence against women, and chair of the Aceh Women Volunteers for Humanity (RPUK). She is currently the Aceh Program Director of International Center for Transitional Justice (ICTJ). See also, Ashoka (2006).

14 Farida was awarded Yap Thiam Hien Award in 1998 for her struggle in defending the rights of women and victims of conflict. See Bungong (2007).

15 Robinson (1998, 1278) wrote that during almost ten years of military operation more than 2,000 people were killed, and many others were arbitrarily detained, tortured and raped. There were various reports that provide different figures on the number of people killed, tortured, raped and disappeared. Based on its 26 January 2006 update, Koalisi NGO HAM Aceh reported seven forms of violence, which include enforced or involuntary disappearances, arbitrary arrests, torture and other cruelty, rape and sexual assault, gun shots and burning. The total num-ber of casualties caused by seven forms of violations to human rights was 10,949 people since the Military Operation Status (DOM) in 1989 until the signing of Memorandum of Understanding in August 2005. Between 1989 to 2005, there were 11 types of military operation, which include Military Operation Status or DOM (1989–1998); Post-DOM (August to December 1998); Wibawa Operation (January to April 1999), Sadar Rencong Operation (May 1999 to May 2000); Cinta Meunasah Operation (June 2000 to 15 January 2000); Moratorium (16 January 2002 to 15 February 2002); COHA (9 December 2002 to 17 May 2003); Martial Law 1 and 2 (19 May 2003 to 18 May 2004); Civil Emergency 1 and 2 (19 May 2004 to 18 May 2004); MOU Helsinki (15 August 2005).

16 Unfortunately, soon after that historic event, a new chapter of conflict re-emerged and marked the beginning of another tragic humanitarian disaster in Aceh. Reports suggest that the year 1999 was, in fact, the beginning of one of the bloodi-est episodes in the Aceh conflict. Kamaruzzaman (2000) observed that from January 1999 to February 2000 there were nine massacres in which 132 civilians were killed, 472 wounded, 304 arbitrarily detained and 318 extra-judicial execu-tions and 138 cases of disappearances. In February 1999, more than 250,000 to 300,000 Acehnese became displaced.

17 Schulze (2006, 238) observes that there were repeated reports indicating that GAM had, in fact, played a role in creating massive numbers of refugees in 2001. According to Schulze, GAM forced villagers to leave villages and to stay in camps with the objective of attracting international media coverage, to generate inter-national sympathy for GAM's struggle for independence.

18 For an account of the success of RPUK, and its leadership, see Zeccola (2007).

19 For more accounts on legal cases arising from the tsunami and how it affects women, see for example, Fan (2006), Fitzpatrick (2008) and IDLO Report (no year of publication).

20 There has been no exact record of how many Acehnese men and women were killed by the tsunami. A report by Oxfam (2005) put the ratio of men and women killed at 1:3. The Gender Working Group (2007) reported that about 167,000 people were killed and missing, and about 500,000 people became homeless. Fan (2006, 2) also reported that about 252,323 houses were destroyed, and that about 300,000 parcels of lands were totally or partly damaged.

21 Interview, Banda Aceh, 7 June 2009.

22 Inong Balee was the name first given to women warriors who took up arms against the Portuguese, when the Islamic Kingdom of Aceh was ruled by Sultan Alauddin (1596–1604). These women were widows, as their husbands had been killed earlier during battle against the Portuguese in 1511. Laksamana Malahayati was the first leader of Inong Balee and she led some 2,000 women (*Aceh Magazine* 2007).

23 Financial compensation for those whose lives have been affected by conflict was introduced in 2002 by one of the former governors of Aceh, Azwar Abubakar. At that time, the compensation was to be given to all the immediate kin of people that were killed. It was a strategy to heal the anger of Acehnese and to stop the family members from taking revenge on the Indonesian military by joining GAM. The governor used an Arabic term, *diyat*, in the context of the implementation of Islamic law in Aceh. *Diyat* is a payment made by a killer to the family of the victim (Aspinall 2007, 25).

24 Aceh Monitoring Mission, available at: www.aceh-mm.org/download/english/Helsinki%20MoU.pdf.

25 I am aware that at the district levels there have been also a number of women's NGOs established after the tsunami and conflict. Some of them may have connections with the local NGOs in Banda Aceh but others are purely established by the local women at the district level. In this book, however, I focus my research only on Banda Aceh.

26 The Women's Empowerment Bureau (Biro PP) is the only governmental official bureau that has the authority to coordinate the development of regional governmental policies pertaining to the issue of women empowerment in the province (IDLO Report 2008). The International Development Law Organization's report explains that BIRO PP of NAD was first established in 1999 through Governor's Decree No. 58 of 1999, but the office was only officially launched in 2000. To outline the authority of this bureau, the Provincial Government enacted Regional Regulation (or PERDA) No. 3/2001. According to this PERDA, the bureau is assigned to work under the structure of the Provincial Secretariat, which means it must report and liaise to the Secretariat before taking any action or endorsing a policy platform (IDLO Report, 30 January 2008).

References

Aceh Magazine 2007, 'Tragedi Inong Balee', June, Banda Aceh.

Al-Chaidar, Ahmad, S.Y. and Yarmen, D. 1999, *Aceh Bersimbah Darah: Mengungkap Penerapan Status Daerah Operasi Militar (DOM) di Aceh 1989–1998*, Penerbit Al-Kautsar, Jakarta.

Almubarok, Zaky 2006, '191 Kasus Pelanggaran HAM Terhadap Perempuan Aceh Pascatsunami', *Tempo interaktif*, 22 April, available at: www.tempointeraktif.com/share/?act (accessed 20 March 2007).

Alvarez, Sonia E. 1999, 'Advocating Feminism: The Latin American Feminist NGO-Boom', *International Feminist Journal of Politics*, vol. 1, issue 2, pp. 181–209.

Amir, Iwan Dzulvan 2002, 'Inong Aceh: An Analysis on the Changing Position of Women in Aceh', MA Thesis, Research School of Pacific and Asian Studies, Australian National University, Canberra.

Amiruddin, Hasbi 2004, 'Women in the Acehnese Society: A Lesson from History', in Ahmad Sunawari Long, Jaffary Awang and Kamaruddin Salleh (eds), *Proceeding of the International Seminar on Islamic Thoughts: Islam Past, Present and Future*, 7–9 December 2004, available at: http://alambuku.tripod.com/pdf/ISoITCD%20XP.pdf#page=546.

Amnesty International 1993, *Indonesia: Shock Therapy Restoring Order in Aceh 1989–1993*, United Kingdom.

Andaya, Barbara W. 1995, 'Women and Economic Change: The Pepper Trade in Pre-Modern Southeast Asia', *Journal of the Economic and Social History of the Orient*, vol. 38, issue 2, pp. 165–192.

Ashoka 2006, 'Innovators for the Public', available at: www.ashoka.org/fellow/5174 (accessed 15 April 2009).

Aspinall, Edward 2003, 'Modernity, History and Ethnicity: Indonesian and Acehnese Nationalism in Conflict', in Damien Kingsbury and Harry Aveling (eds), *Autonomy and Disintegration in Indonesia*, RoutledgeCurzon, London and New York, pp. 128–147.

Aspinall, Edward 2006, 'Violence and Identity Formation in Aceh under Indonesian Rule', in Anthony Reid (ed.), *Verandah of Violence*, ISEAS, Singapore, pp. 149–176.

Aspinall, Edward 2007, 'From Islamism to Nationalism in Aceh, Indonesia', *Nations and Nationalism*, vol. 3, issue 2, pp. 245–263.

Basu, Amrita 1995, 'Introduction', in Amrita Basu and Elizabeth McGregory (eds), *The Challenge of Local Feminisms: Women's Movements in Global Perspective*, Westview Press, Colorado, pp. 1–21.

Basu, Amrita 2000, 'Globalization of the Local/Localization of the Global Mapping Transnational Women's Movements', *Meridians*, vol. 1 no. 1, pp. 68–84.

BBC News 2003, 'Schools Torched in Aceh Conflict', 20 May, available at: http://news.bbc.co.uk/2/hi/asia-pacific/3042211.stm (accessed 12 April 2007).

Beckwith, Karen 2000, 'Beyond Compare? Women's Movements in Comparative Perspective', *European Journal of Political Research*, vol. 37, pp. 431–468.

Beckwith, Karen 2005, 'The Comparative Politics of Women's Movements', *Perspective on Politics*, vol. 3, no. 3, pp. 583–596.

Beckwith, Karen 2007, 'Mapping Strategic Engagements: Women's Movements and the State', *International Feminist Journal of Politics*, vol. 9, no. 3, pp. 312–338.

Bianpoen, Carla 2000, 'Aceh's Women Show the Road to Peace: Reflections on International Women's Day', *Inter-Asia Cultural Studies*.

Blackburn, Susan 2004, *Women and the State in Modern Indonesia*, Cambridge University Press, Cambridge.

Blackburn, Susan 2008, 'Indonesian Women and Political Islam', *Journal of Southeast Asian Studies*, vol. 39, issue 1, pp. 83–105.

Boserup, Ester 1970, *Women's Role in Economic Development*, Allen & Unwin, London.

Bowen, John R. 2003, *Islam, Law and Equality in Indonesia: Anthropology of Public Reasoning*, Cambridge University Press, Cambridge.

Bungong 2007, 'Farida Handayani: Tidak Ada Guna Uang Selama Hati Terluka', no. XI I December.

Chafetz, J.S. 1990, *Gender Equity: An Integrated Theory of Stability and Change*, Sage Publications, Newbury Park.

Cooke, Miriam 2000, 'Multiple Critique: Islamic Feminist Rhetorical Strategies', *Nepantia: Views from South*, pp. 91–110.

Crisis Management Initiative 2006, *The Aceh Peace Process: Involvement of Women*, a report by CMI, UNIFEM and CCDE.

Davies, Sharyn G. 2005, 'Women in Politics in Indonesia in the Decade Post-Beijing', *International Social Science Journal*, vol. 57, issue 184, pp. 231–242.

Dijk, C. van 1981, *Rebellion under the Banner of Islam: The Darul Islam in Indonesia*, Nijhof, The Hague.

Djohar, Zubaidah 2003, 'Peran Organisasi Perempuan Aceh dalam Proses Penyelesaian Konflik Bersenjata di Aceh', Unpublished MA Thesis, Magister Humaniora, Program Kajian Wanita Pasca Sarjana, Universitas Indonesia.

Eye on Aceh 2004, 'Victims and Witnesses: The Women of Aceh', *Analysis*, April, available at: www.acheh.eye.org (accessed 16 August 2006).

Fan, Lilianne 2006, 'The Struggle for Land Rights in Post-Tsunami and Post-Conflict Aceh', paper presented at the World Bank Land Policies and Legal Empowerment of the Poor conference, 2–3 November, available at: www.internal-displacement. org/8025708F004CE90B/(httpDocuments)/6B228134BFD97F67C12572DB00366 AE5/$file/struggle+for+land+rights+nov06.pdf (accessed 20 January 2010).

Feener, Michael R. 2002, 'Indonesian Movements for the Creation of a National Madhhab', *Islamic Law and Society*, vol. 9, no. 1, pp. 83–115.

Feener, Michael 2007, *Muslim Legal Thought in Modern Indonesia*, Cambridge University Press, United Kingdom.

Fitzpatrick, Daniel 2008, 'Women's Rights to Land and Housing in Tsunami-Affected Aceh, Indonesia', *Working Paper: Asia Research Institute*, ARI, Singapore, no. 3.

The Globe Journal 2009, 'Tahun 2009, Perceraian Meningkat di Aceh Besar', *Beranda*, 28 October, available at: www.theglobejournal.com/kategori/sosial/tahun-2009-perceraian-meningkat-di-aceh-besar.php (accessed 23 March 2010).

GWG 2007, 'Évaluasi Situasi Perempuan tahun 2006 di Aceh', unpublished paper.

ICTJ 2008, 'Kasus Keterlibatan, Exxon Mobil di Pengadilan karena Perannya dalam Pelanggaran Hak Asasi Manusia di Aceh', *Briefing Paper*.

IDLO Report 2008, *The Role of the Women Empowerment Bureau (Biro PP) of the NAD Province in Increasing the Welfare of Women*, 30 January, available at: www. idlo.org/DOCNews/RoleOfWoman.pdf (accessed 20 February 2009)

Inayatillah 2009, 'Peren perempuan dalam lembaga Pendidikan Tinggi Islam di Aceh', paper presented at International Conference on Aceh and Indian Ocean Studies II Civil Conflict and Its Remedies, Banda Aceh, Indonesia, 23–24 February.

Jayawardena, Chandra 1977, 'Achehnese Marriage Customs', *Indonesia*, vol. 23, pp. 157–173.

Kamaruzzaman, Suraiaya 1999, *Hak Asasi Manusia dan Kekerasan Terhadap Perempuan di Aceh*, Ureca, Aceh.

Kamaruzzaman, Suraiaya 2000, 'Women and the War in Aceh: Those Women Want to Silence All the Guns, Whether Indonesian or Acehnese', *Inside Indonesia*, vol. 64, available at: www.insideindonesia.org/content/view/521/29/ (accessed 2 April 2009).

Kamaruzzaman, Suraiaya 2006, 'Violence, Internal Displacement and its Impact on the Women of Aceh', in Charles A. Coppel (ed.), *Violent Conflicts in Indonesia: Analysis, Representation, Resolution*, Routledge, London and New York, pp. 258–268.

Kaptein, Nico J.G. 2004, 'The Voice of the *Ulama: Fatwa's* and Religious Authority in Indonesia', *ISEAS Working Paper*, vol. 2, Institute of Southeast Asian Studies, Singapore, available at: www.iseas.edu.sg/vr22004.pdf (accessed 2 May 2006).

Kell, Tim 1995, *The Roots of Acehnese Rebellion 1989–1992*, Cornell Modern Indonesia Project, Southeast Asia Program, Cornell University, Ithaca, New York.

Kumar, Krishna 2001, 'Introduction', in Krishna Kumar (ed.), *Women and Civil War: Impact, Organizations and Action*, Lynne Rienner Publishers, Boulder and London, pp. 5–26.

Molyneux, M. and Razavi, S. 2002, *Gender Justice, Development and Rights*, Oxford University Press, Oxford.

Morris, Eric, 1985, 'Aceh: Social Revolution and the Islamic Vision', in Audrey R. Kahin (ed.), *Regional Dynamics of the Indonesian Revolution: Unity from Diversity*, University of Hawaii Press, Honolulu, pp. 83–110.

Noerdin, Edriana 2002, 'Customary Institutions, Syariah Law and the Marginalisation of Indonesian Women', in Kathryin Robinson and Sharon Bessell (eds), *Women in Indonesia: Gender, Equity and Development*, ISEAS, Singapore, pp. 179–186.

Noerdin, Edriana 2005, *Politik Identitas Perempuan Aceh*, Women Research Institute, Jakarta.

Noerdin, Edriana 2007, 'Women against Islam-based Nationalism in Aceh: A Discourse Analysis on Language, Social Institutions and Subjectivity', available at: www.wri.or.id/?q=node/71 (accessed 15 June 2008).

Oxfam Briefing Note 2005, *The Tsunami's Impact on Women*, Oxfam International, March, available at: www.oxfam.org.uk/what_we_do/issues/conflict_disasters/downloads/bn_tsunami_women.pdf (accessed April 2008).

Poverty Assessment Report 2008, *The Impact of the Conflict, the Tsunami and Reconstruction of Poverty in Aceh*, The World Bank, BRR, NAD Government.

Rai, Shirin M. 2003, 'Introduction', in Shirin M. Rai (ed.), *Mainstreaming Gender, Democratizing the State? Institutional Mechanisms for the Advancement of Women*, Manchester University Press, Manchester, pp. 1–11.

Ray, R. and Korteg, A.C. 1999, 'Women's Movements in the Third World: Identity, Mobilization, and Autonomy', *Annual Review of Sociology*, vol. 25, no. 4, pp. 47–71.

Reid, Anthony 1979, *The Blood of the People: Revolution and the End of Traditional Rule in Northern Sumatra*, Oxford University Press, Kuala Lumpur and New York.

Reid, Anthony 1988, *Southeast Asia in the Age of Commerce 1450–1680*, Yale University Press, New Haven.

Reid, Anthony 2003, 'War, Peace and the Burden of History in Aceh', *Asia Research Institute Working Paper Series*, ARI, Singapore.

Reid, Anthony 2005, *An Indonesian Frontier: Acehnese and Other Histories of Sumatra*, Singapore University Press, Singapore.

Reid, Anthony (ed.) 2006, *Verandah of Violence: The Background to the Aceh Problem*, Institute of Southeast Asian Studies, Singapore.

Ricklefs, M.C. 1993, *A History of Modern Indonesia since c.1300*, Macmillan, Houndmills, pp. 145–146.

Ricklefs, M.C. 2001, *A History of Modern Indonesia since c.1200*, Palgrave, Basingstoke.

Riddell, Peter G. 2006, 'Aceh in the Sixteenth and Seventeenth Centuries: "Serambi Mekkah and Identity"', in Anthony Reid (ed.), *Verandah of Violence: The Background to the Aceh Problem*, National University Press, Singapore, pp. 38–51.

Robinson, Geoffrey 1998, 'Rawan is as Rawan Does: The Origin of Disorder in New Order Aceh', *Indonesia*, vol. 66, pp. 127–157.

Safril, Isra 2008, 'Perempuan Aceh Belum Bangkit', *Harian Aceh*, 25 December, available at: www.harian-aceh.com/opini/85-opini/1595-perempuan-aceh-belum-bangkit.html (accessed 5 April 2009).

Salim, Arskal and Nurlaelawati, Marcoes-Natsir, Lies and Sayuti, Wahdi 2009, *Demi Keadilan dan Kesetaraan: Dokumentasi Program Sensitivitas Jender Hakim Agama di Indonesia*, PUSKUMHAM, Jakarta.

Schulze, Kirsten E. 2004, 'The Free Aceh Movement (GAM): Anatomy of a Separatist Organization', *Policy Studies*, vol. 2, East-West Center, Washington, DC.

Schulze, Kirsten E. 2006, 'Insurgency and Counter-Insurgency: Strategy and the Aceh Conflict, October 1976–May 2004', in Anthony Reid (ed.), *Verandah of Violence: The Background to the Aceh Problem*, National University Press, Singapore, pp. 225–271.

Schulze, Kirsten 2007, 'From the Battlefield to the Negotiating Table: GAM and the Indonesian Government 1999–2005', *Asian Security*, vol. 3, no. 2, p.80.

Serambi Indonesia 2008, 'IDLO: A Review of the Position of Women in Aceh', 19 April, available at: www.idlo.org/DocNews/220DOC.pdf (accessed 20 May 2008).

Serambi Indonesia 2010, 'Gugat Cerai Tinggi Karena Emosional tak Terkendali', 18 January, available at: www.serambinews.com/news/view/22049/gugat-cerai-tinggi-karena-emosional-tak-terkendali (accessed 23 March 2010).

Siapno, Jacqueline 2000, 'Gender, Nationalism, and the Ambiguity of Female Agency in Aceh, Indonesia and East Timor', in Marguerite R. Waller and Jennifer Rycenga (eds), *Frontline Feminisms: Women, War and Resistance*, Garland Publishing Inc., New York and London, pp. 275–295

Siapno, Jacqueline 2002, *Gender, Islam, Nationalism and the State in Aceh: The Paradox of Power, Co-optation and Resistance*, Routledge, London.

Siegel, James T. 2000, *The Rope of God*, The University of Michigan Press, Ann Arbor.

Siegel, James T. 2005, 'Peduli Aceh', *Indonesia*, no. 79, pp. 165–167.

Sjamsuddin, Nazaruddin 1985, *Republican Revolt: A Study of the Acehnese Rebellion*, Institute of Southeast Asian Studies, Singapore.

Sukma, Rizal 2004 'Security Operations in Aceh: Goals, Consequences and Lessons', *Policy Studies*, no. 3, East West Center, Washington, DC.

Sulistiyanto, Priyambudi 2001, 'Wither Aceh?', *Third World Quarterly*, vol. 22, no. 3, pp. 437–452.

UNFPA 2005, 'Gender-Based Violence in Aceh, Indonesia', *Consultative Meeting*, Bucharest, Romania, 17–20 October.

UNIFEM 2005, 'Aceh, Tsunami's Women Survivors Demand Greater Role in Recovery and Reconstruction Efforts', 23 June, available at: www.unifem.org/news_events/story_detail.php?StoryID=251 (accessed 12 January 2008).

Vianen, Inge 2006, 'Working Women, Gender and Work in Nanggroe Aceh Darussalam', Working Paper, available at: www.ilo.org/public/english/region/asro/jakarta/download/genderinaceh.pdf (accessed 10 November 2006).

Waylen, Georgina 1993, 'Women's Movements and Democratization in Latin America', *Third World Quarterly*, vol. 14, no. 3, pp. 573–587.

World Bank 2008, *Aceh Poverty Assessment 2008: The Impact of the Conflict, the Tsunami and Reconstruction on Poverty in Aceh*, available at: www-wds.worldbank.org/servlet/WDSContentServer/IW3P/IB/2008/01/09/000020953_20080109160816/Rendered/PDF/421010Aceh0Pov1nt0P010437501PUBLIC1.pdf.

Zeccola, Paul 2007, 'A Heroine for Humanity', *Inside Indonesia*, vol. 90.

4 Conversation on equality and rights

Introduction

The freer political environment in post-tsunami Aceh has helped women activists to engage in debates about how best to interpret the Islamic doctrines as the basis to form Islamic law. They referred to the historical practices found in Aceh when it was an Islamic kingdom in the thirteenth century. The public sphere in the city of Banda Aceh became very lively as people freely discussed their religion and how it should be positioned and used to create a better Aceh. Thus, the work of Acehnese women activists in response to the implementation of Islamic law developed alongside Aceh's broader social and political transformation, both responding to and influencing it.

In trying to understand the responses of Acehnese women activists, two women's networks are worth looking at. These two women's networks were established after the Islamic law was introduced. They were JPUK or Jaringan Perempuan Untuk Kebijakan (the Women's Policy Network) and the Gender Working Group (GWG). Both JPUK and GWG represented local women's movements in Aceh whose members were NGO workers from both local and national branches of NGOs working in the province, academics and government officials. They voluntarily joined the networks, united by the agenda of the movement, to advance women's call for justice and equality under the implementation of Islamic law. The advocacy and activities carried out by these two networks made them part of the major civil society movements in socio-political and legal reform in Aceh.

Literature on women's movements has acknowledged the difficulty of strictly defining what should be considered to be 'women's movements'. 'Women's movements can be seen as [a process] of women's mobilization based on appeals to women both as a constituency and as an organization' (Ferree and Mueller 2004, 577). Women's movements bring women's political activities to empower women to challenge limitations to their roles, and create networks among women that enhance women's ability to recognize existing gender relations as oppressive and in need of change (Ferree and Mueller 2004, 577). Gandhi and Shah (cited in Bystydzienski and Sekhon 1999, 11) characterize women's movements in the late twentieth century as 'fluid, diverse, fragmented, sporadic, issue-oriented and autonomous, employing different ideological thought and strategies'. Thus, women's movements encompass a great variety of organizations, NGOs, other groups or actions, many of which 'emerge in response to the needs of and are firmly anchored in local communities'. Margolis (1993, 379) argued that every women's movement follows a distinctive course, developing its unique agenda in response to local circumstances.

As mentioned, women's movements can consist of women activists of Muslim-based organizations or women's NGOs. NGOs, unlike women's movements, are run by specialized, paid and professional staff with only a small number of volunteers (Alvarez 1999, 185–186). In terms of funding, NGOs obtain the support of international or national donors. They engage in pragmatic and strategic planning which aims to influence public policy. Unlike NGOs, women's movements are largely made up of volunteers, who are sporadic participants rather than 'staff'. They also have more informal organizational structures and operate on a smaller budget. Women's movements and their actions are guided by 'more loosely defined, conjectural goals or objectives'. Based on this discussion, I categorize women's movements in Aceh as encompassing all kinds of women's activism, including women's organizations involved in human rights, research and advocacy, women's NGOs and women members of religious, mass-based organizations attempting to enhance women's awareness of gender relations, and to initiate change and reform to both social norms and Islamic legal doctrines.[1]

JPUK and GWG were the two major women's networks that existed in Aceh during post-tsumani reconstruction that not only actively demanded reform of the *Qanun* but also attempted to advance the socio-economic and political interests of Acehnese women. These two networks used and navigated different strategies and targeted different audiences while they shared similar goals. They attempted to develop public awareness of women's rights in Islam to challenge discriminatory practices in the implementation of Islamic law. Women's movements demand that religious leaders and government institutions include women in rereading the sources of Islamic law, so that *Qanun* will not discriminate against women but instead guarantee equality. They worked to teach the local communities, both male and female, how to understand Islamic texts, about the history of revelation of the *Qur'an* and *Sunna*, and how Islamic texts become the rules of the people. The social interaction of the local activists with those from outside Aceh has contributed to the different views they offered over particular topics pertaining to women's issues, gender equality and the issue of justice and rights.

Women's Network for Policy (JPUK)

There are a number of regulations that fundamentally change the way politics was carried out in Aceh alongside Indonesia's democratization. It started with Law No. 44/1999 on Autonomy, which granted the province the right to organize and manage its own religious, cultural and educational affairs and granted the religious leaders a greater role in policy-making as recognition of Aceh's uniqueness (Miller 2004, 333).[2] In 2001, the Special Region Status under the Autonomy law allows the Acehnese to directly elect their local leaders. Thus, the granting of autonomy to the local government in Aceh in 1999 and the Special Region Status of Aceh in 2001 provided the Acehnese greater opportunity to participate in public policy-making.[3] In the later development, the widening participation of Acehnese into politics was also granted in the Helsinki Peace Agreement signed in 2005. The MOU stipulated that Aceh can have local political parties (unique among all Indonesian provinces) and can directly elect its local leaders: Article 1 (2) of the MOU on Political Participation, paragraph (1), provides that:

> As soon as possible and not later than one year from the signing of this MOU, GOI (Government of Indonesia) agrees to and will facilitate the establishment of Aceh-based political parties that meet national criteria.

Paragraph 2 adds:

> The people of Aceh will have the right to nominate candidates for the positions of all elected officials to contest the elections in Aceh in April 2006 and thereafter Acehnese are also granted the freedom to elect its governor, regents and mayors.

Paragraph 6 further provides:

> Full participation of all Acehnese people in local and national election will be guaranteed in accordance with the Constitution of the Republic of Indonesia.

The MOU also provided that the local legislature would redraft the Law on the Governing of Aceh as written in Article 1 (4). This meant that after the signing of the MOU, the local legislature would create new regulations to be enacted as part of the process of political reform. Article 1 (4) requires the new law to include universal principles of human rights. It provides that:

> The legislature of Aceh will redraft the legal code for Aceh on the basis of the universal principles of human rights as provided for the United Nations International Covenants on civil and political rights, and on economy, social and cultural rights.

These legal developments provided Acehnese men and women with the opportunity to play much wider roles and to take part in local politics to reform the existing regulations, the sharia law and other future regulations. Activists, as the basic guidelines for their activism, have used the inclusion that the future law in Aceh should refer to the universal principles of human rights.

This background prompted women activists in Aceh who were part of Jaringan Perempuan untuk Kebijakan (JPUK, Women's Policy Network) to advocate changes to some of the laws already enacted and to influence the drafting of the future laws. JPUK was created in 2004 by dozens of women activists and academics who shared concerns over the small number of women in the bureaucracy and local parliament.[4] The small representation of women in parliament would give serious impact to the formulation of local regulations that lack gender interests. In the 1999 general election, no women were elected as members of local parliament, and in the 2004 general election only six women were elected. This means women constituted only 4.3 per cent of 69 members of local parliaments.[5] This development led women activists from various local NGOs such as Syarifah Rahmatillah, the leader of local women's NGO Mitra Sejati Perempuan Indonesia, Khairani Arifin from RPUK, and female academics from Syiah Kuala University and State Institute of Islamic Studies (IAIN) Ar-Raniry to organize into JPUK.[6]

When created in 2004, the founders of JPUK expected the network would provide Acehnese women (such as women activists, women academics, women judges and women religious leaders) greater opportunity to influence the formation of local regulations. One JPUK activist said that the network aimed to provide the legislature and the bureaucracy with recommendations on issues related to gender and women's interests (interview, Banda Aceh, 4 March 2007).

JPUK activists were mostly leaders of local women's NGOs or other women's mass-based organizations such as Aisyiyah, the women's wing of the moderate Muslim organization Muhammadiyah or Fathayat, the women's wing of Nahdhlatul Ulama. Most of the activists at JPUK were graduates of the Faculty of Law of Syiah Kuala University. There were also women activists with a background in Islamic studies, such as the female IAIN Ar-Raniry lecturer and activist Dr Nurjannah Ismail; a woman judge from the Mahkamah Syariat, Roosmawardani; and Soraya Devi, the head of IAIN Ar-Raniry's Center for Women's Studies.

To women activists at JPUK, the legal provisions mentioned above were political openings that allow women activists to ensure that women's gender interests will be included in new laws. Apart from the points mandated in the MOU, Law No. 10/2004 on the Mechanism of Creating Legislation also supports women's public participation, and Article 238 of the Law on Governing Aceh (LOGA) provides that the public has the right to give both oral and written suggestions within the process of deliberation of *Qanun*, and that public participation is guaranteed at every stage of drafting the *Qanun*. Chapter 25 of *Qanun* No. 3/2007 on the making of *Qanun* is also a basis for a public participation, as it provides that public participation can take the form of seminar, workshops, focus group discussions and public hearings (Novianan and Yudiansyah 2009).[7]

During the process of preparing the LOGA, which was finally enacted in 2006, JPUK proposed 26 themes related to women's issues to be included in the new Law for Aceh. Of these, only six were finally included into the LOGA. They include: Article 75 on the requirement of local political parties to have 30 per cent of women's participation; Article 231 on the role of the governor and deputy vice governor in gender mainstreaming efforts; Article 138 on women's representation at the MPU; Article 154 (3) on women's access and government credit for women's business; and Article 215 (2) on the role of education in women's empowerment and the role of government and Acehnese society protecting women's rights (UNIFEM 2007).

JPUK also played a significant role in the process of drafting the Law on Governing Aceh (LOGA) or RUUPA (Rancangan Undang-Undang Peraturan Aceh), finally enacted as Law No. 11/2006. LOGA was promulgated as implementing the MOU between the Gerakan Aceh Merdeka (GAM, the Free Aceh Movement) and the Indonesian Government in Helsinki in 2005.[8]

Immediately after the 2006 Law on Governing Aceh was enacted, the local parliament planned to enact 59 *Qanun* during the period of 2007 to 2012 (UNIFEM 2007). Of these 59 *Qanun*, there were draft *Qanun* that occupied the attention of activists at JPUK. They included a *Qanun* on the making of *Qanun*; a *Qanun Jinayah* on criminal law; a *Qanun* on women's empowerment; a *Qanun* on land ownership; a *Qanun* on the implementation of Islamic law; and a *Qanun* on local political parties and local elections (UNIFEM 2005). JPUK attempted to ensure that these *Qanun* would pay attention to women's needs and would not discriminate against women or ignore women's gender interests. They also wanted to ensure that any policy or *Qanun* produced by the local government led to gender equality and justice.[9]

There were two events than can be used to see JPUK's achievements in lobbying and advocating for women's interests to be included into the new law. The first was its attempt to lobby for changes to the draft *Qanun* on local leader elections, or PILKADA. JPUK demanded the local parliament revise the draft *Qanun*, saying that it discriminated against women. The draft provided in Article 1 that:

> Everyone has the right to be elected in the election; everyone has the right to nominate oneself as a political party candidate to be nominated by a political party or join other candidates from a political party or to be nominated by a coalition of political parties (Article 41 Article 1).

JPUK criticized Article 1 of the draft *Qanun*, arguing that it did not clearly mention 'women' but used only the non-gender specific word *setiap orang* or 'everyone'. JPUK saw this as too vague and demanded that the article deliberately mention *perempuan dan laki-laki*, 'woman and man', so it was clear that both have equal rights to be elected.

JPUK also demanded changes to Article 2, which, according to them set limits on how one can be elected. The article required that all candidates:

> Have the ability to apply sharia law, can recite the *Qur'an* and are able to become *Imam* (leader) in the prayer and can deliver the sermon (*khatib*).

JPUK argued that this article intentionally limited women's opportunities to participate in the election, since, when enacted, the *Qanun* would require political candidate in the election to be capable of being an *Imam* and a *Khatib*. In the local context of Aceh, women are strongly prohibited from acting as an *Imam* or leading a congregation in prayer or becoming a *Khatib* (one who delivers the sermon after the prayer). JPUK saw that if the *Qanun* was passed it therefore would preclude women from running as candidates. Women activists did agree, however, that both men and women candidates should be required to be able to recite the *Qur'an*. JPUK, therefore, demanded that the article read:

> Be able to follow sharia law and can read from the *Qur'an* if they are a man or woman, and if they are man, be able to lead prayer.

JPUK was successful and its demand for changes to these drafts was accepted and incorporated into the *Qanun*, which was finally enacted as *Qanun* 7/2006 on the Election of Local Leaders. Since JPUK was concerned about the under-representation of women in the local parliament, it proposed two articles for inclusion in the LOGA:

> Local political parties can be established and formed by at least fifty Indonesian citizens who are over twenty-one years old of age with at least 30% of them women who are domiciled in Aceh (paragraph 2).
> The leadership of political parties should at least consist of 30% (thirty percent) of women (paragraph 5).

These two articles were finally enacted as part of Chapter XI, Article 75 on Local Political Parties of Article No. 75 of LOGA.

Successful in influencing the formation of the LOGA, JPUK also played a crucial role in the process of drafting *Qanun* on women's empowerment and the protection of children, which began in 2007. This *Qanun* was introduced by the Women's Empowerment Bureau (BIRO Pemberdayaan Perempuan) of the province of Aceh and prepared by the Law Division within the Governor's Office. In particular, JPUK argued for the need to include three issues that were not adequately addressed in the draft *Qanun* on women's empowerment, domestic violence, and gender mainstreaming and gender empowerment. JPUK was supported by Oxfam in its attempts to support and promote the enactment of this *Qanun*. It organized a series of workshops involving activists, academics and government officials to discuss several points that it believed required the attention of policy-makers. To gain more insight, JPUK invited activists from Jakarta and used Law No. 12/2006 on Citizenship (*Kewarganegaraan*) and Law No. 13/2006 on the Protection of Witnesses and Victims as the basis for its recommendations. The draft *Qanun* was eventually amended on the basis on JPUK's requests as regards women's rights, education, women's health, labour issues, women's public participation, economy, social security, women's empowerment and social participation. The *Qanun* on Women's Empowerment was finally enacted as *Qanun* No. 9/2009 on Women's Empowerment and Protection.

Besides advocating and promoting gender equality through political institutions as elaborated above, women's activists from JPUK continued to work to develop gender awareness among the members of parliament, the bureaucracy, and within the religious community. Through its activism and advocacy, this women's network had been able to significantly influence the making of public policy. Activists of JPUK argued that although individual women's NGOs may have been working to advocate public policy-making, coalitions of local women's NGOs, academics, women religious leaders and other members of civil society organizations were more likely to produce significant contributions to the betterment of Acehnese women.

The JPUK women's network has also helped in forming new perceptions among Acehnese men and women regarding their rights under Islamic law. The work of JPUK can be seen from the fact that it had been successful in introducing the issues of women's equality and women's rights not only to the local government, the local legislature and bureaucracy, and religious leaders, but also to the people of Aceh. Gender equality, women's rights and the need for a reinterpretation of Islam did, in fact, become a standard part of public discussions among Acehnese at that period of time. This demonstrated a positive trend for women and their movements within the context of women's struggles for equality under Islamic law. This demonstrates that JPUK has the ability to set its own goals, agenda and choose its own forms of struggle, while continuing to develop networks with women's movements in Jakarta and working with international organizations and foreign NGOs.

Gender Working Group

The second women's network that had significant influence in promoting gender equality and women's rights within the implementation of Islamic law in Aceh was the Gender Working Group, known by activists as GWG. The GWG was established immediately after the tsunami in 2005. International institutions and foreign donors, such as USAID, UNIFEM and UNFPA together with the Agency for the Rehabilitation and Reconstruction of Aceh and Nias (BRR)[10] and the Women's Empowerment Bureau (Biro PP), supported its creation. At its initial establishment, the major objective behind the establishment of GWG was to support the work of the Women's Empowerment Bureau of the Province of Nanggroe Aceh Darussalam (NAD) since many members of its staff were killed by the tsunami, making it difficult for the Bureau to provide assistance to Acehnese women who were victims of the tsunami.[11] In its later development, GWG's work did not only focus on providing support to women affected by the tsunami, but also attempted to promote gender equality and protect women from discriminatory practices justified by reference to the Islamic law.

Different from JPUK, GWG applied a clearer structural system, as a result of it being under the Bureau of Women's Empowerment. The head of the Bureau, Lailisma, automatically became the leader of GWG. She expected all women's organizations working in Aceh to join GWG, but some local women's NGOs did not join. They held regular meeting organized by the Bureau office. The head of the Bureau always opened the meeting. On average, the meeting was attended by about 10–12 activists. Interestingly, some of the audience were also male activists. In an interview, Lailisma in fact expected more activists to actively join GWG in order to push their agenda forward into government agenda (interview, Banda Aceh, 14 December 2007). Arabiyani, the manager of the Women and Children's Unit at BRR, however, expressed her doubts as to the level of commitment of women activists to the cause of women's movements when it was under the government apparatus. Many activists saw the agenda of GWG as being closely inclined to the local government's agenda, giving some doubts to women activists that working within GWG would advance women's interests and promote gender equality.

It was obvious then that there were significant differences between GWG and JPUK. In terms of its members, active members of GWG were mostly younger activists who are staff of new local women's NGOs, for example, from Beujroh, Rifka An-Nisa, Balai Syura Ureung Inong Aceh, Bungong Jeumpa and Sri Ratu. Many of these activists were in their late twenties and early thirties. Interestingly, these activists mostly knew each other quite well because they came from the same student movement groups, active in the late 1990s and early 2000s. Unlike JPUK, activists from the Jakarta-based NGOs such as Kapal Perempuan and international organizations such as UNIFEM, UNFPA or the World Bank were also involved in GWG activities.

The history behind the establishment of GWG make it look like the *perpanjangantangan* or 'extension' of the bureaucracy. This can be seen for example in how the head of the Bureau attempted to direct the kind of programmes that GWG conducts. If JPUK has demonstrated its ability to influence policy-making, GWG's activities were more inclined to building grassroots and public awareness on women's issues. For example, in 2007 and 2008, to celebrate International Women's Day, GWG organized a long march attended by hundreds of Acehnese men and women. In 2007, the march ended in front of the local parliament building. Activists met with members of local parliament to convey their assessments of the various issues that challenged Acehnese women in post-tsunami and post-conflict Aceh and that needed government attention. In 2007, GWG released a report that summarized their assessment of the problems still confronting Acehnese women in post-tsunami and post-conflict Aceh. The report was critical towards the local government policy resulting in a series of incidents in which women were discriminated against in the context of the implementation of Islamic law. From various conversations, it was clear that some GWG activists believed that problems facing Acehnese women in post-tsunami and post-conflict Aceh were exacerbated by the discriminatory application of Islamic law.

In their meetings, women activists at GWG discussed various problems Acehnese women have to deal with in their lives, including issues that were still considered to be very sensitive in Aceh, such as polygamy, domestic violence and homosexuality. They talked about how difficult it is to be an Acehnese woman nowadays, as they are tasked not only with helping with their children's homework at night, since their husbands choose to spend their time in local coffee shops and only returning home at midnight, but also they need to support the household. Still, women have to accept the fact that their husbands are taking second wives and also that they are being discriminated against in taking socio-economic and political roles in the public sphere.

Thus, one issue that became the subject of discussion among activists at GWG was polygamy. However, it was interesting to see how activists showed their different views and perspectives on the issue of polygamy. While some activists agreed that polygamy is a form of domestic violence, others rejected the idea that it has to be categorized as domestic violence. The latter argued that Islam does not prohibit polygamy. In all these discussions, women activists at GWG usually referred to the views of Islamic feminists from Jakarta, such as Musdah Mulia. Musdah Mulia, a professor at the State Islamic University Syarif Hidayatullah Jakarta, works for the Ministry of Religion and is a prominent Muslim woman activist who believes that gender equality is taught in Islam. She has criticized the practice of polygamy, and the use of Islamic texts to justify polygamy (*The Jakarta Post* 2006).[12]

The many topics that GWG activists were interested in have caused concern to the head of the Bureau and GWG leader, Lailisma. In her opinion, some of the discourse has stretched the limits of Islamic conservatism. Lailisma would rather see GWG's activities more in line with the Bureau's agenda, which is to advance women's interests along with the implementation of Islamic law. There was one incident, however, which I will describe in more detail, which shows how members of GWG and the head of the Bureau view the problems confronting women's movements from very different perspectives.

There was a meeting that the Bureau called to be organized on 29 January 2008. It was two days after hundreds of students of *Dayah* and traditional *Ulama* from *Dayah* organized a mass rally in front of the Grand Baiturrahman Mosque. The rally demanded the dissolution of women's NGOs in Aceh, on the grounds that women's NGOs work for Western interests to destroy Islamic values in Aceh and disrupt the implementation of Islamic law. Lailisma saw this movement as a serious threat to the women's struggle because the *Dayah* community has strong support in villages across Aceh. Her great concern was the fact that the traditional *Dayah* community may not allow women's NGOs and activists to work with villagers across the province. The rejection by conservative *Ulama* of the activities of women's movements could jeopardize the agenda of women's movements and, if this is not dealt with in a careful way, it may create greater resistance within conservative religious communities.

Confronted by this fact, the head of the Bureau along with women activists in Aceh expressed disappointment at the fact that conservative religious communities were still suspicious of the activities of women's movements. Lailisma told dozen of activists sitting in the meeting room how disappointed she was when learning about such events. She said she immediately contacted several prominent figures, including the Head of the Office of Islamic Sharia, several government officials, a number of members of local parliament and senior women's activists. Without explaining what was discussed, she said that the conversations she had with key figures led her to think that women activists needed to respond this development by taking a softer approach in implementing the women's movement agenda so that there will be no further resentment from the *Dayah* community. According to her, the head of Dinas Syariat Islam, Professor Alyasa Abubakar, was of the view that part of the resistance of the *Dayah* community was because people in *Dayah* and in the villages had no clear idea of what it is that women activists are trying to do with their campaign on 'equality'. They did not understand why they were suddenly being taught that women need to be 'equal' with men.[13] Other activists in the room were in silence listening to the explanation of the head of the Bureau.

Lailisma also said that the resistance in the community to women activists was also driven by the fact that some of the activists have been too fervent in introducing the idea of gender equality in the training programmes they organized. She therefore reminded women activists at the meeting of the need to be 'extra cautious' in disseminating their programmes on issues of gender equality, especially when relating it to religion and local culture. She has pointed out that some activists, in particular those from Jakarta, often do not wear a scarf or *jilbab* when they reached out to villagers, carried out programmes, and met villagers, which according to many local Acehnese was a breach of the law and against local culture. This, she said, was one of the reasons why the appreciation of the work of women's NGOs and activists was so minimal among the conservative religious communities. She also referred to foreign NGO activists who came and worked in villages and talked about gender equality without having an adequate understanding of local traditions. To her, introducing the idea of 'equality' to a strongly patriarchal community like Aceh must be done in a way that paid attention to the 'culture of the people' or *'memperhatikan budaya masyarakat'*. She referred to the use of the term 'gender equality', or 'kesetaraan antara laki-laki dan perempuan', the catchword among women's activists. She said that if not properly explained, the world 'equal' or 'kesetaraan' would be understood by many Acehnese as *sama* or 'same' in English. Thus, the term gender equality could be understood as an attempt to make men and women 'the same', while 'equal' would mean *seimbang* or that it refers to 'role' or *peran* rather than the physical objective of being equal. But, this complication with the terminology was not being explained and delivered adequately to the people in the villages.

The head of the Bureau also told a story, as an example. She said she heard from a report, which involved a health-based NGO working in several villages, that its workers talked to Acehnese villagers about female circumcision.

They told villagers that circumcision to female babies must not be carried out and explained that there are no health benefits from doing it.[14] Listening to this information, the community was shocked because they had long believed that female circumcision is part of the tradition and part of observing Islamic religious piety. Thus, what they heard easily caused anger among the community. Lailisma said it is this type of activity and information that led many Acehnese to think that the work of NGOs is 'un-Islamic' and corrupted Islam as a religion.

After telling this story, the head of the Bureau asked women activists to be very cautious with what they were telling villagers. In addition to that, Lailisma also warned the activists that it is very important for them to not question the implementation of Islamic law as, for her, all Acehnese activists should accept and support the process. In her words, 'It is a pity if any of the Acehnese women activists still question the implementation of Islamic law'. She said that women activists must reject any accusations that Acehnese women have experienced a setback since the implementation of Islamic law. In light of this, it is obvious that Lailisma, as part of the government bureaucracy, must support the policies of the local government, including the implementation of Islamic law. Thus, any attempt to promote 'equality' and women's rights within the agenda of the Bureau must be framed in terms of Islamic law.

An activist from An-Nisa, a new local women's NGO, showed her support for Lailisma's statement, saying that it is important that local women activists in Aceh understand how gender should be defined and how to disseminate the idea of gender equality to a strongly Islamic and patriarchal society. According to her, if women activists and their gender-related programmes aim to create equal social, economic and political opportunities for men and women, then they should be clear what 'equal' means in the context of Aceh. She argued that it would be hard, if not impossible, for women activists to achieve their goals if references are made to 'equality' as in the West. Any women activist who dreams of totally changing the character of Acehnese women to follow what woman in the West practise should leave Aceh, she said. She further argued that she was strongly against the attitude of some of her fellow activists from outside Aceh and who claimed to be working to advance women's interests but did not pay attention to sensitive cultural issues such as veiling. She said she understand that many women activists believe that Muslim women have the right to choose either to veil or not because they understand the different interpretations of sharia, but that is not the case for many Acehnese. She argued that many Acehnese men and women still cannot accept a woman who does not cover her hair or who wears dress that is considered to be un-Islamic. Likewise, those who live in the villages have not yet been exposed to *Fiqh* knowledge as those activists had. Many Acehnese women, especially those who live in the villages, only understand that women are required to cover their hair and to wear a loose dress to cover their *aurat*, and perceive that it is what Islam requires. Thus, she suggested that her fellow activists should negotiate their own understandings on these matters with those subscribed to by most Acehnese. She said, 'Even though you disagree with how the *Qanun* on Muslim dress has been implemented, we still need to pay attention to it if we want society to accept us'. This argument is significant, because, as for many other Muslim women in Indonesia, Acehnese understandings of Islam are mainly based on how Islam has been taught by religious leaders, mostly men. As a result, it becomes difficult to differentiate the 'real teaching of Islam' as activists may see it from what is believed to be the local tradition.

Apparently not everyone at that meeting agreed both with the head of the Bureau or the activist whose views I have first described. One activist, the Head of Women's Studies Center of the Syiah Kuala University, Sri Walni, disagreed with what had been discussed. She said that, to her, it is the task of women activists to introduce the real teachings of Islam. It is the real challenge for activists or NGO workers to change the mindset of the community and the understanding of people in the villages. She further argued that the Acehnese need to be informed that they cannot rely only on the interpretations of Islam and social practices taught to them, because those interpretations and practices that have lived and practised in the society often derive only from local (patriarchal) cultures and not from Islam. To her, the reality that had been mentioned was the background for women activists to work in introducing new understanding to men and women.

From the above discussion, it was clear that women activists in Aceh were struggling to define how they should promote equality, women's status and women's rights while facing resistance from the conservative religious community. The different background and exposure among the activists themselves made it even more difficult for them in defining the strategy and approach they should use to achieve their goals.

The difficulty women activists face in challenging the conservative religious community stems, to an extent, from the lack of women activists' knowledge of Islam itself. This is because most women activists come from secular educational backgrounds, which makes it difficult for them to base their arguments within an Islamic framework. However, there were indications that local women activists have begun to reread the Islamic texts, the *Qur'an*, *Hadith* and *Fiqh* commentaries, and learn from similar movements that have appeared in other Muslim societies and even from what has developed in other provinces in Indonesia (Anwar 2001; Othman 2006).

As in many post-colonial societies, local activists in Aceh as described above were reluctant to acknowledge that their struggle for equality is, to a certain extent, inspired by feminism. Basu (1995, 6), for example, observes that many women in the Third World are uncomfortable with the concept of feminism because of the widespread belief that its inspiration, origins and relevance are 'Western' and 'bourgeois'. She further argues that many women narrowly associate feminism with certain 'ideologies', 'strategies' and 'approaches'.

Fitri, an activist from Flower Aceh, an organization well-known for its struggle for human rights during military conflict, denies, however that the struggle for gender equality in Aceh follows feminist ideas (interview, Banda Aceh, 10 March 2007). According to her, feminism is not in line with the teaching of Islam. Fitri herself was not wearing proper *jilbab*, as she only covered her hair by draping a shawl and let her red-dyed hair fall on her back uncovered. Certainly, she was not the only activist in Aceh who strongly rejects the idea that women's movements in Aceh are driven by feminism, despite rejecting the way the Islamic law has been enforced.

The Head of the Centre for Gender Studies of Syiah Kuala University, Sri Walni, was aware of this situation, but argued that resistance to outside values arises precisely because some women activists were being too cautious about using terms associated with the 'Western'. She said that if lay people are critical of the terms 'gender' and 'feminist' because both are seen as 'Western', then women activists should show the Acehnese that 'gender' or 'feminism' is no different to 'burgers', 'Kentucky Fried Chicken' or 'Pizza Hut', all Western products that have increasingly become popular in Aceh. By saying this, she wanted to assure her colleagues that, as activists, they should not be over-cautious in introducing new understandings that can benefit women.

The meeting at the Women's Empowerment Bureau's office took almost two hours and at the end some activists were still not happy with what had been discussed. The head of the Bureau was still trying to demand that activists consider what she had said. When the meeting was over, I saw disappointment in the faces of many young activists. They resented the fact that, in their view, the Bureau had not listened to their concerns, instead wanting to co-opt women's movements, as they saw it. One activist who sat next to me said, 'See, I do not know where our movement will go from here'. She seemed to be deeply disappointed by the fact that the activities of women's movements have to be subject to the approval of the authorities.

There were, however, some interesting developments at GWG in 2008. After my fieldwork finished, the Women's Empowerment Bureau began the process of transforming to become a government agency. In Indonesia's bureaucratic system there is a significant difference in terms of the administrative structure and authority between a government bureau and a government agency. The first has limited authority while the latter has wider administrative authority. One of the obvious differences is that a government bureau sits under the administrative structure of the local government, while as an agency it is directly responsible only to the Governor of Aceh. This transformation of the Bureau into an agency was the result of women's activists' intensive lobbying. Women activists perceive that given the complexities of gender problems, there is a need for a government agency that has the authority to address problems autonomously. As a government agency, the new institution no longer works under the supervision of the local government secretariat, and will be allocated a larger budget.

The transformation of the Bureau into an agency provides the institution with greater capacity to deal with the complexity of gender issues. It will, for example, have the authority to provide protection to children. In an interview I had with Lailisma, the head of the Bureau in 2007, she said that the transformation will be very helpful because under the current administrative structure her office was only given limited room to initiate policies and allocated a very small budget. In addition, all policies also need to be approved by the Provincial Secretariat. Problems appear as the Provincial Secretariat did not see women's issues as its priority.

Despite the different perspectives of women activists and the head of the women's Bureau, women activists (especially at GWG) expected Lailisma to lead the new institution. Compared to other women leaders in Aceh, Lailisma was one of the more moderate government figures and for that reason activists expressed their strong preference for her to fill the new post. Women activists were therefore disappointed when she was not appointed. Instead, Irwandi Yusuf,[15] the Governor of Aceh, on 10 March 2008, assigned Raihan Putri to lead the new government body.[16] This created bewilderment among women activists, especially those who were active members of the GWG, because Raihan,[17] formerly the leader of the Center for Women Studies at the IAIN Ar-Raniry and a lecturer at IAIN, was considered by activists to be very conservative. Raihan had often attacked women activists and accused them of ignoring Aceh's traditional values and Islam in promoting gender equality. Many local activists were therefore worried that the election of Raihan Putri would create a setback for women's movements. In an interview before she was elected, Raihan had, for example, expressed her concern at the activities of women's NGO activists (Banda Aceh, 5 March 2007). She mentioned, for example, that at one event she attended, organized by an NGO, the activist who opened the forum did not greet the meeting with *Assalamu'alaikum* (peace be upon you), the Islamic greeting, and instead, said, *Selamat Pagi*. To many Acehnese, including her, it is important that people greet each other with *Assalamu'alaikum*. This incident strengthened her argument that some activists ignore Islam and local traditional values and have their agenda of changing Acehnese culture. One activist told me that one of the reasons for the appointment of Raihan Putri over Lailisma was based on the answer she gave to a question asked by the governor during the interview process (interview, Banda Aceh, 7 June 2008). Both were asked about their views on polygamous marriage. It was circulated among activists that Raihan Putri said she accepts polygamy and that she understands Islam allows polygamous marriage. A different answer was, however, given by Lailisma. She said Islam inherently prohibits polygamous marriage and that the practice of polygamy disadvantages women.

In 2009, GWG has ended its affiliation with the Government Agency for Women and Children's Protection. Raihan said there are too many differences in how GWG and her office view women's issues in Aceh. According to her, one of the characteristics of women's empowerment programmes in

Aceh is that they need to be in accordance with Islamic law so that gender empowerment advocacy efforts must focus on creating *Qanun* that are gender-responsive based on Islam (interview, Banda Aceh, 27 January 2007). During my visit in June 2009, Raihan criticized some activists and women's NGOs in Aceh for not paying attention to the special status of Aceh, that is, the application of Islamic law. She said that her agency has been trying to ensure that it advocates an 'Islamic' gender mainstreaming programme.

In 2008, soon after the agency was established, it published a book entitled *Relasi Gender Dalam Masyarakat Aceh (Perspektif Islam)* (Gender Relations in Acehnese Society (Islamic Perspective)). The book was written by Raihan herself, who also has a Master's degree in Education from IAIN Ar-Raniry. The book explores several *Qur'anic* verses that outline how Islam guarantees equality between men and women and assigns the respective roles of men and women. In its preface, Raihan wrote that the book can be used as a reference in understanding 'gender', which has become increasingly popular among the Acehnese. She said, 'gender' in Aceh has to be understood within the framework of *syari'at*, which means that gender relations carry with them both the concepts of 'equality' and that of 'differences' among men and women. She wrote, 'Islam strongly opposes Western principles of gender that advocate "free for all action"'.

Resistance and challenges

While activists claim that their work is to advance women's interests and promote better status for women, the above discussion on resistance towards women's NGO work in Aceh proved otherwise. Many Acehnese, including women, whose rights the activists are fighting for, have no idea about some of the issues. Lila Abu-Lughod (2010) criticized the work of the 'rights' activists and questioned how activists can claim their works are in the interests of women. When working in the villages, NGO activists encounter resistance, as their agenda might not be what the Acehnese women need at that time.

Suraiya Kamaruzzaman, a woman activist in Aceh and former leader of the NGO Flower Aceh, argues that since women's movements were established in Aceh, they have consistently worked to promote women's rights (interview, Banda Aceh, 14 December 2007), because many Acehnese women continue to be targets for human rights violators. During conflict, women were violently targeted by the military and GAM, and under the implementation of Islamic law, women were targeted by the WH.

Kamaruzzaman also identified several issues that impeded women's movements in Aceh during that period. Many women's NGOs (which she considered as the backbone of local women's movements) did not have a strong basis at the grassroots level. They did not understand the needs of the grassroots. This contributed to the difficulty for women activists to disseminate new understandings of gender equality and women's rights. Villagers were not familiar with the activists who came to their villages and told them how to do things. It is also worth mentioning that the history of military conflict made many Acehnese suspicious when receiving people they were not familiar with. Thus, a special approach was needed to work with the larger community.

Despite the approach used by activists, Kamaruzzaman also considered problems with women's movements in Aceh that stemmed from the lack of adequate organizational capacity of many local women's NGOs. She said, 'these organizations are weak, they are not driven by a voluntary vision to support and work with Acehnese women'. Lacking the organizational skills and capacity, she believed, would easily bring women's organizations to end their programmes, especially without sustainable financial support. She said, 'when there is no longer support available for local women's NGOs, they would disappear'. This assessment seems to be quite right. Many of the local women's NGOs that were there during the post-tsunami reconstruction are no longer active. This is especially true since foreign donors that previously worked in Aceh under the reconstruction project left the province in 2011.

In regards to the resistance from the religious community towards the issues that women's movements in Aceh was trying to introduce, Kamarruzzaman saw this as one of the serious challenges to the local movements. The lack of understanding towards the issue of sharia, women's rights and status in Islam, the definition of *Fiqh*, and the teaching of Islamic texts among the women activists themselves is what made the movement difficult to work out. The lack of understanding of the issues mentioned above meant women activists often failed to deliver their message to their audience, especially to the religious community. While proclaiming to be activists, many, however, have only worked for women's NGOs for a short while, and had no previous training on gender let alone on Islamic jurisprudence. These activists are dispatched to villages and to meet with the community to deliver and introduce 'gender' or 'equality' as part of their NGO's programme but they lack the necessary knowledge, and, failing to acknowledge local wisdom, they only create confusion.

These all created resistance among traditional communities. Many thought that their social structure would be distorted by the new 'gender equality' programmes introduced by women's NGOs and their activists. Suspicion from the community was also addressed towards the agenda of women's movements of 'empowering' Acehnese women. This notion of 'empowering' is understood by some conservative Acehnese men as an attempt to make women equal to men, thus threatening local social structures and endangering the religious establishment in Aceh. The conservative religious male community perceived the concept of 'equality' or 'empowerment' as not in line with the teachings of Islam.

Kamaruzzaman explained to me a story of how she was confronted by one *Ulama* from a *Dayah* after she finished delivering a speech in a village. He accused her of introducing 'Western' values to the Islamic society. Kamaruzzaman said to me that she used all her knowledge of Islam and the teachings in the *Qur'an* with which she was familiar to convince the *Ulama* that 'equality' is not strange to Islam. She also reiterated the *Qur'anic* verse which says, 'What makes men and women different in Islam is only their religious observance'.[18] In addition, she also used the story of women's roles when Aceh was an Islamic kingdom in the seventeenth and eighteenth centuries. She said that after this long explanation she felt the *Ulama* could see her point of view. Finally the *Ulama* said to her 'then I support you ... I wish I knew this from the beginning'. From this incident, Kamaruzzaman argued that it is necessary for women activists in Aceh to think more carefully how they should deal with the religious community. She said, 'In Aceh, we can not imitate the understanding of gender of A, B, or C from other places, it has to be "gender Aceh"'.

In many training courses, seminars or workshops on gender-related issues, I often see this tension and resistance among the participants. During introductory sessions when participants are introduced to the meaning of 'gender mainstreaming' or 'gender equality' most reject it. In a seminar organized by Yayasan Insan Cita Madani in Banda Aceh on 23–25 January 2008, for example, I heard participants (mostly men) asking the speakers to stop using the word 'gender' during the session. They suggested that the speaker find other words from the local language, with a similar meaning to the word 'gender'.

When faced with resistance on 'gender', local women activists show their uncertainty as to how they should approach this problem. Kamaruzzaman argued that this happens as local activists still have no common understanding of how to define and understand 'gender'. Kamaruzzaman could be correct, because during my fieldwork I often encountered women activists involved in long debates about whether they need to find a local term to replace 'gender', or whether they should continue using 'gender' as it is used in other places in Indonesia. To a senior activist like Kamaruzzaman these developments have disadvantaged women's movements in Aceh and differences among local women activists, she says, will only weaken women's solidarity.

Foreign NGOs, according to Kamaruzzaman, have contributed to these problems. Many Acehnese feel that foreign NGOs activists who work in Aceh are the ones who have introduced the term 'gender'. That is why 'gender' is associated with 'foreign' or 'Western'. These foreign activists have not anticipated the potential for resistance from the Acehnese, forgetting that the Acehnese have a long history of resistance to 'foreign' powers.

In response to the debate on the 'sensitivity' and 'foreignness' of the term 'gender', activists at Aceh Institute introduced the local term *Timang*, to replace the term 'gender'. Mahdi and Zein (2008, xviii) define *Timang* by reference to multiple meanings: *lurus* or straight, *sejajar* or parallel, *adil* or just, and *setara* or equivalent. *Timang* also refers, however, to *mempertimbangkan* or to 'reconsider' and *menganalisa* or to 'analyse' reality objectively. In any case, *Timang* later became the title of a book, launched by Darwati A. Gani, the wife of the current Governor of Aceh, Irwandi Yusuf. In her remarks, Gani expresses her gratitude that the Acehnese have finally found a local term for 'gender' and use it to promote *kesetaraan hubungan* or equal relations between men and women. She says, the word 'gender' is not only 'foreign', but at certain point also irrelevant in the local context. To her, the term *timang* or *kesetaraan hubungan* (equal relations) is easier to accept. Yuval-Davis (1997, 9) has also pointed out the need to invent a word for 'gender' for a non-English-speaking countries, arguing that unless there is a separation between the discourse of sex and that of gender, biology will be constructed as destiny in the political discourse.

One pro-democracy activist, Mashudi (2006), observed that to him, women's movements in Aceh have not yet been successful in developing women's awareness of the need for women to participate in political reform. He referred to an incident where only two women participated in the local leadership election but failed to meet the requirements of being able to read the *Qur'an*. He observed that from the 19 districts and municipalities that conducted local elections, there were only five women political candidates out of 258 candidates, so that only 1.94 per cent of total candidates were women. This small number of women participating in the local election, Mashudi argues, demonstrates the failure of local women's movements to endorse women and facilitate women's participation in local politics. Local women's movements have failed to benefit from the political reform, which has guaranteed women's public participation in politics. He suggests women activists expand their activities to reach women at the grassroots.

Mashudi may be correct, but to assess the success of women's movements only by looking at how many women have participated in the local election is misleading. There is a need to take into account other problems that prevent women from taking public roles, such as whether or not women are supported by their families and the community. So far, women's movements in Aceh have, in fact, been quite successful in developing people's awareness about the need to 'support' women to take up public roles, and they have attempted to ensure that legal regulations in Aceh accommodate women equally with men.

Networking

The proliferation of women's NGOs in Aceh and the variety of issues they were working on were, in part, the result of the arrival of foreign NGOs and international institutions, which originally came to Aceh to provide humanitarian assistance to the Acehnese. As part of the 'building back' spirit, they also introduced various programmes emphasizing the need to pay attention to 'gender'.

An officer working for a UN organization said that although at the beginning many international NGOs came simply to assist in the physical reconstruction of Aceh, they were later 'required' by their donors to include gender mainstreaming within their programmes (interview, Banda Aceh, 12 March 2007). Thus, when international institutions such as the UN or other international NGOs work with local women's NGOs, they created a 'gender mainstreaming' component in their programmes. With dozens of foreign donors supporting local organizations to work on 'gender', 'gender mainstreaming' suddenly became a 'buzzword', occupying the attention of many Acehnese, both in villages and towns. Thus, there were criticisms over this development, arguing that the gender campaign in Aceh has been primarily the creation of Western NGOs, as local NGOs will not receive support if they do not include a 'gender' element in their programmes (Mahdi and Zein 2008, xviii).

Before the arrival of foreign NGOs in Aceh, women's issues were primarily dominated by the state's gender ideology, as discussed in Chapter 3 (Brenner 2005; Suryakusuma 1996; Robinson 2009). Although already established, local women's NGOs in Aceh played a minimal role in promoting women's issues in public during the conflict.

The changing policy of the state towards women cannot be separated from the role of the international donor community, which introduced new strands of aid policy as foreign NGOs intervene, challenging the assumptions and priorities, in this case demanding that women's interests to be taken into account (Kabeer 1991, 45). The effects of this trend can be seen, for example, in the policies of aid donors to Bangladesh who began to earmark separate budgets for women's programmes and for research on women's issues (Kabeer 1991, 45). These developments had positive effects in the Bangladesh context as they introduced a 'new' and 'progressive' vocabulary – such as women's emancipation – into official discourse on women. A similar development occurred in Aceh with the arrival of international institutions and foreign NGOs who introduced local activists and government officials to the need to pay attention to gender problems, women's rights and the equal representation of women.

In the context of Aceh, along with the ongoing political reform and the implementation of Islamic law, foreign institutions and international NGOs introduced new discourses such as 'political participation', 'empowerment' 'women's rights in Islam' and 'gender perspective'. This can be seen from the role of foreign funding in disseminating new ideas to women activists, for example in JPUK or GWG, as discussed earlier. Although the idea of creating JPUK came from local women activists, JPUK also receives support from foreign donors such as the Asia Foundation and international organizations such UNDP (United Nations Development Program) and UNIFEM (United Nations Development Fund for Women).

The Asia Foundation is one foreign NGO that openly attempts to increase women's participation in politics, democracy and good governance in Indonesia. For example, it considers it important for local women activists at JPUK to participate in local politics. In the context of the implementation of Islamic law, the Asia Foundation introduced local activists to a comprehensive understanding of women's rights in Islam and how women's rights are guaranteed by the international norms such as CEDAW. It also considers it necessary to introduce local women activists in Aceh to developments in Islamic feminist discourse in other places in Indonesia, such as Jakarta, for example.

In 2007, the Asia Foundation facilitated a workshop for 19 Acehnese women activists on understanding women's rights in Islam. The workshop aimed to introduce the Acehnese activists to attempts made by Indonesian Muslim feminists and reform-minded Muslims to reinterpret the basic sources of sharia; the *Qur'an* and *Hadith*. This workshop was held in Cirebon, West Java, on 15–21 March 2007, and was called the *Kursus Islam dan Gender untuk Aktivis Perempuan Aceh* (Workshop on Islam and Gender for Acehnese Women Activists).

The training or *pelatihan* was organized by Fahmina Institute, an NGO based in a *pesantren* located in Cirebon. Fahmina is one of the leading Muslim organizations working on the need to reinterpret Islamic religious doctrines, in particular, those pertaining to women's roles within the family and in public (Bowen 1998; Feener 2007). Most Fahmina activists are *kyais* (*Ulama*)[19] with a background in Islamic law. This organization mainly focuses its efforts on promoting gender equality within the *pesantren* community, which has strong conservative and traditional understandings of Islam. The Asia Foundation considers that in order for Acehnese women activists to have better under-standing on how to read the sources of Islamic law, they need to understand methodological issues in interpreting sharia principles. One activist, Soraya Devy, who participated in the training recalled that, in his welcoming speech, Faqihuddin, a *kyai* and activist at Fahmina, said that the training aimed to listen to how Acehnese women experience the implementation of Islamic law (interview, Banda Aceh, 23 March 2007). He explained to the participants that both men and women have equal opportunities to form the legal regu-lations such as Islamic law in Aceh. For that reason, he said it is important for women activists to understand their rights in Islam and what Islam says about women and Islamic law. Among the themes covered at the workshop were discussions about polygamy, divorce, marriage and inheritance, empha-sizing that all these practices need to be understood and revisited by rereading Islamic texts.

Devy said after the training she has a better picture of the position of women within Islam, and became more confident that *Qanun* must not dis-criminate against women. She wondered, however, if she and her fellow activ-ists at JPUK will be able to share their new knowledge with local *Ulama* (religious leaders) or people in the *Dayah* (traditional Islamic boarding school in Aceh), because religious leaders in Aceh, in her view, often perceive their knowledge of Islam as more advanced than other Indonesians and the idea of letting them know they learned it from Javanese *kyai* would further jeopardize women activists' goals.

UNIFEM was another international institution that worked closely with local women's NGOs and women activists in Aceh. In a meeting at her office, the director of UNIFEM explained that when they came to Aceh in 2005, the agenda was to provide support and protection to women affected by the tsu-nami and they had no mandate to work on issues pertaining to the implemen-tation of Islamic law (interview, Banda Aceh, 25 March 2007). One way to support women in recovering from the tsunami was, however, for UNIFEM to focus on working with the local government to ensure that the spirit of good governance is applied. To this end, good governance was translated as guaranteeing women and other disadvantaged groups better support. Thus, when it started talking about good governance, UNIFEM had to deal with issues such as transparency, justice and equality, leading it to touch on the issue of the implementation of Islamic law. Its work was confined to how to ensure that the implementation of Islamic law could promote clean governance and transparency. If these aims were fulfilled, then women's rights will be protected. In the director's opinion, Acehnese women, in particular women activists, made tremendous efforts during their transition from conflict and in post-tsunami. She said:

> Aceh is a special place, it has Islamic law, and it has its customary law and also the special autonomy status, which are not present in other areas in Indonesia.

She believed Aceh can be a progressive place where men and women have equal opportunity, as they live under Islamic law. To her, Aceh can be a place to showcase how Islamic law can promote women's rights, good governance and transparency because of the availability of democratic mechanisms. In 2008, UNIFEM introduced Acehnese activists to CEDAW by supporting local women's NGOs activists with training on CEDAW. This was the first forum to allow local activists to learn about international norms that guarantee women's rights and equal opportunity.

Like the Asia Foundation, UNIFEM also sought to provide Acehnese women activists with the skills necessary to allow them to influence policy-making. From 8–10 January 2008, for example, UNIFEM supported JPUK to conduct a workshop on legal drafting. JPUK found that both civil society in Aceh and the legislature still lack the ability to create effective and coherent legal products, as is seen by the continuing creation of discriminatory *Qanun*. JPUK's workshop on legal drafting for activists was expected to equip the activists with a better understanding of the law-making process in Aceh, the position of *Qanun* within the hierarchy of Indonesia's legal system, and international legal and human rights norms.

An interesting debate took place during the legal drafting workshop. Some activists questioned why in drafting the *Qanun*, the speaker, who was a foreigner, did not suggest the *Qur'an* and *Hadith* as the primary references. From their perspective, since they are drafting an Islamic law, the *Qur'an* and *Hadith* should be the primary source of the rules of law. For example, Teungku Daniel from Lhoksemauwe explained that in formulating *Qanun*, the primary source must be the *Qur'an* and *Hadith*, and that requires an understanding of Islamic theology and methodology of interpreting Islamic texts in order to form *Fiqh*, which later becomes the basis of the law. For him, 'Islam is not the aspiration but Islam is the inspiration'. Teungku Daniel was also troubled with the explanation given by a speaker at the workshop, a woman activist based in Malaysia, who advocated that CEDAW needs to be used as the basic principle in creating *Qanun*. According to Teungku Daniel, considered one of the most moderate Acehnese *Ulama*, 'It is not time to localise global theory such as CEDAW, but how to globalise local norms such as those embraced by most Acehnese'. One result of the workshop was therefore increased tension between groups of activists who accept the need to make international norms the primary reference and those who resist such a perspective.

The increasing awareness by Acehnese women of their rights in politics and in Islam was later manifested in the creation of a Charter of the Rights of Women in Aceh, the development of which was supported by GTZ, the German aid agency. Nine public institutions in the province of Aceh, including the Governor of Aceh, the Chairman of the Provincial Parliament of Aceh (DPRA), the judiciary, the police, representatives of Islamic institutions and local NGOs signed the Charter:

> We, the signatories of the Aceh Charter on Women's Rights, believe that fair treatment of women is in line with the principles of Islam.[20]

Khairani, a woman activist, says that the creation of this Charter is timely, considering the many problems that Acehnese women face (IDLO, 5 July 2008). She underlined that although the creation of this Charter was inspired by the principles contained in CEDAW, it pays more attention to the rights of women from a local perspective. Policy-makers and government institutions were expected to refer to the Charter in developing their policies in the future of Aceh. This Charter sets out, among others, the rights of women to life and security, freedom from discrimination, intimidation and violence, the rights of women in education, the rights to legal protection and equality before the law, the rights of women within the family, the rights of women to organize and express opinions, and rights of access to, and control of, resources, and political rights.

In addition to activists, international organizations have also contributed to developing gender awareness among Acehnese academics and researchers. One example was the activities introduced by the Aceh Research Training Institute (ARTI), an initiative of universities in Australia and Indonesia. Since its arrival in Banda Aceh after the tsunami, it has worked to develop the academic capacity of young Acehnese academics and researchers.[21] ARTI's programmes are designed to develop critical skills in order to produce high-quality and relevant research. With the support of the Myer Foundation and the Australian aid agency (AusAID), ARTI supports young Acehnese academics and researchers from different disciplines and introduces the need for them to understand gender analysis. In addition, ARTI also offers international academics the opportunity to become involved and collaborate with local Acehnese academics.

When I visited Banda Aceh in 2008, I was very fortunate because Professor Virginia Hooker from the Australian National University (ANU) led a course on Gender and Society, from 14 to 25 January 2008. In addition to Professor Hooker, Muslim feminists such as Musdah Mulia, Lies Marcoes-Natsir, Nina Nurmila and Muhammad Faqih also participated in the course. About ten male and female academics and researchers from different universities in various districts participated in the programme. Participants were introduced to the need to use a gender perspective when conducting research. Participants were also introduced to the methodology available in interpreting the *Qur'an* and *Hadith*. It is hoped that Acehnese academics will contribute in developing gender awareness in their own educational institutions. They were also, later, expected to participate in contributing to the process of drafting *Qanun*, so that the *Qanun* will guarantee justice, equality and gender-sensitivity.

Local women's NGOs have not only developed networks with international institutions and foreign NGOs. They also work with the national NGOs, for example, Kapal Perempuan (Women's Ship), Koalisi Perempuan Indonesia (or Indonesian Women's Coalition), and many others. Siapno (2002, 173), however, found that some women activists in Banda Aceh 'resist being integrated into a progressive-national feminist agenda'. According to Siapno, the resentment of Acehnese activists continues to be nurtured and replicated in the way that local Acehnese activists think about their fellow women activists from Jakarta. She says that Acehnese women activists are often careful to not follow any ideology that is subscribed to by activists in Jakarta.

From the discussion above, it is clear that the resentment of local women activists towards Jakarta-based activists that Siapno (2007) observed has not disappeared. During numerous interviews and personal communications, I often heard expressions of contempt towards women activists from Jakarta, although many of the interviewees had worked collaboratively with them. One activist told me, for example, that even though she was very grateful for the support given to Acehnese activists, she needed to be very cautious since she found some of the agenda of activists in Jakarta not in line with her own ideas regarding the struggle of Acehnese women (interview, Banda Aceh, 13 February 2007). Among her concerns is the fact that women's activists in Jakarta have often forced Acehnese activists to accept issues that are still difficult for many Acehnese to deal with. These include same-sex relations or homosexuality. Some activists told me that if tolerance of this behaviour is promoted, resistance to the women's movement in Aceh will increase. I observed, however, that those who are critical still express a willingness to collaborate and continue developing networks with Jakarta.

In relation to the implementation of Islamic law, local women activists acknowledge the success of movements established in Jakarta but are reluctant to pursue a similar approach. In many of their statements, some women activists seem reluctant even to refer to the success of the efforts of activists in Jakarta at all. This is because the nature and characteristics of Acehnese society are seen as not being the same as other Muslims in Indonesia. In other words, Acehnese women activists share a common local idea that Aceh has a separate identity to that of the rest of Indonesia.

Despite the benefits that these international NGOs and foreign institutions have brought to Aceh, there are criticisms still directed towards their work as well. Fatima Sjam, a leader of LBH Apik based in North Aceh, Lhoksemauwe, for example, said that the presence of international NGOs has, in fact, weakened local capacity (interview, 12 March 2007). She referred to two cases. The first is the 'cash for work' programme introduced by the World Bank immediately after they arrived in Aceh. The programme asked villagers to clean their villages of rubbish and paid them for cleaning up their own houses, gardens and mosques. Fatima Sjam sees this practice as having changed the attitude of Acehnese towards their village. Ever since the 'cash for work' programme was introduced the villagers have been reluctant to clean up their villages unless they are paid for it, she argues. Worse, according to Fatima, since these foreign institutions always give money to the Acehnese, they become more materialistic. They always expect to get financial rewards for anything they do, even if it is for their own benefit. For local women's NGOs this means that they also need to give money to villagers whenever they seek to work with them. She said that when her NGO initiated a programme to introduce *Qanun* to villagers in North Aceh, she was disappointed, as the village leader immediately told her that it would be impossible to ask villagers to sit and listen to her unless she brings money for them.

Second, many international NGOs come to Aceh, Fatima Sjam said, without having adequate knowledge of Aceh's social and cultural setting. When they start working in the area most of these organizations recruit locals. Some of these local people have a professional background in women's issues, but there are many who do not. Since international NGOs offer a big salary, often 15 times more than local salaries, many activists quickly leave their local NGOs to work with the international ones. According to Fatima, international organizations and foreign NGOs in Aceh have thus caused what she calls a 'brain-drain' for the staff of local women's NGOs.

The international NGOs are also criticized for introducing a culture of consumption to Aceh. Seminars, workshops and other programmes are most often organized in hotels in Banda Aceh. Shadia Marhaban, a woman activist of LINA, for example, argues that instead of spending so much to pay for hotels, money saved could be used to support Acehnese women, whose lives are still difficult.

Conclusion

Despite some restraints on women's public appearance due to the implementation of Islamic law, Acehnese women have demonstrated that they have been able to manoeuvre to advance women's interests. The implementation of Islamic law has not totally impeded women from appearing in public and challenging the local government over various discriminatory practices against women. Local women activists have, in fact, been able to organize into women's movements by creating two key women's networks, the Women's Network for Policy (JPUK) and the Gender Working Group (GWG). Both of these networks have attempted to introduce wider Acehnese society to the need to participate in politics and understand their rights in Islam. To do this, local women activists equip themselves with new skills and knowledge pertaining to legal mechanisms and the theological basis for their call for the reform of Islamic law.

The interaction of local women activists with those from outside Aceh has been influential in introducing new discourses among local women activists. Despite this, local women activists are still struggling to come to terms with how they should promote equality. This is not only because of resistance from the conservative religious communities, but also because their own encounters with these issues are still relatively recent. However, as the process continues, Acehnese activists will be able to direct their struggles more effectively.

All these developments have happened alongside the political democratization of Aceh, which has offered women activists greater opportunity to participate in the public sphere, as can be seen from the increasing influence they have on local politics. By working with the legislature and religious leaders, women activists have continued to advance women's interests, as has been demonstrated by JPUK's activities. As followers of Islam, local women activists in Aceh acknowledge that their gender activism is based on Islamic teachings and the Acehnese *adat* (customs), and they therefore seek a more familiar discourse within which to locate their activities.

The next chapter offers a case study of one local women's NGO in Aceh and its key members, to illustrate these points.

Notes

1 Beckwith (2000, 435) acknowledges that there have been no major conceptual frameworks that can be used to define women's movements. In her article, she shows how scholars have defined them in different ways.
2 III Article 3 (d) of Law No. 44/1999 provides that the *Ulama* have roles in forming and deliberating the local regulation. This point is to reinstate the 'specialness' of Aceh and reinstate the former roles of Ulama.
3 The Law No. 18/2001 on the Special Autonomy for the Province of Aceh Special Region on the Province of Nanggroe Aceh Darussalam was ratified by the Indonesian president, Megawati Sukarnoputri, on 9 August 2001. The Law allows the transfer of power and resources from the central to the provincial government. It allows Aceh to receive more revenues from the economic activities of its natural resources. Aceh is also given the autonomy to run its internal affairs to redesign local government in line with local tradition. The central government is only responsible for Aceh's foreign political relations, external defence and monetary affairs. For more on the Autonomy Law, see ICG Report (2001) and Miller (2004).
4 At the national level, during the period of 1999–2004 the representation of women at the national parliament or DPR RI was only 9 per cent. The total representation of women from all DPRD throughout Indonesia was 350 out of 10,250. See http// wri.or.id/files/Representasi_05_BAB-2.pdf.

5 The six women members of parliament represented Golkar Party, the National Mandate Party (PAN), the Star and Crescent Party or Bulan Bintang, the Partai Demokrasi Indonesia Perjuangan (Indonesian Democratic Party of Struggle) and the Partai Persatuan Pembangunan (United Development Party).
6 Syarifah was speaking on a seminar organized by the Women's Research Institute in Jakarta on 9 March 2005. The seminar was organized to discuss women's representation in local parliament in Aceh. For more details see: www.wri.or.id. MISPI is one of the local women's NGOs that is going to be the case study of this research. It will be elaborated in the next chapter.
7 All *Qanun* enacted by the local government of Aceh can be viewed at the Aceh Provincial website: www.acehprov.go.id.
8 Prior to the promulgation of LOGA, legislative responsibility was largely in the hands of the military and National Executive. LOGA gives the local legislature more responsibility and it mainly concerns three major issues: revenue allocation, the establishment of local political parties, and independent candidates (UNDP Report 2006).
9 All of the information in this section was mostly gathered from JPUK's minutes of meetings and its reports, since its establishment in 2004. Copies on file with the author.
10 BRR is the official Indonesian government bureau with responsibility for the process of the reconstruction and rehabilitation of Aceh in the post-tsunami period. BRR gender policy has been developed in recognition of the need to identify effective ways to integrate gender-responsive actions in the process of rehabilitation and reconstruction and to support the Aceh and Nias local governments and the government of Indonesia's efforts to ensure gender equality within this process (BRR Policy Strategy 2006).
11 Almost half of the staff at this Bureau were killed by the tsunami. This prompted the Governor's Office to move staff from other departments to the women's bureau without them having the necessary background on women's issues. On the other hand, the devastation hugely affected women's lives, which needed immediate attention. It was based on these considerations that international institutions supported the creation of GWG.
12 For more accounts on the role of Musdah Mulia in introducing gender equality, see Robinson (2007), Budiman (2008) and Bowen (2003).
13 Blackburn (2004, 14) observed that in other places in Indonesia, she also found a resistance among Indonesian women towards the term 'feminism', because it is seen as having Western connotations. This resistance, according to Blackburn, is heavily influenced by Indonesia's nationalism, Islam and New Order ideology.
14 Rizvi *et al.* (1999, 14) argue that 'female circumcision' has no place in Islam, and it is restricted to only a few Muslim countries. They argue that female circumcision is a social custom rather than a religious practice. In Indonesia, female circumcision remains part of the wider debate within Islam. Feillard and Natsir (1998) argued that female circumcision among Indonesian Muslims remains surrounded by a certain amount of secrecy but it is also minimized as purely a symbolic gesture. Feillard and Natsir (1998, 337) have demonstrated that compared to other Muslim ethnic groups in Indonesia, female circumcision in Aceh is considered a secret matter.
15 Irwandi Yusuf was a former spokesperson of GAM. He was elected as Governor of Aceh in the first democratic election for local leadership in Aceh on 11 December 2006. Together with Muhammad Nazar, now the Deputy Governor, they won 40 per cent of the votes (Reid 2006, xiv). This election was the first in Indonesia where non-party candidates were allowed to compete.
16 It was reported that Lailisma was not appointed because she could not fulfil the administrative requirements. By law, a government body has to be headed by government officials who have already reached a certain level within the hierarchy

of employment. This has been one of the issues that women activists have been trying to address for some time, because it is difficult to find women in Aceh who have reached high levels in the bureaucracy. Women activists argue that the lived experience of Acehnese women and the political situation during the conflict had prevented many women from pursuing higher education and participating in public life.

17 It is common in Aceh and elsewhere in Indonesia that a person is called only by her/his first name.

18 Kamaruzzaman is referring to Surah Al-Hujurat (13), which says 'O mankind! We created you from a single (pair) of a male and a female, and made you into nations and tribes, that ye may know each other (not that ye may despise (each other). Verily the most honoured of you in the sight of God is (he who is) the most righteous of you. And God has full knowledge and is well acquainted (with all things)' (Al-Quran: Al-Hujurat:13).

19 Kyai is a Javanese term used for *Ulama* or religious leaders. Mostly they lead *pesantren*, or traditional Islamic boarding schools in Java.

20 See the Charter at: http://piagamhakperempuanaceh.org/en/Default.aspx.

21 Professor Michael Leigh at the University of Melbourne is the Director of ARTI. The ARTI office in Banda Aceh is situated around the Darussalam complex, where two major universities are located, namely, IAIN AR-Raniry and University Syiah Kuala.

References

Abu-Lughod, Lila 2010, 'The Active Social Life of Muslim Women's Rights: A Plea for Ethnography, Not Polemic with Cases from Egypt and Palestine', *Journal of Middle East Women's Studies*, vol. 6, no. 1, pp. 1–45.

Alvarez, Sonia E. 1990, *Engendering Democracy in Brazil: Women's Political Movements in Transition Politics*, Princeton University Press, Princeton.

Alvarez, Sonia E. 1999, 'Advocating Feminism: The Latin American Feminist NGO-Boom', *International Feminist Journal of Politics*, vol. 1, issue 2, pp. 181–209.

Anwar, Zainah 2001, 'What Islam, Whose Islam? Sisters in Islam and the Struggle for Women's Rights', in Robert W. Hefner (ed.), *The Politics of Multiculturalism: Pluralism and Citizenship in Malaysia*, University of Hawai'i Press, USA, p. 227.

Basu, Amrita 1995, 'Introduction', in Amrita Basu and Elizabeth McGregory (eds), *The Challenge of Local Feminisms: Women's Movements in Global Perspective*, Westview Press, Colorado, pp. 1–21.

Beckwith, Karen 2000, 'Beyond Compare? Women's Movements in Comparative Perspective', *European Journal of Political Research*, vol. 37, pp. 431–468.

Blackburn, Susan 2004, *Women and the State in Modern Indonesia*, Cambridge University Press, United Kingdom.

Bowen, John R. 1998, 'Qur'an, Justice, Gender: Internal Debates in Indonesian Islamic Jurisprudence', *History of Religions*, vol. 38, issue 1, pp. 52–78.

Bowen, John R. 2003, *Islam, Law and Equality in Indonesia: Anthropology of Public Reasoning*, Cambridge University Press, Cambridge.

Brenner, Suzanne 1996, 'Reconstructing Self and Society: Javanese Muslim Women and the Veil', *American Ethnologist*, vol. 23, issue 4, pp. 673–697.

Brenner, Suzanne 2005, 'Islam and Gender Politics in Late New Order Indonesia', in Andrew C. Wilford and Kenneth M. George (eds), *Spirited Politics: Religion and Public Life in Contemporary Southeast Asia*, Cornell University Southeast Asia Program, Ithaca, NY, pp. 93–118.

BRR Policy Strategy 2006, 'Promoting Gender Equality in the Rehabilitation and Reconstruction Process of Aceh and Nias', Bureau of Rehabilitation and Reconstruction for Aceh and Nias, September, unpublished.

Budiman, Manneke 2008, 'Treading the Path of the Sharia: Indonesian Feminism at the Crossroads of Western Modernity and Islamism', *Journal of Indonesian Social Sciences and Humanities*, vol. 1, pp. 73–93.

Bystydzienski, J.M. and Sekhon, J. (eds) 1999, *Democratization and Women's Grassroots Movements*, Indiana University Press, Bloomington.

Feener, Michael R. 2007, *Muslim Legal Thought in Modern Indonesia*, Cambridge University Press, Cambridge.

Feillard, Andree and Natsir, L.M 1998, 'Female Circumcision in Indonesia: To Islamize the Ceremony or Secrecy', *Archipel*, vol. 56, pp. 337–367.

Ferree, Myra Marx 2006, 'Globalisation and Feminism: Opportunities and Obstacles for Acetivism in Glocal Arena', in Myra Marx Ferree and Aili Mari Tripp (eds), *Global Feminism: Transnational Women's Activism, Organizing and Human Rights*, New York University Press, New York and London, pp. 3–23.

Ferree, Myra Marx and Martin, P.Y. 1995, *Feminist Organizations: Harvest of the New Women's Movement*, Temple University Press, Philadelphia.

Ferree, Myra Marx and Mueller, C. 2004, 'Feminism and the Women's Movement: A Global Perspective', in David A. Snow, Sarah A. Soule and Hanspeter Kriesi (eds), *Blackwell Companion to Social Movements*, Blackwell Publishing, USA, pp. 576–607.

ICG Report 2001, 'Aceh: Can Autonomy Stem the Conflict', *Asia Report*, no. 18, available at: www.crisisgroupd.org (accessed 20 February 2006).

The Jakarta Post 2006, 'Cleric Aa Gym Rekindles Polygamy Debate', 4 December, available at: www.thejakartapost.com/news/2006/12/04/cleric-aa-gym-rekindles-polygamy-debate.html (accessed 25 January 2007).

Kabeer, Naila 1991, 'The Quest for National Identity: Women, Islam and the State in Bangladesh', *Feminist Review*, no. 37, pp. 38–58.

Mahdi, Saiful and Fajran, Z. 2008, 'Editorial', in Fajran Zain and Saiful Mahdi (eds), *Timang: Aceh, Perempuan, Kesetaraan*, Aceh Institute Press, Banda Aceh, pp. 1–10.

Margolis, Diane R. 1993, 'Women's Movements around the World: Cross-Cultural Comparisons', vol. 7, no. 3, pp. 379–399.

Mashudi, S.R. 2006, 'Merebak gerak bandul politik perempuan', *Serambi Indonesia: Politik*, 15 December, available at: www.serambinews.com (accessed 29 July 2007).

Miller, Michelle Ann 2004, 'The Nanggroe Aceh Darussalam Law: A Serious Response to Acehnese Separatism?', *Asian Ethnicity*, vol. 5, no. 3, pp. 333–351.

Miller, Michelle Ann 2009, *Rebellion and Reform in Indonesia: Jakarta's Security and Autonomy Policies in Aceh*, Routledge, New York.

Novianan, Nina and Yudiansyah 2009, 'Prolega sesuai amanat UUPA?', *Harian Aceh. Opini*, 2 October, available at: www.harian-aceh.com/opini/85-opini/3783-prolega-sesuai-amanat-uupa? (accessed 5 October 2009)

Othman, Norani 2006, 'Muslim Women and the Challenge of Islamic Fundamentalism/Extremism: An Overview of Southeast Asian Muslim Women's Struggle for Human Rights and Gender Equality', *Women's Studies International Forum*, vol. 29, pp. 339–353.

Reid, Anthony (ed.) 2006, *Verandah of Violence: The Background to the Aceh Problem*, Institute of Southeast Asian Studies, Singapore.

Rizvi, S.A.H., Naqvi, S.A.A., Hussain, M. and Hasan, A.S. 1999, 'Religious Circumcision: A Muslim View', *BJU International*, vol. 83, suppl. 1, pp. 13–16.

Robinson, Kathryn 2007, 'Islamic Influences on Indonesian Feminism', in Tony Day (ed.), *Identifying with Freedom: Indonesia After Soeharto*, Berghahn Books, New York and Oxford, pp. 39–48.

Robinson, Kathryn 2009, *Gender, Islam and Democracy in Indonesia*, Routledge, United Kingdom.

Siapno, Jacqueline 2002, *Gender, Islam, Nationalism and the State in Aceh the Paradox of Power, Co-optation and Resistance*, Routledge, London.

Siapno, Jacqueline 2007, 'Precarious Reconstruction(s), Contested Development(s): Decolonizing Gender Discourse(s) and Reading Competing Islamist Presentations and Re-presentations in Aceh', *First International Conference of Aceh and Indian Ocean Studies*, Banda Aceh, Indonesia, 24–27 February, available at: www.ari.nus. edu.sg/docs%5CAceh-project%5Cfull-papers%5Caceh_fp_jacquelinesiapno.pdf (accessed 20 March 2007).

Suryakusuma, Julia 1996, 'The State and Sexuality in New Order Indonesia', in Laurie J. Sears (ed.), *Fantasizing the Feminine in Indonesia*, Duke University Press, Durham, NC and London, pp. 93–119.

UNDP Report 2006, *Access to Justice in Aceh: Making the Transition to Sustainable Peace and Development in Aceh, Indonesia*.

UNIFEM 2005, 'Aceh, Tsunami's Women Survivors Demand Greater Role in Recovery and Reconstruction Efforts', 23 June, available at: www.unifem.org/news_events/ story_detail.php?StoryID=251 (accessed 12 January 2008).

UNIFEM 2007, 'Qanun and Aceh', *e-news*, vol. 1, available at: www.unifem-eseasia. org (accessed 15 June 2008).

Yuval-Davis, Nira 1997, *Gender and Nation*, Sage Publication, London.

5 MISPI, agency, identity and the reform of Islamic law in Aceh

Introduction

The previous chapter highlighted how local women's NGOs and activists have responded to the implementation of Islamic law in Aceh. As discussed, women activists and women's NGOs in Aceh developed and mobilized to become women's movements with the objective of broadening women's opportunities to take up public roles and promote women's status and gender equality within an Islamic framework. They start having conversations on equality, and on women's economic, civic and political rights. They weigh up what they should take and what they should reject from the secular Western/feminist movements. Some women activists still find it problematic to combine Islamic teachings and Aceh's cultural values with international norms, in particular, women's rights. They are engaged in a conversation about what they think will fit with their own tradition and culture, which are strongly entrenched in Islam.

This chapter is a case study of one local women's NGO in Aceh. It aims to demonstrate how this NGO and its activists respond to the implementation of Islamic law. It will show that MISPI (Mitra Sejati Perempuan Indonesia or the True Partner of Indonesian Women) responds by introducing Acehnese women to the notion of equality, rights in Islam through a wide range of programmes and activities. MISPI understands that there is resistance from some segments of Acehnese societies to new ideas such as gender equality and women's rights. In particular, MISPI is aware of the resistance from religious authorities who are unwilling to approve women's advances in public life. Understanding this situation, it chose to develop networks with male-dominated religious authorities or *Ulama* represented by the MPU, patriarchal gender-insensitive government officials including members of the local legislature, and the broader religious community at the grassroots. Even though MISPI works closely with government institutions, it has not abandoned its principles, and continues to criticize policies that it sees as gender-biased and discriminatory towards women. Instead, MISPI's strategy of developing networks with government institutions and religious authorities should be seen as part of women's agency taking active roles in the public sphere.

This chapter intends to confirm that MISPI's strategy and agency has mirrored what Waylen (1996) has argued about women's political participation and agency in promoting social change. The strategy of working with government is, in many ways, empowering, and enables women's organizations to actively engage in public (Waylen 1996, 19–20). This chapter shows that different systems represent different kinds of patriarchal bargains for women, including different rules of the game and the differing strategies women can use to maximize women's security and life options (Kandiyoti 1988). This understanding, according to Kandiyoti, helps explain 'why some women act in certain ways, which may superficially seem to be in conflict with their long term interests'. This chapter will show that even though MISPI works closely with government institutions, it has not abandoned its principles in promoting reform of Islamic law in Aceh and introducing awareness of women's equality and status in Islam.

Background

MISPI was established in August 1998, just months after the fall of President Suharto in May 1998. Among women's civil society organizations in Aceh, MISPI is considered to be one of the most established, as I will show later. Both national and international donor institutions that work in Aceh, especially those working on women and gender issues, greatly respect the role MISPI has played among the wider civil society movements in the province.

The establishment of MISPI came from a dream that Syarifah and her colleagues shared to build a better Aceh for its women. According to Syarifah, the original intention behind the creation of the organization was simple. In the 1990s, while Aceh was still in conflict, she and her colleagues imagined that in the future Aceh might have an organization that could serve as a resource organization to benefit Acehnese women. Based on their experiences during conflict, she believes that a resource organization could pave the way for the creation of an 'all Acehnese women's network'. She dreamed that, once created, the network would become a forum for Acehnese women to mobilize, promote their agenda and to advance their status. It could become a place for women of different backgrounds, women's activists, academics and bureaucrats, all sharing an interest in improving the status of Acehnese women to work together. She explains that this idea derived from the fact that although there were already women's organizations working in Aceh at that time they had not demonstrated the capacity to mobilize Acehnese women.

Syarifah and her colleagues, however, acknowledged the complexity of the problems facing Acehnese women. Women who are victims of conflict need both legal protection and economic support. Many Acehnese women have become widows and have had to take the role of sole breadwinner for their families. They thus need to be given wider access to the economy. During the conflict, women had limited space while the government did not support women to gain better access to the economy. The way Syarifah and her colleagues saw this problem was that it is important to have more women in politics so the interests of Acehnese women can be considered in policy-making. This is what prompted Syarifah to establish an organization focusing on advocacy in policy-making. According to Syarifah, the situation in Aceh needs to be addressed cautiously and to do so women need a forum as an avenue to organize and voice their interests. If women want their voices to be heard, they need to mobilize into movements to create public awareness. She expects that the establishment of women's NGOs could contribute to the development of a robust Acehnese civil society. To achieve these objectives she and some of her colleagues founded MISPI, imagining that in the future it could initiate legal, economic and political reform, and bring about the social transformation of Acehnese society and Acehnese women.

Politics

According to Syarifah, its establishment cannot be separated from the political opportunities that arose in Aceh following the fall of Suharto in 1998.[1] Many Acehnese saw the end of Military Operation Status (DOM) and political reforms at the national level as chances to demand justice, and force the government to investigate gross human rights violations in their province.[2] Demands for justice for the Acehnese did not receive an immediate response from Jakarta, and this caused new resentments and disappointment among Acehnese. This disappointment later manifested in the creation of ethno-nationalist demands (Bertrand 2004, 175). The Free Aceh Movement (GAM) saw this as a political opportunity to generate more support for their cause of Acehnese independence. This created tension among the society, because not all Acehnese supported the idea of independence, including many students (former student activists, interview, 10 March 2008). Student movements in 1999 to 2000, according to Aspinall (2009, 123), were not initially interested in independence, but were part of national student movements centred in Jakarta, with an agenda of bringing down Suharto, demanding political reforms and demanding punishment for those who violated human rights. In addition, the Acehnese students also used the moment to put pressure on the central government in Jakarta to grant political concessions and address human rights violations.

As the central government in Jakarta remained unable to control the military, abuses against Acehnese civilians continued. This situation finally led to a fresh radicalization of Acehnese students, which Aspinall (2009, 123) argues turned them into 'committed nationalists'. In addition, Aspinall also saw novelty in these movements, 'as in many ways, [they are] not similar to the earlier movement, GAM'. These student movements reframed their struggle as one striving for national independence through democratic mechanisms, which emphasized 'human rights, an inclusionary national identity and relations with Indonesia'. These students did not believe in armed struggle but relied on discourses of Aceh's unique Islamic heritage and the Jakarta administration's betrayal of the Acehnese cause of independence. In February 1999, groups of students from across Aceh formed SIRA (Sentral Informasi Rakyat Aceh or the Aceh Referendum Information Centre), which later demanded 'self-determination based on independence, freedom and justice', to allow the Acehnese to choose either to be independent or to remain part of Indonesia (Reid 2003, 10).

Reid (2003, 10) indicates that there were, however, some Acehnese who were not keen to see a separate Aceh, independent of Indonesia. Reid, however, observed that as the public mood for independence was huge, those who opposed the idea of independence were reluctant to express their views openly. Likewise, Siegel (2000, 337) observes that Acehnese elders were, in fact, wanting Aceh become a 'federation', so that its rights were better guaranteed. Different views on the future of Aceh, according to Syarifah, also appeared among Acehnese women. While some women, such as the *Inong Balee*, were eager to see Aceh separate from Indonesia,[3] there were many others who hoped that Aceh would remain part of Indonesia.

It is this political situation that inspired women like Syarifah and her colleagues to do something for Acehnese women. They considered it to be a crucial time for Acehnese women to take a role and express their views within broader civil movements, to represent women's silent voices. In addition, Syarifah was aware that there were many Acehnese women who were forced to support one view over the other while, in fact, many women felt that both sides had perpetrated similar violence against women. Siegel (2000, 388–389), for example, observes that some Acehnese women fear GAM as they experienced being targeted by GAM because their physical appearance closely resembles the Javanese, which is the largest ethnic group in Indonesia and is strongly associated with the Indonesian military. In other words, women were exploited by both the Indonesian military and GAM. Syarifah explains that the situation at that time became intense as Acehnese divided into two factions: those who supported Aceh to remain part of Indonesia, and those who were in favour of independence (that is, they supported GAM). According to Syarifah, many women considered that supporting either side would have its own risks.

During my conversations with Syarifah it became clear that Syarifah holds the view that Aceh should remain part of Indonesia. One women activist from Balai Syura Inong Aceh (Aceh Women's Forum) expressed similar views to Syarifah's. She said, 'If Aceh is ruled by GAM, the future for women is bleak' (interview, Banda Aceh, 8 March 2007).[4] However, the intensity of the political situation from 1998 to 2000 made it impossible for women like Syarifah to publicly express their views. For example, Syarifah describes how both GAM and the Indonesian armed forces often physically targeted her after the Humanitarian Pause was agreed in 2000. Both sides were suspicious that she was supporting one side over the other. She recalls that she had to hide many times to avoid being kidnapped by either one of the parties.[5] She imagines that other Acehnese women had similar experiences during the military emergency status or *Darurat Militer* that began in 2003. Despite all the threats she received, however, Syarifah continued to develop her new organization. During this tough period no one talked about women's rights and women's needs, so Syarifah saw this as an opportunity for MISPI to play that role.

Regarding this political situation, Dana Lubis, a former member of HMI, explained that the creation of a women's organization with a strong national-ist and Islamic character had strategic importance, especially in the context of growing demands for a referendum and independence from Indonesia.[6] He and his fellow HMI activists believed that, if not handled cautiously, the situation could lead to a serious civil war within Acehnese society that would, again, badly affect women. He acknowledged injustices and human rights violations perpetrated by the Indonesian military, but at the same time he was even more frightened of the idea of independence, with Aceh ruled by GAM. He argued that civil society in Aceh did not want civil war, and preferred Aceh to remain part of the Republic of Indonesia.

He and his colleagues were aware, however, of the challenges facing women who wanted to join a civil society organization. According to him, women at that time were still treated unequally, in particular as regards their pub-lic roles. He acknowledged that other women's activists have protected other Acehnese women during severe military conflict, but he contended that the existing women's organizations had failed to end the isolation of women from the peace process. He therefore supported his fellow women members of KOHATI in establishing MISPI.

Naming

Under these political circumstances, Syarifah and her colleagues believed that 'naming' their organization was another important challenge, in addition to outlining their organizational strategy, their platform and the direction they wanted to take. They considered it important that the name of their new organization reflect the organization's identity and agenda. Hilhorst (2000) argued that establishing meaning is 'central for an organization, as it underlies the kind of decisions and actions that will later define it'.

MISPI's members expected that their organization should occupy a 'mid-dle position' in the political conflict at that time, despite their political view of the situation. This is because they believe that only by doing so could they be sure that they can work with both sides in order to advance Acehnese women's interests. However, I argue that since MISPI was created by a group closely attached to national Islamic based organizations, it must be in the position to support the idea that Aceh remains under the Indonesian govern-ment, and become part of the broader Indonesian Muslim sisterhood. I argue that MISPI's rhetoric of wanting to be in the middle of two warring parties is mainly part of its organizational strategy.

The choice to name the organization Mitra Sejati Perempuan Indonesia, which literally means The True Partner of Indonesian Women, clearly demonstrates this point. Syarifah said that it is true that she wanted to show the rest of Indonesia that many Acehnese women see Aceh remaining part of Indonesia in the future, and to show that not all Acehnese women are happy to be labelled as separatists. This, Syarifah argued, is because she and many of her fellow Acehnese women were aware that the rest of Indonesia doubted Aceh's commitment to the Republic, and simply labelled them 'rebellious'. By naming her organization 'MISPI', she hoped that Indonesian women would perceive them as 'their true friends' and not question Acehnese women's 'Indonesian-ness' (*keIndonesiaan*).

Dana Lubis, a former leader of HMI,[7] also argued that the name would bring strategic benefits to the new women's NGO (interview, Banda Aceh, 10 March 2008), and he was among the first to support the name. He acknowledged the consequences that MISPI might bear for including the word 'Indonesia' in its name: GAM and other Acehnese who were critical of Jakarta might accuse MISPI of being an agent of the Indonesian government. Despite that possibility, he argued, it was also important to confirm that not all women in Aceh wanted to see Aceh separate from Indonesia. In its later development, as I shall show in the next section, MISPI continues to align itself more towards the government while, at the same time, maintaining its critical character as an NGO.

Ethnography

There have not been many academic writings on Aceh that mentioned women's organizations other than Flower Aceh. Flower Aceh has often received more of both national and international recognition. Literature on Aceh mention Flower Aceh but no other local women's NGOs when discussing issues relating to women. Local women activists were aware of this and they have expressed concern that this could create the perception that Flower Aceh is the only local women's NGO. Some activists resent the fact that the national and international media frequently refer to and quote Flower Aceh's leader, Soraya Kamaruzzaman, as she spoke at many national and international events about the suffering of Acehnese women. Many activists I talked with do not rule out the role of Flower Aceh; however, their concern was rather on the need for outsiders to acknowledge that women's organizations are not only Flower Aceh and there is a dynamic within women's movements in the province.[8] My observation reveals that this has possibly occurred because the discourse within women's movements in Aceh in the 1990s was highly focused upon the suffering of Acehnese women in the midst of military conflict. Flower Aceh is, indeed, one of the local women's NGOs that were most active during the early 1990s, meaning that the development of MISPI, as well as other local women's NGOs whose works at that time focused on improving women's economic status, went relatively unnoticed.

Since it was officially established in 1998, MISPI has been able to maintain and even expand its programmes. The organization began from the activities of Syiah Kuala University activists and graduates who were concerned about the life of Acehnese women. In the early stages, MISPI works on improving women's access to economy. It received its first grant from the Canadian International Development Agency (CIDA) in 1998 to work on improving Acehnese women's economy. In fact, the idea among activists at MISPI at that time was to work on policy advocacy. However, that was apparently not considered important by donors who worked in Aceh at that time. Through its activities, MISPI continues to win support from locals, as well as gaining national recognition. Its activities started to expand from working on women's economic capacity to providing legal assistance for both women in the village and in the city. With the social and political developments, in particular since 2000, MISPI has started to receive support to work on advocacy and policy reform. It then demonstrated a leading role in advocating policy reform, both at the local legislative and government levels. MISPI has also experienced steady growth in terms of its professional capacity, as it employs more of both local volunteers and professional staff compared to other local women's NGOs.

One reason to select MISPI as the case study is the fact that compared to other local women's NGOs, MISPI has demonstrated a unique character in the broader context of promoting women's awareness of their status, such as equality in Islam and women's civic and political rights. MISPI has, for example, actively sought to advocate public policy reform while at the same time introduce the rights of women in Islam since Islamic law was introduced in 1999. MISPI believes that women are a social group that could be disadvantaged by the implementation of Islamic law. In pursuing this agenda, MISPI has organized various programmes from training law-makers on legal drafting and gender awareness, organized seminars and workshops with religious male and female *Ulama*, jurists, scholars and civil society activists, on issues pertaining to women and sharia, as well as providing legal aid to female victims of violence.

Organizational capacity

At the time of my research, MISPI employed seven professional staff. Three of them were working as administrative officials, while three others were responsible for running programmes, and one of them was a lawyer. MISPI also employed four casual staff that provided litigation advice and support for women facing legal problems. Most of the staff at MISPI have undergraduate degrees in law, with some being graduates of the Law Faculty of Syiah Kuala University in Banda Aceh, and some from the Sharia (Islamic law) Faculty of IAIN Ar-Raniry, also in Banda Aceh.

MISPI's office is located at Simpang Lima, in the heart of the city of Banda Aceh, walking distance from the landmark Grand Mosque of Baiturrahman,[9] and close to the central market of Banda Aceh.[10] MISPI's new office is in a three-storey building that it has rented since the tsunami. MISPI's previous office was destroyed by the tsunami, causing huge losses to its archives.

The arrival of foreign NGOs and international donors has allowed MISPI to develop more networks, with the result that MISPI has been inundated by various projects. In my observation, many of the international donors and foreign institutions have more interest in working and building cooperation with MISPI than with more newly-established women's NGOs. One official of an international NGO said that the decision to work with MISPI was based on the assessment that MISPI has demonstrated its capacity to run programmes on women's issues (interview, Banda Aceh, 12 March 2007). In addition, foreign donors regard MISPI as one of the local women's NGOs that has gained wider recognition among the local Acehnese, including that it has a wide network with policy-makers and the government offices. This can be understood as international NGOs often just want to be practical and make sure that their programmes will run well. They do not want to take the risk of working with a new, untested organization. So, for example, the country manager of UNIFEM (interview, Banda Aceh, 23 March 2007) said that international NGOs have to make a pragmatic decision in choosing a local partner because they are responsible to donors to ensure their money is well spent.

Inundated by programmes from donors, MISPI usually organizes two or three consecutive trainings and seminars in a given week. It was remarkable for me to see how effectively a relatively small number of staff can organize these training and workshops, designed for different audiences and on different issues. For example, on the first three days in one week, I observed MISPI organize and deliver training on empowering local women *Ulama* in different districts in Aceh. Over the next three days, it organized training on building women's peace networks with Acehnese men and women of different social backgrounds. In the following week, MISPI organized a seminar on empowering women members of local parliament. From these activities, MISPI works heavily in line with the campaigns on women's equality, which in this case is equality based on Islamic teachings and women's civil and political rights.

All the seminars, workshops and training that MISPI organizes are usually held in three- or four-star hotels in Banda Aceh. However, as explained, this really depends on the support they receive from donors. MISPI provides participants with hotel accommodation, especially for those who come from outside Banda Aceh. MISPI also reimburses participants for transportation costs incurred and they also receive an honorarium, about IDR 150,000 per day, equal to AUD$ 90.[11] I asked an official of an international NGO about paying money to those who participate in these seminars, and it was explained that the money is to compensate for the time that the participants have to spend to attend seminars, instead of at their usual activities (interview with IDLO staff, Banda Aceh, 12 March 2007). Other expenses incurred from these activities include the cost of renting the venue, provision of food during the training and honoraria for speakers. During the time of my fieldwork, MISPI obtained support from foreign NGOs including the Asia Foundation,

UNDP (United Nations Development Program), UNIFEM (United Nations Development Fund for Women) and Yayasan TIFA, as well as several other foreign NGOs. The Asia Foundation has been working with MISPI since early 2000. The Asia Foundation is one of the first international NGOs that worked with MISPI after it was established. Yayasan TIFA is another Indonesian-based NGO that works to promote an open society which respects diversity and honours the rule of law, justice and equality. Unlike other local women's NGOs, MISPI most often conducted its events at four-star hotels, such as the Hermes Hotel or the Sultan Hotel, both in Banda Aceh. This suggests that MISPI probably receives greater funding compared to other women's NGOs.

Leadership

Effective NGO leaders are able to balance a range of competing pressures from different stakeholders in ways that do not compromise their individual identity and values (Hailey and Rick 2004, 343). Since NGOs work for the marginalized and disadvantaged members of communities, the leadership of NGOs face extraordinary challenges as they work with very limited resources, in uncertain and volatile political situations and economic circumstances. Based on this, it becomes important to analyse the leadership of MISPI in order to understand how MISPI has obtained legitimacy from a range of institutions such as local governments, donors and its grassroots constituency.

The success of MISPI in organizing seminars, workshops and training cannot be separated from the role of Syarifah Rahmatillah, the current leader of MISPI. Syarifah is considered one of the most important female figures in Aceh during the post-tsunami reconstruction period. In her capacity as the leader of MISPI, Syarifah has tried to represent herself as an Acehnese Muslim woman who strongly upholds her religious and cultural values, as I will explain later.

From a number of conversations I had with activists, government officials and lawmakers, Syarifah's family are believed to be the descendants of the Prophet Muhammad. This belief derives from the Acehnese tradition that only descendants of the Prophet can name their daughter 'Syarifah'. Although they cannot really prove if this is true, almost everyone I talked with about Syarifah agreed that her family are the descendants of the prophet. This, according to some Acehnese, gives the leader of MISPI credit because people perceive her to be a strict adherent of Islam, a pious Muslim. Syarifah's appearance strengthen the argument about her religious piety. Unlike many other women activists, Syarifah always wears long skirts with loose *baju kurung* and she also wear socks. Her *jilbab* covers loosely into her chest. This, many women activists believe, makes it easy for Syarifah to gain acceptance from the religious community. Certainly, Syarifah is known for her skills in working with various elements in Aceh, including government officials at all levels, members of the local legislature and *Ulama*. Few other women activists have so large a network.

Syarifah's identity as an NGO activist is influenced by her previous involvement in the 1990s student movements. She started her activism while taking a law degree at Syiah Kuala University, having completed her primary and secondary education at a public school in Banda Aceh. When she was at the university, she became involved in the university student association (Badan Executive Mahasiswa or BEM), the Faculty of Law Student Senate and also the university-level Student Senate. She later joined KOHATI (Korps HMI-Wati), a women's wing of the nationally based Muslim Student Organization or Himpunan Mahasiswa Islam (HMI), before being elected as head of the organization. When she graduated, Syarifah continued her activism by joining ICMI (All Indonesian Union of Muslims Intellectuals), created in December 1990 in Malang, East Java.[12] Syarifah is married to the former leader of HMI Banda Aceh, who later became a lawyer and in 2004 was elected as a member of a local legislature representing Partai Bulan Bintang (PBB or the Crescent Star Party).[13] Syarifah then became a civil servant (PNS or Pegawai Negeri Sipil) at the Badan Pertanahan Nasional or Indonesian National Land Agency in Banda Aceh. Before the 2004 general election, Syarifah became a member of the KPU (Komisi Pemilihan Umum or the General Election Commission).[14] Although a public official, her enthusiasm for social activism did not stop, as she was then involved in Duek Pakat Inong Aceh (Aceh Women's Congress), being elected to its steering committee, and later its board.

Many believed that Syarifah's HMI activist background and her strong network among former members of HMI in the government bureaucracy and in civil society organizations have influenced her rise in civil society activism. This is probably true, as I observed that in her capacity as the leader of MISPI, Syarifah used her HMI and KOHATI networks to develop her organization. For example, she recruited only those who have KOHATI backgrounds to work at MISPI. To this, Syarifah argued she had to be pragmatic in terms of recruiting former HMI- KOHATI activists. With limited resources, MISPI did not have enough resources to train women to be activists. These HMI-KOHATI activists already understand civil society activism, are familiar with problems faced by women, and know what it is like to work in an organization. Her position at KPU also further enhanced her access among government officials from the district to provincial level. All these links add to Syarifah's credentials, and boost her leverage among other local women activists.

Islamic piety

This section discusses how personnel at MISPI express their religious piety. This is because it is important to understand how MISPI staff understand their religion, and how it is reflected in their work as NGO activists.

As mentioned earlier, at the time of my research there were about six permanent and four casual staff working at MISPI. As in all other women's

NGOs in Aceh nearly all the staff at MISPI are women. There is only one male employee, and he works as a general helper, with tasks that include cleaning the office and acting as a porter. This is interesting. MISPI is actually not the only women's organization that employs men as the office general helpers. One of the staff told me that it is part of their campaign that male employees are engaged to do all the general household jobs, when normally in Indonesia these jobs are assigned to women and are perceived to be 'women's jobs'.

As said before, MISPI activists come mostly from a KOHATI-HMI background. Religious piety is clearly visible in the everyday activities of the office. At every prayer time, all staff members perform the prayer. After lunch, staff will queue to perform the ablutions required before prayer. In the afternoon, before they go home, they also perform *Ashar* or afternoon prayer at the office. Everyone brings their own prayer clothing. There is no special room for them to pray so they just do it next to their desks. Even during busy times, for example, in the middle of training, they still perform their prayers, in turn.

Women who work at MISPI wear Islamic dress, like other Acehnese women: skirt, blouse, tunic and *jilbab*. In her research on RAHIMA, a Muslim women's organization based in Jakarta, Rinaldo (2008, 4) observes that women activists at RAHIMA wear a different style of Muslim clothing. She observes that the younger staff at RAHIMA wear a more 'stylish ensemble of Muslim clothing' such as tight jeans with tight shirts, while the senior workers wear more modest clothing. I noticed a different situation at MISPI. Staff that work on a casual basis, many recent graduates from university, wear more conservative Muslim attire. This difference might be attributed to the desire of the younger generation to abide by the Islamic law or it may also be understood as a result of Acehnese youth wishing to express a higher level of Islamic piety than Muslim youth in Jakarta.

Smith-Hefner (2007) writes on her research in Yogyakarta that Muslim women use different styles of Muslim dress, including wearing headscarves with jeans. At MISPI, women also express their religiosity through different styles of Muslim fashion. As mentioned earlier, those who have recently joined MISPI tend to choose stricter Muslim attire. They wear the *jilbab*, which Smith-Hefner (2007, 390) describes as 'a large square piece of fabric, which is drawn tightly around the face to cover hair, ears and neck completely'. The large fabric square may cover the shoulders and chest, although some hang down to the navel. Women mix Muslim attire with wearing loose blouses that cover down to their knees, and ankle-length skirts and socks. During my time in the field, I never saw younger or newly-employed staff wearing pants.

The senior staff, however, prefer different ways of wearing their Muslim attire. Unlike the younger ones, these senior staff (most in their early and mid thirties) rarely wear skirts, nor do they wear the same style of big *jilbab*. Although their *jilbab* is typically made of the same kind of fabric, they wear smaller versions, which only cover their hair, ears and neck. Their blouses are not loose and on occasion some choose to wear tight or 'fitted' clothes. Senior staff also demonstrate a strong passion for creative Muslim fashion, and seem to be obsessed with wearing fake-branded handbags and watches.[15] In fact, it becomes part of their lunch conversation about going to Medan, in North Sumatra province, a 30-minute flight from Banda Aceh, to buy these fake handbags, Gucci and Louis Vuitton. To me this simply reflects Smith-Hefner's argument that veiling can also be seen as a symbol of women's engagement in a modern, albeit deeply Islamic, world (2007, 395).

Syarifah, however, has her own style of Muslim attire. She often wears a traditional, Aceh-type *baju kurung*, which consists of a loose-fitting tunic draped down to her knee and loose skirts that cover up to her ankle. Unlike her casual staff, she chooses bright colours, and complements the *baju kurung* with silk or chiffon colourful *jilbab*. She matches her *jilbab* with her clothes, and puts a matching and colorful brooch on her *jilbab*. She also always wears a small amount of makeup. One of the staff once told me that Syarifah is actually very strict on the Muslim dress issue. So, for example, she always warns her staff not to wear tight blouses, tight pants or small *jilbabs*. She especially emphasized this to those staff that are responsible for organizing events. She does not want participants who attend MISPI's events to judge them by their clothing. This is because the conservative religious community, including the *Ulama* and government officials, still believe that women can be divided into good/bad Muslims only by looking at the way women choose their dresses and how they cover their hair.

MISPI staff are aware that their clothing attracts the attention of people at the events they organize. In one of the workshops attended by men and women *Ulama* at the Hotel Sultan in Banda Aceh in January 2008, Murni, one member of the MISPI staff, received a cynical comment from a male *Ulama* regarding the dress that she was wearing. She was wearing tight jeans, and a tight-fitting blouse with a small *jilbab*, covering only her hair and neck The male *Ulama* whispered to her that she should wear something else. She was annoyed and grunted:

> They called themselves *Ulama*, but they do not understand that there is a verse in the *Qur'an* that calls men to protect their eyes from seeing any [bad] thing.

This teaching is contained in *Surah An-Nur* 30:31 of the *Qur'an*, in which it says, 'Katakanlah kepada laki-laki yang beriman, agar mereka menjaga pandangannya' or 'tell the believing men to watch where they look'. In her understanding, this verse teaches that the *Ulama* or men should avoid looking at her [woman] if he thinks that her dress is inappropriate. Thus, she said to me that she wished she could yell back at the *Ulama*, and tell him to stop looking at her dress.[16] Murni graduated from the Faculty of Sharia of the State Institute of Islamic Studies (IAIN) Ar-Raniry. She understands well the debate on women's clothing in Islam. She is also familiar with the discourse introduced by Fatima Mernissi, Amina Wadud and Asghar Ali Engineer on gender equality message in Islam.

I notice that this issue of women's dress does indeed occupy Syarifah's attention. One day, for example, she told me that she resented the way some of her colleagues in the women's movement show reluctance to wear what she considered to be 'proper' Muslim clothing and *jilbab*.[17] By 'reluctance' (*malas*) Syarifah wanted to say that these activists do not properly wear a modest *jilbab* like she does.[18] Apart from saying that it is part of the Islamic tradition, Syarifah is mostly concerned that for the movement to gain acceptance, they need to first win the hearts and minds of the society, in particular, the religious Ulama. It is, she said, not too hard to be done. Most of the women activists involved in the movement wear small *jilbab* covering their hair into their neck, or *kerudung* or scarf, draped over their hair, and some of them even only wear a shawl and let it drape to their shoulders.[19]

MISPI's position on Muslim clothing as discussed above clearly shows its Islamic credentials, which for many conservative Acehnese is an important gesture. I would add that from her position on the issue of women's clothing and veiling, Syarifah shows that veiling and women's clothing cannot be seen merely as symbols of Islamic traditionalism or domestic confinement. Syarifah's veiling proves that it can be also a vehicle for women to exercise their mobility and to gain public acceptance for their political activism, as Smith-Hefner has argued (2007, 397).

MISPI and Islamic law

This section will discuss how MISPI has responded to the implementation of Islamic law. Syarifah believes that most Acehnese accept the rights of Aceh to implement Islamic law. She mentioned, for example, the overwhelming response of the Acehnese when Aceh was granted the rights to implement sharia law in 1999.[20] According to her, this was because many Acehnese believe that they have already been living under sharia principles anyway, even if they were not legally formalized.

Like other local women activists, Syarifah has criticized discriminatory practices that have occurred in the course of the implementation of Islamic law. However, she always seeks to make it clear that her criticism should not be understood as a rejection of Islamic law being implemented in Aceh.[21] In her view, if there are criticisms of the implementation of Islamic law in Aceh, they should be addressed to government institutions, and not directed against sharia or Islam per se.

According to Syarifah, the problems and disputes that have recently emerged and which have led to a heated discussion on the implementation of Islamic law are the result of a number of factors. First, many Acehnese have different perspectives on how sharia should be interpreted and expressed in the *Qanun*. Second, *Qanun* that regulate Acehnese religiosity are based only on the interpretation by legal authorities and the *Ulama* of the sacred texts. Third, women were not consulted during the process of interpreting sharia and drafting the *Qanun*, so the *Qanun* becomes insufficiently gender-sensitive.

Fourth, the way *Qanun* is being implemented has not been appropriately supported by government institutions.

Syarifah offers several approaches that should be considered in an attempt to address the above matters. First, there is a serious need for Acehnese *Ulama*, academics, policy-makers, and civil society activists to go back to the sources of Islamic law, to reread and reinterpret sharia in the context of Aceh. In the process of rereading the Islamic texts women must be included. This way, she expects that a new form of religious interpretation can be generated and formalized into *Qanun* that is gender-sensitive, promoting justice and equality. Second, although the implementation of Islamic law is still in its early state, the government has to make sure that it supports the process by providing adequate facilities and resources to the institutions responsible for overseeing the implementation.

In response to the implementation of Islamic law, MISPI argues, it needs to be improved in three ways. First, at the institutional government level, MISPI attempts to convince the local government that the current *Qanun* need to be reformulated, because they have not led to justice, as had been expected. Second, MISPI considers it important for women and women's activists to work with religious communities, most importantly with *Dayah* (Islamic traditional educational institutions) and the *Ulama*, in particular the female *Ulama*, and with academics. Third, MISPI believes that in order for the first two strategies to be successful, it needs to promote a rereading of the sources of Islamic law to uncover the egalitarian messages of Islam that MISPI members see as contained in the *Qur'an*, *Sunna* and *Hadith*. MISPI believes if this can be better promoted in patriarchal Acehnese society, women will have better access to equality and will not be the subject of discriminatory religious and social practices. In carrying out its programmes, MISPI needs to continue to work with both national and international partners. MISPI also acknowledges the need for women's NGOs and women activists to collaborate with Muslim intellectuals.

Agency

Maintaining Islamic credentials and Acehnese identity has become one of the key strategies used by MISPI to pursue its agenda in responding to the implementation of Islamic law. MISPI's Islamic credentials have become an important element in it gaining support from the male-dominated government institutions and religious and patriarchal society. MISPI enjoys access to *Ulama*, the MPU, the Office of Islamic Sharia, the local government and members of the local legislature, and expects that this access will enable it to influence legal reform and policy-making.

In my observation, many other local women's NGOs and its activists do not enjoy the access MISPI and Syarifah have to these government institutions or to public figures. For example, one member of local legislature from the Golkar Party[22] mentioned to me that when women activists were invited to attend a public hearing session (*sesi dengar pendapat*) at the DPRA (Dewan Perwakilan Rakyat Aceh, or Aceh's Provincial Parliament), many of them raised their voices, showing a lack of respect for the forum.[23] To him, this kind of attitude makes Syarifah different to other local women activists. Syarifah is seen by members of local legislature as able to maintain her Acehnese culture and tradition by showing respect to others, and she is thus able to deliver her ideas in a culturally acceptable manner. He said, 'Syarifah respects us [local Members of legislature] and above all she respects sharia'. On the other hand, he criticized other local women activists, saying, 'The others, especially the younger ones, are too emotional when they want to share their views with us and they attack sharia'. Another point that is important to him is the fact that Syarifah maintains her Acehnese values and Islamic tradition, for example, by always wearing Islamic dress. He said, 'She always wears what an Acehnese woman has to wear, and what Islam asked women to wear, while other activists are not doing this'. This again demonstrates that the male-dominated government institutions expect Acehnese women activists to maintain both their femininity and their Acehnese or Islamic credentials. A similar view was expressed by one male member of local legislature, the head of Partai Bulan Bintang (the Crescent Star Party) in the DPRA. In his view, Syarifah is a model of the true Acehnese woman activist and her leadership at MISPI has led the organization to focus on women's issues that are based on Islam.[24]

Similar comments have also been made by Professor Alyasa Abubakar, the head of Dinas Syariat Islam until 2008.[25] In his opinion, other activists should follow in the steps of Syarifah and MISPI. He said:

> MISPI has been working to promote women's status, women's rights and gender equality in line with sharia Islam, and Syarifah through MISPI has focused on empowering women within the framework of Islam.

Professor Abubakar added that his office was always in communication with Syarifah and MISPI and he often received updates on developments relating to his office from her. Similarly, unlike other women activists, Syarifah shows respect for Professor Abubakar. During my interaction with her, for example, I never heard Syarifah or MISPI staff criticize Professor Abubakar, while other women's activists often do so.

MISPI realizes that to pursue its agenda it needs not only support from local authorities, but also from foreign donors and international funding. This is interesting because of Syarifah's views on 'Western interests', as I will explain below.

The idea of obtaining foreign support for an Acehnese organization may sound inherently contradictory, because local women activists are often resistant to Western values.[26] In the case of MISPI, however, I argue that Syarifah has been skilful in convincing donors that gender equality or the promotion of women's rights in Aceh can be done only if it is carried out 'her way'. It is difficult for foreign donors or international NGOs to simply ignore MISPI's agency, even if they find MISPI's views on equality and women's rights contradict their agenda. Compared to other local women's NGOs, MISPI has thus proved to be very successful in winning support and acknowledgement from different elements of society, and this cannot be ignored. To me, this demonstrates that MISPI has effectively exercised agency, even in dealing with donors. I argue that MISPI has applied a strategy of 'I take your money, but I do it in my way', and this has worked successfully. Since it was established, MISPI has thus managed to maintain partnerships with various foreign donors, including the Asia Foundation (among the first foreign donors), and in recent times Oxfam, UNIFEM and UNFPA, among others.

Working with, and for, Acehnese women

With the wide support and networks that it enjoys, MISPI considers that it needs to work in particular with two special interest groups: women at the level of policy-making (such as female members of the local legislature, women in the bureaucracy, women academics, and women *Ulama*), and women at the grassroots, whose voices are often not heard. Syarifah argued that this is important, because existing democratic mechanisms have not been able to bond these two elements of society, thus contributing to the failure of the government to produce a policy that is gender-sensitive and not discriminatory.

For women at the grassroots, MISPI has developed a programme to introduce women in the village who are members of *Qur'anic* reading groups or *Majlis Taklim*[27] to issues related to women's rights and gender equality. MISPI chooses to work with *Qur'anic* reading groups because these groups have strong bases in the villages. During the conflict, these groups also proved to be relatively safe from both of the warring parties, as they were able to continue regular meetings at the local *meunasah* or village mosques. Syarifah also adds that the decision to work with women's *Qur'anic* reading groups was based on the perception that these groups are widely considered apolitical.

In one of these workshops for women's *Qur'anic* reading groups that I attended on 9 March 2007, I observed how MISPI introduces new knowledge on equality and justice in Islam. Women members of *Majlis Taklim* invited by MISPI include those who have leadership roles in their *Majlis Taklim* around Banda Aceh and Aceh Besar district. It is expected that these women would later share their new knowledge with other women in their own *Majlis Taklim*. The workshop covered several themes, ranging from how to understand the meaning of the verses in the *Qur'an*, to preaching *akhlak* or (good deeds) in the family, understanding Islamic texts, sharia and *Fiqh*, and a discussion on women's and men's roles in the family, as well as in society, according to Islam.

In her introduction, Syarifah shared her understanding about Islamic texts and sharia. She explained to the participants that sharia is a divine teaching derived from the *Qur'an*, *Hadith* and *Sunna*. She then refers to several verses in the *Qur'an* which, to her, guarantee the equality of men and women, for example, verse 2:228, which says 'and women have the rights similar to those against them in a just manner'. Syarifah also quotes a verse which emphasizes that God creates men and women of different nations, but what differentiates men and women is only their good deeds for God, as written in *Surah Al-Hujurat* 49:13:

> Oh human kind, We created you from male and female and made you into nations and tribes so that you might know one another. Verily the most noble of you in the sight of God is the one with the most *taqwa*.[28]

Having identified Islamic teachings from the *Qur'an* on the equality of men and women, Syarifah then elaborates how Acehnese should understand *Qanun* in Aceh. She explains the process of creating the *Qanun* and explains that, unlike sharia, *Qanun* can always be changed because it is not a divine law but rather simply what the Acehnese *Ulama*, political leaders and government understand in interpreting the divine law as set out in texts made by scholars. She underlines the need for all women to be aware of their rights in Islam, and the process of the creation of *Qanun* and their implementation. She also mentions that in a democratic system, women have equal opportunity to protest against *Qanun*, if they discriminate against them.

In disseminating the idea of equality between men and women, Syarifah tries to avoid using the term 'gender equality'. Instead she uses Indonesian terminology '*kesetaraan hubungan antara laki-laki dan perempuan*' or 'equality between men and women'. She later explained to me that it is part of her strategy that in this activity she would not use the terms '*keseteraan gender*' or 'gender equality'. This is because she is aware that female members of *Majlis Taklim* may be hostile to foreign terms. She does not want to make them feel they are being taught 'foreign' values. For many Acehnese women, the word '*kesetaraan*' or equality implies a situation in which men and women become the same, so that women, for example, must be able to do men's jobs and vice versa. This becomes problematic, as if men and women must be equal in this sense, then they must abandon deeply-held notions that the woman is tasked to be a wife, daughter and mother, while men must be husbands, fathers and brothers.

Syarifah is aware of this problem. Thus, in disseminating the idea of equality she reminds these women that while Islam requires women to be wives, daughters and mothers, it does not limit women from doing other things outside the home, such as obtaining an education and working. She says that it is important for parents to make sure that both their daughters and sons have equal opportunity to go to school and to allow them to pursue their dreams. To make her case, she refers to the Prophet's wives, Khadija, who was a successful businesswoman, and Aisah, who led the Muslim forces to war and become an important political figure after the death of the Prophet. Syarifah also tells how she and her husband manage their household so that they can both pursue their own careers.

What was interesting from this workshop is the fact that MISPI not only provides opportunities for women from *Qur'anic* reading groups to obtain new knowledge, but also allows these women to interact with other women in a new environment, and, most importantly, to learn how to express their own perspectives. I argue that MISPI has thus introduced women participants to the need to be critical of the constructed social values produced by male patriarchal authorities. At the very least, this forum allows women to speak their own voices.

MISPI also reaches out to female members of parliament, academics, lawyers, teachers and women *Ulama*. To accommodate these women, MISPI has participated in creating the Women's Network for Policy (Jaringan Perempuan Untuk Kebijakan or JPUK) and a Women's Network for Peace (Jaringan Perempuan untuk Perdamaian or JPUP) at both the provincial and district levels. As in the case of the agenda it has for female members of the *Qur'anic* reading group, MISPI created these networks to develop women's awareness of their rights in Islam and introduces similar themes through it, such as messages of gender equality in Islamic texts. Through JPUK, MISPI introduces women to the need to understand the legal drafting process, the techniques of diplomacy and good communication skills.[29] They are also taught about the position of *Qanun* within the national hierarchy of laws. By contrast to its programmes for women from *Majlis Taklim*, MISPI also introduces international norms in its work with JPUK and JPUP, in particular human rights and CEDAW (the Convention on the Elimination of All Forms of Discrimination against Women).[30] As discussed previously, some of the activists, both men and women, still find it problematic if in drafting *Qanun* for Aceh, they need to consider international norms, because many see them as incompatible with Islam and Aceh's cultural values.

Another important group that has become a focus of MISPI activity is women *Ulama*. This is because Law No. 44/1999 gave the *Ulama* in Aceh the opportunity to regain power in local politics by having a formal role in the production of regional regulations, as stipulated in Article 1 (8). The social and religious position of *Ulama* in Acehnese society also makes it important for MISPI to work with the *Ulama*. MISPI's agenda for empowering women *Ulama* is based on its concern at the very small number of women who teach in the traditional Islamic boarding schools or *Dayah*, and the lack of acceptance in the Acehnese community of women *Ulama*. Women *Ulama* are clearly still not adequately represented in formal institutions, such as the MPU.

Based on this background, MISPI finds it important to work with women's *Ulama*. During my fieldwork, I attended one training session for women Ulama convened on 30 June to 1 July 2007. This was part of the training series MISPI has organized in the past three months. In total, there were about 137 participants, representing 21 districts around the province. As usual, the training was opened by MISPI staff who also facilitate the training. It then began with every participant introducing each other. Participants were then asked to discuss and write down issues they think seriously challenge their role in the society. They came up with five points they identify to be important to be addressed immediately. First, the confusion among the *Ulama* on the different *madzhab* within *Fiqh*. This, according to them, hinders them from providing clear explanation to the society. Second, the limited roles of the women *Ulama* as many Acehnese consider male *Ulama* to be more authoritative. Third, how to help address problem arising from the implementation of sharia law. Fourth, better access for women to education and employment. Fifth, knowledge on how sharia law is implemented in other areas.

The five problems they have listed were then discussed and recommendations were finally agreed. Women *Ulama* need to be better equipped with the knowledge of the different *madzhab* in attempts to understand *Fiqh*. The more they understand the complexity the better it is for them to disseminate the knowledge and minimize differences. Women *Ulama* need more support from the authorities, including from male *Ulama* to acknowledge their roles in the society. In relation to sharia implementation, they agree that what needs to be done is to involve women's *Ulama* in disseminating the *Qanun* in society and to include them in the process of interpreting Islamic sources before turning them into *Qanun*.

Based on these recommendations, MISPI, with the MPU, published a handbook, entitled *Penguatan Ulama Perempuan di Nanggroe Aceh Darussalam* or 'Empowering Women *Ulama* in Nanggroe Aceh Darussalam'. Prominent religious leaders such as Professor Alyasa Abubakar (former head of the Office of Islamic Sharia), Professor Tgk Muslim Ibrahim (head of the MPU), Dr Nurjannah Ismail, women academics and activists, and other Muslim intellectuals were all involved in the creation of this handbook.[31] It is expected that women *Ulama* in Aceh will use this book as a reference in order to advance their understandings of issues pertaining to sharia. It contains materials such as *Fiqh-ushul Fiqh* (Islamic jurisprudence), good deeds or *akhlak ketauladanan*, *Tafsir Hadith* or interpretation of *Hadith*. It also discusses methodology for interpreting Islamic texts, the position of *Hadith* in legal matters, and the development of Islamic thought. This handbook also addresses the sociology of law in Aceh. It discusses, for example, the definition of *Qanun*, the position of *Qanun* within the Indonesia's hierarchy of law, and the process of enacting, revising and annulling a *Qanun*.

This handbook has become one of the main materials used by MISPI in its workshops with women *Ulama*. One woman *Ulama* who participated in the workshops said that she found it very helpful that she had the opportunity to learn new knowledge. She referred, in particular, to the session in which she was introduced to the various *madzhab* on *Fiqh* and the session on methodology in interpreting Islamic texts. She said that she had only gained Islamic knowledge from her previous training in *Dayah*, so that her knowledge was very limited. The environment during this workshop allows women *Ulama* to question, in distinction to the way they learn Islam from *Teuku*, or Islamic teachers in *Dayah*, who do not allow any discussion to occur. Many women *Ulama* therefore express great satisfaction with the workshop. One participant added that the workshops gave her new experiences, because during the workshop, women *Ulama* sat together at the same table with male *Ulama* and engaged in discussion. To her, this had previously been impossible, because of social attitudes that have it that men and women are not equal. Thus, to her, organizations like MISPI have not only introduced her to new ways of understanding Islam but also allow female *Ulama* to have the same rights to speak as male *Ulama*.

I find this to be similar to what Badran (2008, 9) has described in her research on how women in Nigeria discuss *Hudud* in public and private contexts. According to Badran (2008, 9), the activities organized by NGOs in Nigeria provided women with venues to express their opinions and to engage with men that were not otherwise available.

Resistance

During my interaction with Syarifah in the course of my fieldwork, I often saw her demonstrate her strong personality. I saw that she was very confident with her identity, both as an Acehnese and as a Muslim woman. Like many other Acehnese women that I have talked with, Syarifah is a Muslim woman who does not feel that Islam has put her in an unequal position to men. MISPI activities reveal that Acehnese women now have the forum to exercise their public roles. It has facilitated local women activists, along with many other Acehnese women, to participate and engage in the wider discussion on sharia, Islamic law and women's rights in Islam.

This section argues that although MISPI acknowledges the need to win the support of both national and international partners, it remains critical in its interaction with them. Syarifah told me that she disagrees with the portrayal of Acehnese women as 'victims' of Islamic law. Syarifah describes how annoyed she is when she is asked questions by foreign journalists, international activists or international researchers on issues related to sharia and women. Syarifah said that she is irritated by the fact that most of the questions that were asked of her seem to be based only on preconceptions and an ignorance of Islamic law in Aceh. In her view the perception that Acehnese women are oppressed is an idea created by the West (*Barat*) and to her reflects a lack of understanding that for many Acehnese Islam is more than just a legal regulation but, rather, an integral part of the Acehnese way of life.

Syarifah not only resents the attitude and perception of foreign activists towards the implementation of Islamic law vis-à-vis women, but also the approach of some activists from Jakarta. She resents the fact that some activists come to Aceh with the idea of promoting gender equality, without having an understanding of the culture of the local people. As a result, their attempts to promote gender equality and advance women's status neglect local cultural traditions and in the end only create resistance. One example, she says, is the fact that most of these activists introduce Acehnese women's NGOs and their activists to 'feminism', which for her is simply 'too much' and culturally ignorant. In her view, 'feminism' is a Western value and is not compatible with Islam and Acehnese culture. She explains that even the term 'gender', used by many Indonesians, is still strongly resisted by many Acehnese. Thus, she argued that the Acehnese cannot be expected to easily take in 'feminism', because its values are believed to be in contradiction with Islam. Introducing the idea of 'feminism', in her view, only creates problems in promoting gender equality.

Syarifah's lack of sympathy for people from outside Aceh is clear, especially if these people come to Aceh to explore the issue of Islamic law, as I experienced myself. One day, for example, she told me that she was sick of people who come to Aceh to get to know how Acehnese women live under sharia law. She illustrated her feelings by saying that such people need to be careful when they talk about women and Islamic law in Aceh. She said 'There is something about the Acehnese that connects us with sharia and the people from outside Aceh will never be able to understand that connection'. In particular, she said:

> People come to Aceh to see what is happening and later they make their own conclusion. They write it everywhere. In fact they are not Acehnese, they know nothing about Aceh and Islam in Aceh.

Syarifah's position on the current implementation of Islamic law can also be seen in her criticisms of her fellow local women's activists. On one occasion she attacked her colleagues for being 'contaminated' by outside cultures:

> Sometimes I noticed my friends [activists] have been infiltrated by outside values. Friends [activists] forget our identity as Acehnese. Sometimes they forget to wear proper Islamic clothing and cover their hair while delivering their messages during the training, while their audiences are *Ulama* and villagers. How can we expect people to respect our work if we do not respect our own values and cultures?

According to Syarifah, equality between men and women in Aceh should not be based on foreign values but should be 'extracted' from within Acehnese culture and Islam. She argued that Islam has taught men and women what is proper for them. She fears that 'equality' as it is in the West means that men and women are 'the same', while for her, equality in Aceh is not about 'sameness'. For example, she argues that in Aceh's culture, equality means that men and women share the tasks at home. She describes how her father always helps her mother doing household work, while also being the breadwinner in the family. Her father never hesitates to do the laundry or to cook for the family, she says. She describes her father as wholeheartedly supporting her mother to continue working outside the house, so that she can pursue her own career and be involved in various community activities. In short, she thinks the values lived in her family are Islamic and that it is also what Acehnese tradition has taught. To her, that is what Acehnese men need to do with their families.

A similar argument was also made by Murni, one of the senior staff and activists at MISPI. According to Murni, the patriarchal culture of Acehnese society should be addressed by looking back at the 'real teachings' of Islam and Acehnese local tradition:

> Women are not created from the skull, because women do not want to be above men. Women are not created from the leg bone because women do not want to be trampled on by men. Instead, women are created from the rib bone because women are equal with men.
>
> (Interview, Banda Aceh, 3 March 2007)

In discussing her views, Murni said that she was inspired by the work of Asghar Ali Engineer, Fatima Mernissi and Amina Wadud, whose works have been translated into Bahasa Indonesia. Murni argues that the teaching of the *Qur'an* guarantees that men and women are equal, as is written in the *Qur'an* in 2:228, which says 'and women have rights similar to those against them in a just manner' (Engineer 1992, 43). She also mentioned another verse in the *Qur'an* that talks about the rights of women to earn and to occupy public space, that is in 4:32, which states: 'For men is the benefit of what they earn and for women is the benefit of what they earn.'

As women activists at MISPI refer to the *Qur'an* to generate reasoning for gender equality, it is clear that they engage with Islamic feminist discourse in pursuing gender equality. However, it is quite problematic at the same time to categorize MISPI activists by reference to the rubric of 'Islamic feminists' because of their reluctance to acknowledge that their activism is inspired by 'feminism'. For example, Murni argued that in promoting gender equality in Aceh, MISPI will not refer to anything that is based on foreign values, such as feminism. From here it can be seen that while at one point MISPI engages with Islamic feminism, it also shies away from it. The reluctance to acknowledge that their work is inspired by feminism can be understood as a part of Acehnese resistance to ideas coming from the West. Although Islam itself, as Lindsey (2008) has argued, is not an indigenous concept and Islam was 'imported' to Aceh, to the Acehnese Islam it is now part of their identity.[32] This unwillingness of Muslim women activists to be referred to as 'feminists' is, in fact, not peculiar to the Acehnese. Brenner (2005, 107), for example, has identified a tendency for women activists in Muslim societies not to be called 'feminists'. According to her, this is because for women Muslim activists in Indonesia to be called feminists can be seen as detaching them from Indonesia's moral values. Thus, for Brenner (2005, 101) this understanding has led some Islamic women activists to avoid being called 'Islamic feminists'. In addition, Sadli (2002, 80) observes that the term 'feminist' is considered by many Indonesians as 'non-indigenous' and 'irrelevant' to local values. The common assumption that often attaches to the term is that 'Feminist is a Western/Northern concept, anti-men, sees men as the sources of all gender inequality, promotes the acceptance of lesbianism and so forth' (Sadli 2002, 80).

Syarifah and MISPI activists argue that the promotion of gender equality should be based on Acehnese traditions, which, according to them, are strongly entrenched in Islam. However, I would suggest that Syarifah is also defending her own (Acehnese) form of Islam as she tends to see Acehnese Islam as inherently different to other forms of Islam.

Conclusion

This chapter uses a case study of MISPI and its activists to demonstrate how one local women's NGO and its activists respond to the implementation of Islamic law through rereading Islamic law. It shows that the local NGO, while working for donors, was still able to maintain its own perspective in promoting equality. The discussion also shows that to work in a society where Islam and tradition are strongly entrenched in the people's lives, an NGO needs to ensure that it works within the local context. MISPI is one Acehnese women's NGO that has demonstrated its agency by preserving its Islamic credentials to earn respect from male-dominated government circles, religious *Ulama*, the conservative religious groups and the wider Acehnese community.

In its response to the implementation of Islamic law MISPI has chosen to work with government institutions by initiating collaboration and networking. By working closely with religious leaders and government institutions, MISPI hopes that it can influence the policy-making process and, at the same time, introduce new understandings on equal gender relations in Aceh based on Islam. MISPI understands that in promoting the issue of equality and gender justice to a conservative religious community it needs to make sure that it pays attention to local knowledge and values. Although it promotes Islam's egalitarian messages, MISPI and its activists are still in the initial stages of introducing what they see as Islamic knowledge on gender equality and justice. MISPI's activities have been possible because of the presence of democratic mechanisms that allow freedom of speech and the freedom to associate. At the same time, however, the presence of foreign institutions and international NGOs has also introduced local women activists to international norms on human rights. Despite its resistance to new values coming from the West, MISPI is, in fact, engaging with feminism.

MISPI has demonstrated its agency to promote women's status and gender equality within the framework of Islam because it sees that as the best way to challenge conservative views about women. MISPI maintains its Islamic credentials and Acehnese identity so it is able to negotiate its agenda and gain access to male-dominated government institutions and conservative religious leaders. While it may be seen as supporting the status quo, MISPI's programmes have also empowered women and introduced women to their rights within Islam. MISPI has been successful in bringing women at the grassroots to start talking about equality and understand that Islam guarantees that their rights should be equal to men's. More than that, I argue that MISPI has also brought together women of different social backgrounds to discuss their views on various issues, something that is new for many Acehnese women.

In conclusion, MISPI has introduced Acehnese women to the importance of having their voices heard and to listening to other voices that in the end can have a positive impact on their lives. MISPI allowed Acehnese women to start having their conversation on the issue of equality, women's civil and political rights and how Islam guarantees women's rights. MISPI's strategy has also resulted in gaining leverage among religious and government leaders so that its voices and views are respected. With this strategy Syarifah and MISIPI have been able to exercise influence, which, it is hoped, will ultimately result in legal and social reforms that will better empower women.

Notes

1 See Chapter 3, where I discuss the social and political circumstances surrounding the emergence of local women's NGOs and women's movements in Aceh.
2 For a comprehensive account of these political developments, see Aspinall (2009).
3 See Chapter 4 for discussion of the Inong Balee and their struggles as part of the GAM movement.
4 See also Chapter 5 for details of intimidation of some Acehnese women by GAM followers. In my conversations with various informants it was sometimes argued that GAM is very patriarchal. Informants referred, for example, to various incidents during the initial introduction of Islamic law, when GAM supporters conducted '*razia jilbab*' or *jilbab* raids. Bowen (2003) has similarly revealed that in Central Aceh, GAM often conducted *jilbab* raids and in some cases cut women's hair.
5 See Chapter 4. For further account on how activists were treated by the Indonesian military, see Schulze (2006, 253–254).
6 At the time the research was conducted, Dana Lubis was the head of IMPACT, a local NGO that works to train trainers and facilitators. He was once the head of the HMI branch in Aceh province and when he graduated he worked at WALHI, an environmental national NGO. I interviewed him in the Hotel Sultan, Banda Aceh, on 8 December 2007, where he was a speaker at a seminar conducted by MISPI on developing a network among women leaders and women members of the local legislature from throughout the Aceh region.
7 HMI or Himpunan Mahasiswa Islam is a Muslim Student Organization established in Yogyakarta in 1947. Since its establishment, HMI has been one of the important student organizations until now. Many of the former members of HMI have gained respected position within government circles, for example, becoming members of parliament and ministers and occupying other important and strategic political positions. This organization has its branches in almost all provinces throughout Indonesia, and is usually based in universities across the country. Mukhtar (2006) argues that the cadres of HMI have been involved not only in Islamic or nationalist struggles. As Mukhtar (2006, 2) points out, Azyumardi Azra, one of the respected former members of HMI, has now become one of the most influential moderate Muslim political thinkers in Indonesia. Mukhtar argues that as an organization HMI has a strong political orientation due to its history. Azra (cited in Mukhtar 2006, 2) points out that at the time HMI was launched, Indonesia was in the midst of its struggle to defend Indonesia's national independence and had

to fight against the Dutch colonial government that sought to resume power in the country. In addition, Hefner (1997, 79–81) has observed that the Muslim Student Organization (HMI) was one of the Muslim groups in Indonesia that 'took a less pessimistic view' of the New Order government. This can be seen, for example, in its support of the New Order policy to ban the Communist Party in the 1960s. Hefner argued that, according to the Muslim Student Organization (HMI), the New Order policy to restrict political Islam did not mean that it was against 'cultural' or 'civil Islam'. Hefner has also noted that in the early period of the New Order, some prominent Muslim activists from HMI 'chose to cooperate and work for change' from within the system. The result was that these Muslim activists have been able to influence Indonesian Muslim political attitudes.

8 Interview with Zubaidah Djohar, Banda Aceh, 12 December 2007.
9 Baiturrahman Mosque is the grand mosque in Aceh. People come here not only to pray but also for recreation. It is located in the main area of capital city of Banda Aceh. Many Acehnese believe that the mosque is sacred. It was built by the Dutch colonial administration in 1879. It has now become the city's main landmark and a symbol of Aceh. Perceptions of the sacredness of the mosque increased after the tsunami, as it remained standing despite being hit by the earthquake and tsunami, while surrounding buildings were destroyed.
10 The central market or Pasar Raya in Banda Aceh was completely destroyed by the tsunami. At the time of my research, the market was in the process of reconstruction. It is located by the Krueng Raya River.
11 See Chapter 1, where I discuss how those who participate in various trainings, seminars and workshops, or who are informants in a survey, usually receive financial compensation.
12 Hefner (1993, 13) argues that the creation of ICMI, which received the support of Suharto in 1990, was a sign of a 'deepening Islamisation of Indonesian State and Ideology'. For more accounts on the backgrounds of the creation of ICMI, see Hefner (1993), Ricklefs (2001, 393), Hefner (1997, 75–77) and Azra (2004).
13 Partai Bulan Bintang is one of the many nationally based Islamic political parties that emerged in 1999.
14 KPU is a government body assigned to manage elections. It is an autonomous commission that works on a nationwide scale, with a permanent basis. It has branches at provincial and district level which are called KPUD or Regional Election Commissions (Pratikno 2009, 58–59).
15 In Indonesia, it is very easy to get fake-branded watches or handbags. Many Acehnese women often travel to Medan, North Sumatra, to get fake fashion.
16 See also Mernissi (2003, 31–32), in which she mentioned that an Egyptian jurist and nationalist, Qasim Amin, had argued that men, in fact, should control their gaze rather than expect women to cover up in public space.
17 One women activist told me, for example, that when she travelled with a group of women activists to Cirebon for training organized by the Asia Foundation, some activists began to take off their *jilbab* as soon as their plane departed Medan, the transit airport from Aceh to Jakarta. By the time they arrived in Jakarta, they had completely let down their hair, without any covering.
18 Many Acehnese said they can recognize activists from how they cover their hair. A woman who wears a shawl that is draped loosely over the head and shoulder is most likely an activist.
19 See Chapter 3, in which I discuss the different interpretations that some Acehnese women have given to 'Muslim clothing'.
20 Syarifah is referring to the mass gathering at the Grand Baiturrahman Mosque after Aceh was granted the rights to implement sharia law. For further accounts of this, see Aspinall (2009).

21 Syarifah expresses this opinion on sharia implementation in speeches that she delivers at almost every training, seminar and workshop organized by MISPI.
22 Golkar Party is a national-based political party. It was the political vehicle of the ruling government during Suharto's New Order administration.
23 Interview, Banda Aceh, 24 January, 2008.
24 Interview, Banda Aceh, 7 December 2007. Partai Bulan Bintang is an Islamic political party. In the 2009 general election, Partai Bulan Bintang won only 1.79 per cent of the vote. It has continued to lose the support from the Indonesian Muslims, as can be seen from declining votes. In 1999, it won 13 seats in the national legislature, but only 11 in the 2004 election.
25 Interview February, Banda Aceh, 25 March 2007.
26 See Chapter 5 for a discussion on the resistance of some local NGO activists to the 'West'.
27 For more on Majlis Taklim, see Doorn-Harder (2006).
28 This verse is quoted from Wadud (1999). *Taqwa* is a key *Qur'anic* term that refers to a person's moral integrity and commitment to the teachings of Islam (Wadud 1999).
29 See Chapter 4 for a discussion of JPUK activities.
30 See also Chapter 4 on how women in Aceh react to the international norms.
31 All these religious leaders – Professor Alyasa Abubakar, Professor Tgk Muslim Ibrahim, Dr Nurjannah Ismail – that MISPI is working with are academics at the IAIN Ar-Raniry.
32 See also Riddell (2006, 48–49), in which he described that in forming their Islamic identity in the sixteenth and seventeenth centuries, the Acehnese drew elements form other Islamic areas, such as from India and from Arabia, before adapting them to local contexts.

References

Aspinall, Edward 2009, *Islam and Nation: Separatist Rebellion in Aceh, Indonesia*, Stanford University Press, California.

Azra, Azyumardi 2004, 'Political Islam in Post-Suharto Indonesia', in Virginia Matheson Hooker and Amin Saikal (eds), *Islamic Perspectives on the New Millennium*, Institute of Southeast Asian Studies, Singapore, pp. 133–149.

Badran, Margot 1995, *Feminist, Islam and Nation*, Princeton University Press, Princeton.

Badran, Margot 2008, 'Shari'ah Activism in Nigeria under Hudud', in Carolyn M. Elliot (ed.), *Global Empowerment of Women: Responses to Globalization and Politicized Religions*, Routledge, New York and London, pp. 173–190.

Bertrand, Jacques 2004, *Nationalism and Ethnic Conflict in Indonesia*, Cambridge University Press, Cambridge.

Bowen, John R 2003, *Islam, Law and Equality in Indonesia: Anthropology of Public Reasoning*, Cambridge University Press, United Kingdom.

Brenner, Suzanne 1996, 'Reconstructing Self and Society: Javanese Muslim Women and the Veil', *American Ethnologist*, vol. 23, issue 4, pp. 673–697.

Brenner, Suzanne 2005, 'Islam and Gender Politics in Late New Order Indonesia', in Andrew C. Wilford and Kenneth M. George (eds), *Spirited Politics: Religion and Public Life in Contemporary Southeast Asia*, Cornell University Southeast Asia Program, Ithaca, NY, pp. 93–118.

Doorn-Harder, Nelly van 2006, *Women Shaping Islam: Reading the Qur'an in Indonesia*, University of Illinois Press, Chicago.

Engineer, Ashgar Ali 1992, *The Rights of Women in Islam*, C. Hurts & Co Publishers, United Kingdom.

Hailey, John and Rick, J. 2004, 'Trees Die from the Top: International Perspectives on NGOs Leadership Development', *Voluntas: International Journal of Voluntary and Nonprofit Organisations*, vol. 15, no. 4, pp. 343–353.

Hefner, Robert W. 1993, 'Islam, State and Civil Society: ICMI and the Struggle for Indonesian Middle Class', *Indonesia*, vol. 56, pp. 1–35.

Hefner, Robert W. 1997, 'Islamization and Democratization in Indonesia', in Robert W. Hefner and Patricia Horvatich (eds), *Islam in an Era of Nation-States: Politics and Religious Renewal in Muslim Southeast Asia*, University of Hawai'i Press, Hawaii, pp. 75–128.

Hilhorst, Dorothea 2000, 'Records and Repudiation: Everyday Politics of a Philippine Development NGO', PhD Thesis, Wageningen University.

Kandiyoti, Deniz 1988, 'Bargaining with Patriarchy', *Gender and Society*, vol. 2, issue 3, pp. 274–290.

Lindsey, Tim 2008, 'When Words Fail: Syariah Law in Indonesia: Revival, Reform or Transplantation?', in Penelope Nicholson and Sarah Biddulph (eds), *Examining Practice, Interrogating Theory: Comparative Legal Studies in Asia*, Martinus Nijhoff Publisher, Leiden, pp. 195–222.

Muhktar, Sidratahta 2006, *HMI dan Kekuasaan*, Jakarta, Prestasi Pustaka Publisher.

Pratikno 2009, 'Political Parties in Pilkada: Some Problems for Democratic Consolidation', in Maribeth Erb and Priyambudi Sulistiyanto (eds), *Deepening Democracy in Indonesia? Direct Elections for Local Leaders (Pilkada)*, ISEAS, Singapore, pp. 21–35.

Reid, Anthony 2003, 'War, Peace and the Burden of History in Aceh', *Asia Research Institute Working Paper Series*, ARI, Singapore.

Ricklefs, M.C. 2001, *A History of Modern Indonesia since c.1200*, Palgrave, Basingstoke.

Riddell, Peter G. 2006, 'Aceh in the Sixteenth and Seventeenth Centuries: "Serambi Mekkah and Identity"', in Anthony Reid (ed.), *Verandah of Violence: The Background to the Aceh Problem*, National University Press, Singapore, pp. 38–51.

Rinaldo, Rachel 2008, 'Envisioning the Nation: Women Activists, Religion and the Public Sphere in Indonesia', *Social Forces*, vol. 84, issue 4, pp. 1781–1803.

Sadli, Saparinah 2002, 'Feminism in Indonesia in an International Context', in Kathryn Robinson and Sharon Bessell (eds), *Women in Indonesia: Gender, Equity and Development*, Institute of Southeast Asian Studies, Singapore, pp. 80–91.

Schulze, Kirsten E. 2006, 'Insurgency and Counter-Insurgency: Strategy and the Aceh Conflict, October 1976–May 2004', in Anthony Reid (ed.), *Verandah of Violence: The Background to the Aceh Problem*, National University Press, Singapore, pp. 225–271.

Siegel, James T. 2000, *The Rope of God*, The University of Michigan Press, Ann Arbor.

Smith-Hefner, Nancy J. 2007, 'Javanese Women and the Veil in Post-Soeharto Indonesia', *The Journal of Asian Studies*, vol. 66, issue 2, pp. 389–420.

Wadud, Amina 1999, *Rereading the Sacred Text from a Woman's Perspective*, Oxford University Press, New York.

Waylen, Georgina 1993, 'Women's Movements and Democratization in Latin America', *Third World Quarterly*, vol. 14, no. 3, pp. 573–587.

Waylen, Georgina 1996, *Gender in Third World Politics*, Lynne Rienner Publishers, Boulder.

Conclusion
Islamic feminism, local women's NGOs and women's movements in Aceh

In her research on women Islamist movements in Egypt, Saba Mahmood (2001, 206), defines agency as 'the capacity to realise one's own interests against the weight of custom, tradition, transcendental will or other obstacles'. Based on the experience of rural Acehnese women, Siapno (2000, 278) argues that Acehnese female agency is not articulated in the form of modern, progressive political movements, as often happens with male nationalist movements. According to Siapno, Acehnese women's agency has instead formed as an indigenous form of local feminism, in which women exercise power but not within a 'Euro-American analysis' of gender agency. She points out that women in Aceh have participated actively in the struggles of their times, though not perhaps in publicly visible positions or in an overt form of opposition. In addition, Siapno makes the point that 'women's agency in Aceh has not been passive and silent'. The relative absence of Acehnese female representation in the public domain should be seen as a function of historiography, which places too much emphasis on organized political movements and the nation-state.

My research on how Acehnese women respond to sharia implementation by mobilizing into women's movements reaffirms Siapno's argument that women's agency in Aceh has not been passive and silent. The urban and educated women who have become part of local women's movements have actively attempted to reform Islamic law by challenging the religious authorities and local government. Women are mobilized because of the discriminatory practices against many Acehnese women, those who live in urban and rural areas across Aceh. Based on six months' fieldwork, this research reveals that many Acehnese women demand reform of the Islamic law through rereading and reinterpreting the religious texts.

Since they were established, local women's organizations and NGOs have become the main avenue for many Acehnese women to struggle for peace, to protect women and promote equality, economic and socio-cultural rights and civil and political rights. These local women's NGOs and activists later became the backbone of Aceh's women's movements. Chapters 3 and 4 show that Acehnese women have gained greater opportunities to engage in public spheres since Aceh was granted autonomy as the result of Indonesia's political democratization. The autonomy granted to provincial and regional administration in Indonesia has benefitted women's groups at the local level because it provided them with more freedom to express their views and to organize (Blackburn 2004, 13). On the other hand, this autonomy has also posed a new challenge for Acehnese women, as male religious authority and Islamist groups try to use the available political space to impose their agenda of returning women to the domestic sphere (Brenner 2005; Rinaldo 2006; Blackburn 2004, 2008). This is because political democratization does not always necessarily mean respect for women's rights (Blackburn 2008, 103).

As elaborated in Chapter 2, the implementation of Islamic law in Aceh was initiated in 1999, during the early phase of Indonesia's transition to democracy following the fall of Suharto's authoritarian and militaristic administration in 1998. This introduction ignited debate over the importance of the formalization of sharia, as an Islamic way of life. Since its introduction almost ten years ago, the Acehnese remain divided in their responses to the implementation of Islamic law. While many Acehnese see it as an opportunity to return to the 'local', 'indigenous' and 'authentic' 'values', which will distance them from the domination of Jakarta, others see it mainly as a strategy to displace the earlier demands of Acehnese for justice and an equal economic share in the province's wealth.

Despite these ongoing debates, the introduction of Islamic law has brought the issue of women's equality, women's role and women's rights into the wider debate on Islam, Islamic law and women's rights. Issues relating to women's roles and women's rights in Islam have increasingly been discussed not only among many Acehnese women but also among the reform-minded Acehnese Muslims. Following Bowen (1993, 27), I argue in Chapter 2 that Islam in Aceh has become 'transparent' as it became subject to public scrutiny, not least because many Acehnese participate in both scholarly and private conversations regarding Islam, Islamic law and women's rights.

This research demonstrates that Islamic law in Aceh, which was introduced in 1999, has, indeed, discriminated against women and other groups in society. However, it has not totally impeded women from taking public roles, as is often assumed. Acehnese women have, instead, been able to use the available space to challenge the implementation and the authorities. The presence of local NGOs has facilitated women of different social backgrounds to demand justice. This is because, as I argue in Chapters 4 and 5, the implementation of Islamic law in Aceh has occurred alongside Indonesia's democratic reform, and democracy had provided Acehnese men and women from different levels of society opportunities to engage in debates regarding women, Islam and Islamic law. In addition, the democratic mechanism also provides Acehnese women with the chance to engage in public policy-making, as it is guaranteed by the law. As discussed in Chapter 2, Acehnese men and women participate rigorously in the resulting discussions, ranging from how the sources of Islamic law, the *Qur'an* and *Hadith*, should be interpreted, to who has the authority to interpret them, and to how that interpretation should be implemented in Aceh.

The continuing debates that have emerged over the implementation of Islamic law reflect significant changes that have occurred in the local politics in Aceh. I explore how Acehnese are divided in the way they perceive the implementation of Islamic law in Chapter 3, however, it is important to note that those who are critical of the implementation of Islamic law do not express a total rejection of it; rather they demand the implementation of Islamic law in a way that treats Acehnese men and women more fairly.

For women activists, the implementation of Islamic law has provided them with momentum to examine what they see as the real message of Islam regarding their rights and status in the family and in community. They also look to Aceh's history, when the Islamic kingdom allowed women freedom to take leading roles in the public domain, for example by becoming the ruling queen or leading the navy, or fighting in battle. Local Acehnese women's NGOs and their activists have now begun to develop distinct women's movements in which they demand that Islamic law in Aceh be reformed through a rereading of the Islamic texts and Islamic jurisprudence, based on Aceh's cultural values. This can be seen, for example, in the Charter of the Rights of Women in Aceh, signed on 11 November 2008. The signatories of the Charter believe that fair treatment of women is entirely in line with the basic principles of Islam.

The demands of local women's NGOs and women's movements in Aceh for legal reform through rereading the *Qur'an* mirror what Muslim women in many other Muslim societies have been arguing. In Muslim societies, such as in Malaysia, the struggle of Muslim women for equality is also derived from within Islam, and is often referred to as 'Islamic feminism'. Thus, what local women's NGOs and women's movements in Aceh have demonstrated can be contextualized within broader women's movements in the Muslim world. As believers in Islam, Acehnese Muslim women challenge patriarchal social norms of Aceh's male-dominated society and their legal doctrines by combining their knowledge of Islamic teachings and Aceh's *adat* with feminist ideas.

The arrival of international institutions and foreign NGOs following the tsunami of 26 December 2004 strengthened local activists' capacity to promote women's rights, as the international institutions and foreign NGOs introduced international norms regarding human rights. The presence of foreign and national NGOs has also, however, prompted Acehnese women activists and reform-minded Muslims to engage in discussions regarding gender in Islam. This is in line with the argument made by Saptari and Utrecht (1997, 319), who observed that the international community has significantly advanced women's NGO activities in Indonesia. It is international NGOs and foreign institutions that have enabled them to strengthen their lobbying and organizational skills, and have provided access for Indonesian women's NGOs to transnational women's movements. So, local women's NGOs in Aceh, have, for example, now been introduced to Muslim women's networks, such as Women Living under Muslim Laws (WLUML) and Musawah. Likewise, in 2009, leading Acehnese women activists such as Dr Nurjannah Ismail attended an event organized by Musawah in Malaysia. Musawah is a global Muslim women's movement for equality and justice in the Muslim family.

As discussed in Chapter 4 local women's movements strategize to negotiate with local authorities including religious institutions, the *Ulama* and local government. The two women's networks, JPUK and GWG, employ different approaches to problems. These differences result from the fact that activists within these two movements come from different backgrounds, and have experienced different patterns of activism. One women's movement, JPUK, which consists only of local activists, has taken an approach of maintaining local *adat* and culture in negotiating with Acehnese male authorities. It focuses its activism on influencing policy-making. The other women's movement, GWG, has a more diverse background. It includes nationally based and foreign activists in its ranks, and they tend to be more confident in discussing new ideas. Compared to JPUK, GWG focuses more of its activities on developing public awareness of gender equality and women's rights.

My case study of MISPI shows how this local women's NGO chose to take a 'local' approach in promoting equality and women's rights in the context of the implementation of Islamic law. As mentioned, its strategy has proven successful. MISPI's Islamic piety has generated respect from religious authorities, the legislature, the government bureaucracy and conservative religious communities. In conducting its activities, MISPI works hard to maintain Islamic credentials, as can be seen, for example, in how it deliberately seeks to express the religious piety of its members. This choice to maintain Islamic credentials is derived from an understanding that resistance from the conservative religious communities can only be challenged by using Islam. The result is that MISPI continues to exercise more leverage than many other local women's NGOs. MISPI has thus demonstrated its ability to exercise agency in advancing women's status through strategizing and manoeuvring with at least three institutions: local authorities including the *Ulama*, activists from national-based NGOs, and the international community. I argue that in a society with a strong patriarchal culture like Aceh, women need to strategize and negotiate with the state and with social structures in a way that is acceptable in that society (Waylen 1996). The moves taken by MISPI are thus in line with what Afshar (1996, 1) has argued, namely that women in the Third World negotiate with the state and this does not have to be equated with weakness, nor should their strategies be classified as either temporary or unimportant.

MISPI is one of many local women's NGOs in Aceh that has attempted to employ ideas of 'equality' derived from Islamic feminist movements that have appeared in places like Malaysia, and in the Middle East or North Africa. They have also learned from similar movements that have been present in Jakarta since the 1990s. Their interaction with outside communities, both with Indonesia-based and foreign NGO activists, has equipped local women activists with knowledge of the rights of women both within Islam, and by reference to international norms such as CEDAW.

My research also reveals that the attempts of local women's NGOs to reform Islamic legal doctrines will continue to be reliant on their interaction with nationally based NGOs, as well as their ability to access funds and support from international donors or foreign NGOs. Also likely, Indonesia's democratization and the achievement of peace in Aceh will allow local women's NGOs to develop and have the freedom to continue to advance women's status within the confinements of Islam. This thesis foresees that local women's NGOs activisms in Aceh will continue to affect the future of the implementation of Islamic law. Equally, possible threats towards women's advances in public life will continue to be driven by the use of Islam by male authorities under the rubric of 'Islamic resurgence'.

The work of local women's NGOs and women's movements in Aceh has certainly been subject to criticism. This is especially directed at NGOs working on issues related to '*syari'at*', women's rights and women's empowerment. Some Acehnese accuse local women's NGOs of exchanging their Islamic and Acehnese traditions with Western ideology or Western feminism. Other challenges to the work of women's NGOs and women's movements in Aceh come from within their own movement. As mentioned in Chapter 4, in 2008 local activists have found a local term (*timang*) to replace 'gender', as 'gender' is considered foreign and had created resistance among the Acehnese. *Timang* was presented as referring to the concept of 'equal relations' between men and women as enshrined in Islam and entrenched in Acehnese tradition.

Observing Indonesia's women's movements, Blackburn (2004, 11) observes that conflicts of interest contribute to hampering their work. Women's movements in Aceh have encountered this problem. Local women's NGOs and women activists within the women's movement still have to struggle to define how they should promote women's rights. While some assert the need to maintain Acehnese and Islamic identity, others are starting to see that accepting international norms is not necessarily a violation of Aceh's *adat* and Islamic values. There are groups that still believe certain norms within the international law are not compatible with their values, while others are starting to think differently.

In the literature on women and politics there has been a debate about who is represented by women's NGOs and women's activists in politics. It is argued that women's NGOs and activists come mainly from the middle and upper class, and that they thus represent only this group. This is also what Rinaldo (2003) points out based on her research on women's movements in Indonesia that women's movements are unable to escape from the fact that they are mainly represented by middle- and upper-class women. She writes that women activists have acknowledged that the recent outcome of Indonesia's legislative elections has shown that their activism has not connected with the grassroots, and they have been concentrating on issues that do not affect most women. A similar problem, I argue, also confronts local women's NGOs in Aceh. In the 2009 legislative election, for example, some women activists nominated themselves as candidates, but failed to win the votes of Acehnese women. Aceh, in fact, has among the lowest women's participation in the local parliamentary election with only 28.8 per cent of women participating in the election, that is less than the 30 per cent quota set by the Indonesian election regulation (Puskapol 2013).

Local women's movements in Aceh, I argue, still lack a strong social basis in Aceh, partly because women's movements in Aceh do not have sufficient connection with Islamic institutions such as *Dayah*, the traditional Islamic educational institution in Aceh. This can be seen from the difficulty of including *Teungku* or religious leaders in their work. It may thus be worthwhile for local women activists in Aceh to study similar attempts in Java, where gender equality has been introduced and disseminated by male religious leaders from *pesantren*. Although such trends are not common in Aceh, MISPI has begun to experiment with similar initiatives.

While women activists acknowledge that the reform of interpretation of the *Qanun* requires a rereading of the two sources of sharia, the *Qur'an* and *Hadith*, few efforts have yet been made to address this. They have not yet focused their energy on the field of *Qur'anic* interpretation or exegesis (*tafsir*) and so have not been able to find effective ways to explicate an egalitarian message from the text of the *Qur'an*. Among local activists, there is only one, Dr Nurjannah Ismail, who has the capacity to deal with the issue of interpretation (*tafsir*), but she has so far had little opportunity to influence the whole movement.

The struggle of local women activists in Aceh is made difficult because many activists obtained their education mostly from public schools, which are secular. Unlike Muslim women activists in Jakarta, most Acehnese women activists do not have previous training on Islamic education, for example, from traditional *pesantren*, and only a small number of them trained in Islamic higher educational institutions such as IAIN. The majority of the prominent NGO activists, as mentioned in the previous chapters, obtained their education from secular educational institutions, such as Syiah Kuala University. Activists such as Soraya Kamaruzzaman (founder of Flower Aceh), Samsidar (founder of YPW), Syarifah Rahmatillah (MISPI), Raihani Arifin (RPUK), Norma (Balai Syura), Azriana Noerdin (Balai Syura), Shadia Marhaban (LINA), Fatima Sjam (LBH Apik), Raihan Diani (Beujroh) and Hasdiana (Yayasan Matahari) were all educated in non-Islamic educational institutions. During my research I met female academics from IAIN Ar-Raniry (Dr Nurjannah Ismail, Eka Srimulyani, who also works as a consultant for LOGICA-AIPARD, an Australian-based NGO, and Soraya Devy, the head of IAIN's Women's Centre, Roosmawardani, the founder of Putro Kandee and Rasyidah) who have taken part in local women's movements. However, only Eka Srimulyani, Soraya Devy and Roosmawardani have the resources and access to work directly with Acehnese women. Otto Sjamsuddin Ishak says:

> Of all the women activists, only Dr Nurjannah Ismail who has the capacity and knowledge to reveal the egalitarian message of Islam, however, she has only limited access and opportunity to do so.
>
> (Interview, Banda Aceh, 17 March 2007)

In addition, there has been also lack of support from male Muslim scholars from IAIN Ar-Raniry for the women's movement.

The limited knowledge of women activists on Islamic legal matters has contributed to the difficulties they face in engaging with Islamic texts and challenging the conservative religious community. Due to their secular background, the conservative religious community perceive activists as lacking either capacity or authority in reinterpreting religious texts. In addition, activists face problems in deciding how they should embrace the *Dayah* community and reach out to religious leaders. Because of this, it becomes important for women activists to develop strong networks with institution like IAIN AR-Raniry. At the same time, Islamic scholars from IAIN Ar-Raniry are also challenged to moderate the conservative understandings of Islam predominant among the Acehnese. They need to introduce the same 'renewal' movement (*gerakan pembaharuan*) as scholars of the UIN/IAIN in Java have showed (Hefner 1993; Feener 2007).

It should be remembered, however, that prolonged conflict has also contributed to the relatively limited opportunities that Acehnese women have had to engage with these issues. Thus, there is, I argue, a need for local Acehnese women's activists to learn from the experience of other Muslim women's movements and activists in Java. Although women's movements operate in very different circumstances within and outside Aceh, it is still important for them to look at similar movements for guidance.

Finally, this book shows that women's NGOs in Aceh have been able to engage their Islamic and Acehnese identity with a 'Western' framework on women's rights. In doing so, women's NGOs have become the most visible avenue for Acehnese women to exert their agency to challenge the sociopolitical and religious structures. To do so, they need to receive support from both national and international NGO communities.

References

Afshar, Haleh 1996, *Women and Politics in the Third World*, Routledge, London.

Blackburn, Susan 2004, *Women and the State in Modern Indonesia*, Cambridge University Press, Cambridge.

Blackburn, Susan 2008, 'Indonesian Women and Political Islam', *Journal of Southeast Asian Studies*, vol. 39, issue 1, pp. 83–105.

Bowen, John R. 1993, *Muslims through Discourse*, Princeton University Press, Princeton.

Brenner, Suzanne 2005, 'Islam and Gender Politics in Late New Order Indonesia', in Andrew C. Wilford and Kenneth M. George (eds), *Spirited Politics: Religion and Public Life in Contemporary Southeast Asia*, Cornell University Southeast Asia Program, Ithaca, NY, pp. 93–118.

Feener, Michael 2007, *Muslim Legal Thought in Modern Indonesia*, Cambridge University Press, Cambridge.

Hefner, Robert W. 1993, 'Islam, State and Civil Society: ICMI and the Struggle for Indonesian Middle Class', *Indonesia*, vol. 56, pp. 1–35.

Mahmood, Saba 2001, 'Feminist Theory, Embodiment, and the Docile Agent: Some Reflections on the Egyption Islamic Revival', *Cultural Anthropology*, vol. 12, no. 2, pp. 202–236.

Puskapol 2013, 'Pencalonan 30% Perempuan Pada Pemilu 2014', 18 April, available at: www.puskapol.ui.ac.id/press-release/1325.html (accessed 1 February 2014).

Rinaldo, Rachel 2003, 'Ironic Legacy: The New Order and Indonesian Women's Groups', *Outskirts*, vol. 10, available at: www.chloe.uwa.edu.au/outskirts/archive/volume10/rinaldo (accessed 14 December 2008).

Rinaldo, Rachel 2006, 'Feminism in Uncertain Times: Islam, Democratization and Women Activists in Indonesia', Globalization Conference, University of Chicago.

Saptari, Ratna and Utrecht, Artien U. 1997, 'Gender Interests and the Struggle of NGOs Within and Beyond the State: The Experience of Women Organizing in Indonesia', *Journal fur Entwicklungspolitik*, vol. XIII, no. 3, pp. 319–339.

Siapno, Jacqueline 2000, 'Gender, Nationalism, and the Ambiguity of Female Agency in Aceh, Indonesia and East Timor', in Marguerite R. Waller and Jennifer Rycenga (eds), *Frontline Feminisms: Women, War and Resistance*, Garland Publishing Inc., New York and London, pp. 275–295

Waylen, Georgina 1996, 'Analysing Women in the Politics of the Third World', in Haleh Afshar (ed.), *Women and Politics in the Third World*, Routledge, London, pp. 8–25.

Postscript

After the completion of my fieldwork in mid-2009, significant developments took place in Aceh.

On 14 September 2009, just months before members of the DPRA (the local legislature) for the period of 2004–2009 ended their tenure, 69 local MPs from eight factions unanimously passed a *Qanun* on Criminal Law (Rancangan Qanun Jinayat) and *Qanun* on Sharia Criminal Procedure (Rancangan Qanun Acara Jinayat), both drafted in 2007. The first bill regulates, among other thing, stoning to death for adultery and whipping for homosexuality. When passed, the *Qanun* on Sharia Criminal Procedure will provide legal framework to prosecute the offenders of the four other *Qanun* on sharia. Supporters of sharia law in Aceh believe the passing of the two *Qanun* will lead to a total implementation of sharia law (*penerapan Syariat secara kaffah*). On the other hand, civil society activists and reform academics are adamant that the two *Qanun* contradict the higher regulations in Indonesia's legal system. Women and other civil society activists strongly rejected the draft *Qanun*, as many of its regulations were believed to be against the spirit of equality and human rights (Waspada Online 2009). Fifteen activists from Gender Working Group (GWG), for example, submitted a position paper to the Supreme Court in Jakarta on 10 September 2009 that opposed these harsh punishments (Radzie 2009). Other civil society organizations showed their objection to the bill by organizing a mass demonstration in front of the local parliament building. The bill is considered to contravene the national legislation No. 39/1999 on Human Rights, and contradicts the principles of CEDAW which the Indonesian government ratified in 1984.

Although the *Qanun* on Criminal Law has been passed by the local legislature, the Governor of Aceh at that time, Irwandi Jusuf, refused to sign the bill because of the controversial death penalty it authorizes (Liputat6, 28 October 2009). Article 24 of the bill stipulates that an 'unmarried couple found of adultery will be whipped 100 times, and for an married couple will be whipped 100 times/stoned to death'. The Deputy Governor Muhammad Nazar said that the local administration objected to passing the bill and would not implement it (*The Jakarta Post* 2009). Almost a month after the bill was passed by the local legislature reported that Governor Jusuf remains adamant that he will 'never' sign the bill because it violates and contradicts the national law (*Tempo interaktif* 2009).

Supporters of sharia law criticized the governor for showing little commitment to the 'total implementation' of Islamic law (*pemberlakuan Syariat secara kaffah*) by refusing to sign and pass it into a *Qanun*. This development has raised concerns about the possible clash between the proponents of the new *Qanun* (such as the activists from KAMMI (Kesatuan Aksi Mahasiswa Muslim Indonesia, or the Indonesian Student Action Muslim Union) and the Prosperous Justice Party) and its opponents among human rights and women's rights activists (Rahmad 2009). There has been an attempt to bring the bill to the Supreme Court for review to determine whether it is in breach of national legislation, with the Aceh Coalition of NGOs for Human Rights stating its willingness to apply to the Supreme Court if the newly-elected legislature of Aceh continues to support the passing of the *Qanun* (*The Jakarta Post* 2009). Until he finished his term in April 2013, the governor did not change his mind.

Salim (2009) reveals doubts about the future of the implementation of Islamic law in Aceh, especially in relation to the application of the *Qanun Jinayah*, first, because of the reluctance of Governor Irwandi to sign the draft *Qanun* on Criminal Law, and, second, because of the poor support the *Ulama* Consultative Assembly of Aceh (MPU) has shown for the bill. Salim argues that this lack of support from the MPU is because it is currently dealing with significant internal problems. A high-ranking *Ulama* within the MPU, Amirul Hadi, a lecturer at IAIN Ar-Raniry who graduated his postgraduate studies at McGill University, agrees with this, saying that tensions among the *Ulama* at the MPU emerged due to their different religious affiliations. According to Hadi, there are now two groups of *Ulama* represented within the MPU. The first are *Ulama* with an IAIN background, while the other are *Ulama* with a traditional religious background. *Ulama* from *Dayah*, who enjoy wide public support (especially in rural areas) claim that those who graduated from IAIN cannot be considered to be true *Ulama*. To reduce these tensions, the MPU has now tried to include both groups in the organization's leadership, to share equal control over the organization (interview, Banda Aceh, 7 July 2009).

Salim also mentions that after eight years of implementation, the jurisdiction of the sharia courts still overlaps with other jurisdictions, including those of customary law and civil court. All of these developments potentially hold back the implementation of Islamic law, Salim argues.

Despite these developments, civil society in Aceh, and, in particular women activists, are concerned about the future of women's rights and gender equality. The institutionalization of sharia may have weakened at the formal level, but Acehnese society continues to experience an Islamic resurgence, which often targets women. For example, in October 2009, the Mayor of West Aceh district announced that starting from 1 January 2010, women in West Aceh were forbidden to wear trousers (*Serambi Indonesia* 2009). The West Aceh district administration has since prepared 7,000 skirts to be distributed to women in Western Aceh.

The election of former GAM leader Zaini Abdullah and Muzakkir Manaf, in the 2013 election, gives new hope since both leaders do not set total implementation of sharia as their priority. In December 2013, the local parliament and the governor approved the *Qanun* on Sharia based Criminal Procedure or *Qanun Acara Jinayat*, which becomes *Qanun* No. 7/2013. This *Qanun* provides regulation and implementation of the four sharia-based Criminal Codes. Interestingly, the authority adamant that the *Qanun* applies to all Acehnese regardless of whether they are Muslim or not (Simanjuntak 2014). Rights activists strongly criticized the passing of the bill as it regulates, among other things, criminalization of homosexuality and a penalty of death by stoning for convicted adulterers.

Many believe that the future of Islamic law in Aceh depends very much on who gets elected to the local parliament. During my last visit to Banda Aceh in 2009, just a few days before the national presidential election, local women activists shared their concerns at the result of the legislative election. Partai Aceh, the new political vehicle of GAM,[1] won 33 seats out of 69, with only one of them held by a woman. It is now the strongest party in the local parliament. Some Acehnese activists consider GAM very patriarchal and conservative. They refer to the very small number of women that the party nominated in the general election. Some Acehnese men and women activists also speak of incidents in the past where followers of GAM intimidated Acehnese women. As mentioned in Chapter 5, one informant recalled that in the early phase of the introduction of Islamic law, GAM members actively conducted '*jilbab* raids' (*razia jilbab*) in many places. Similarly, Bowen (2003, 232) has observed that in Gayo highlands in Central Aceh, GAM declared that all women must wear *jilbab* when outside of their houses, and mentions incidents in 1999 when girls had their hair cut for not wearing *jilbab*.

On the other hand, previous studies have argued that Islam has never been the platform of the GAM's leadership, that GAM's struggle for Aceh's independence is not driven by the idea of creating an Islamic state, and that it did not base its struggle on Islam. The former Governor of Aceh, Irwandi Jusuf, a former senior advisor to GAM, clearly showed his position towards the Islamic law with his reluctance to support the 'total implementation' of Islamic law, when he refused to sign the new *Jinayah Qanun*. It is this background that has led some Acehnese and observers to think that GAM's position as the strongest party in the local legislature will eventually change the direction of the formal implementation of Islamic law in Aceh. To this, Professor Abubakar argues that even though Partai Aceh or GAM is secular, and is not based on a religious platform, Partai Aceh could not win the election without the support of traditional *Ulama* based in *Dayah* at the village level across the province (interview, Banda Aceh, 4 June 2009). Thus, he believed it would be premature to suggest that the direction of the implementation of Islamic law in Aceh will change abruptly simply because of the dominance of Partai Aceh in the legislature.

Another interesting development can also be seen in the result of the presidential election in July 2009. Almost 96 per cent of Acehnese voted for Susilo Bambang Yudhoyono, a retired general who once declared martial law in Aceh in 2003. He defeated Jusuf Kalla, who, by contrast, had played a crucial role in bringing the two warring parties to peace talks in January 2005 and signed the peace agreement in August 2005 (Aspinall 2006; *Tempo Online* 2009). This result was quite surprising, given that some political pundits predicted that Jusuf Kalla could win the majority of votes of Acehnese, not only because of his role in peace talks, but also because he was seen having more appeal to Islamic voters. During the campaign, the issue of his wife's veiling was used to generate support from Islamic voters. The result of the presidential election can thus be seen as supporting the notion that Islam is no longer so important an element in Aceh's politics.[2]

These political developments will definitely affect the institutional capacity of the local government structures whose role is central in the implementation of Islamic law, such as the Wilayatul Hisbah (WH). As discussed in Chapter 2, the WH faced problems at its initial establishment, including limited resources and restricted areas of authority. In the beginning, the WH was organized under the Office of Islamic Sharia. Under the Law on Governing Aceh (LOGA or UUPA No. 11/2006), Article 244, paragraph 2, WH was integrated into the civil Satpol PP or Public Order Enforcers (Satpol PP or Satuan Polisi Pamong Praja) and the Governor of Aceh passed *Qanun* No. 2/2008 to legally enforce this. As a result, in February 2008, WH and Satpol PP became officially integrated, with the WH having to wear the same uniform as Satpol PP, and share the same office. The only difference between them is now a badge on their uniform. Although the integration of WH into Satpol PP was intended to improve the effectiveness of WH, it, in fact, created more problems. The field commander of WH in Banda Aceh explained to me his resentment at the decision that WH should wear the same uniform as the Satpol PP (interview, Banda Aceh, 4 June 2009). According to him, people now tend to assume that all incidents involving public order offences are perpetrated by WH.

WH officials also feel that the local government has not seriously supported the WH in implementing its obligations. In Banda Aceh, the WH now has 60 officers, including 14 women. They work 24 hours, seven days a week in two shifts. Women officers, however, work only from 8 a.m. to 5 p.m. and their numbers are small. Because no women personnel are tasked to work in a night shift, the male personnel have to deal with cases that involve women and this has caused serious problems. On 8 January 2010, for example, Acehnese were shocked to hear that three WH Officers in Langsa district had raped a female student who was caught violating *Qanun* No. 14/2003 on *Khalwat*. The incident took place at night, after she and her partner were detained and placed in different rooms at the WH Langsa district office (*Tempo*, 19 January 2010). Therefore, it would be better if women officers are tasked to deal with women perpetrators so that they can be protected by WH women officers. But when

I asked the WH officer why the female personnel are not assigned the night shift, he replied that Acehnese still find it hard to accept women working at night with male colleagues.

Another issue resented by many WH officials is that there are many WH members who have not yet been promoted to be government officials or Pegawai Negeri Sipil (PNS) and remain casual employees. Sadly, all the 14 female personnel are still employed casually, even though they possess undergraduate degrees from either the Sharia Faculty of the IAIN AR-Raniry, or from the Faculty of Law at Syiah Kuala University. For example the leader of the female personnel, who has worked for five years, is yet to be promoted to be a PNS. To this welfare issue, the field commander said 'For me, it is not hard to understand local government's commitment to implementation of Islamic law, just look at how they treat us'. By saying this, he was implying that to him the local government of Aceh is not really interested in supporting 'a total implementation' of Islamic law as mandated in the LOGA.

All these developments lead women activists to believe that promoting women's roles in public life and asserting women's rights will not be without obstacles. In fact, they believe that the struggle for Acehnese women activists to advance women's status and gender equality is becoming more difficult. This is because despite the recent efforts made by women activists in promoting gender awareness in their programmes from village to city in Aceh, the numbers of votes that women give to women candidates remain very low. This means that women's representation in the local legislature remains very low too. Women activists therefore predict that they will need to continue their struggle to promote just and non-gender biased policies for the foreseeable future. The struggle for equality will also require women activists to change social attitudes in regards to women's leadership and women's public roles more broadly. Women activists believe that the role of the religious authorities in changing this attitude remains important, and that they therefore need to continue working with religious communities in Aceh.

Notes

1 Aspinall (2009, 8) discussed at great length the transformation of GAM into a peaceful political movement. GAM is now known by Acehnese as KPA (Komite Peralihan Aceh or the Aceh Transitional Committee), a committee responsible for accommodating former GAM combatants.
2 In the 2009 national general election, the Democratic Party, which is the political vehicle of incumbent President Susilo Bambang Yudhoyono and a nationally based political party, won 12.73 per cent of the votes in Aceh. This put the party in second place after Partai Aceh, the local political party founded by GAM in 2007, which won 43.40 per cent. Meanwhile, the Golkar Party, the party led by Jusuf Kalla, achieved only fourth position, with just 4.86 per cent (Hilman 2010). This was quite shocking for Golkar as in 2004 it was the majority in the local parliament with 128 seats, while the Democratic Party then occupied just 55 seats.

References

Aspinall, Edward 2006, 'Violence and Identity Formation in Aceh under Indonesian Rule', in Anthony Reid (ed.), *Verandah of Violence*, ISEAS, Singapore, pp. 149–176.

Aspinall, Edward 2009, *Islam and Nation: Separatist Rebellion in Aceh, Indonesia*, Stanford University Press, California.

Bowen, John 2003, *Islam, Law and Equality in Indonesia: Anthropology of Public Reasoning*, Cambridge University Press, Cambridge.

Hilman, Ben 2010, 'Political Parties and Post-Conflict Transition: The Results and Implications of the 2009 Parliamentary Elections in Aceh', *CDI Policy Papers on Political Governance*, available at: www.cdi.anu.edu.au/.IND/2009-10/D/2010_02_RES_PPS7_ACEH_Hillman/2010_02_PPS7_Hillman.pdf.

The Jakarta Post 2009, 'NGOs to File Review of Aceh Stoning Bylaw', 19 October, available at: www.thejakartapost.com/news/2009/10/19/ngos-file-review-aceh-stoning-bylaw.html (accessed 20 March 2010).

Khumaini, Hayatullah 2009, 'Raqan Jinayah Kesampingan Hukum Positif', *Modus Aceh*, 16 July, available at: www.modusaceh.com/html/read/kolom/1752/raqan_jinayah_kesampingkan_hukum_positif.html/ (accessed 20 March 2010).

Liputan6, 'Gubernur Aceh Tetap Tolak Qanun Rajam', 28 October, available at: http://news.liputan6.com/read/249131/gubernur-aceh-tetap-tolak-qanun-rajam (accessed 24 November 2011).

Radzie 2009, 'Kaji Ulang Qanun Jinayah: Koalisi NGO', *Acehkita.com*, 9 September, available at: www.acehkita.com/berita/kaji-ulang-qanun-jinayah-koalisi-ngo (accessed 20 February 2011).

Rahmad, Yuli 2009, 'Ragam Jinayah, Aktivis Perempuan Kecam PKS dan KAMMI', *The Globe Journal*, 10 September, available at: http://theglobejournal.com/hukum/ragam-jinayah-aktivis-perempuan-kecam-pks-dan-kammi/index.php (accessed 23 December 2009).

Salim, Arskal 2009, 'Islam and Modernity: Syariah, Terrorism and Governance in Southeast Asia', *ARC Federation Fellowship*, Melbourne, Melbourne Law School.

Serambi Indonesia 2009, 'Bupati Aceh Barat Larang Perempuan Bercelana Panjang: Celana Ketat akan Digunting', 27 October, available at: www.serambinews.com/news/view/16482/bupati-aceh-barat-larang-perempuan-bercelana-panjang (accessed 27 October 2009).

Simanjuntak, Hotli 2014, 'Aceh Full Enforces Sharia', *The Jakarta Post*, 7 February, available at: www.thejakartapost.com/news/2014/02/07/aceh-fully-enforces-sharia.html (accessed 10 April 2014).

Tempo interaktif 2009, 'Qanun Jinayah Belum ditandatangani Gubernur Aceh', 28 September, available at: www.tempointeraktif.com/hg/nusa/2009/09/28/brk,20090928-199694,id.html (accessed 29 September 2009).

Tempo Online 2009, 'Pemilihan Presiden 2009: Terbelah di Serambi Mekah', *Halaman Utama*, 22 June, available at: http://majalah.tempointeraktif.com/id/arsip/2009/06/22/NAS/mbm.20090622.NAS130655.id.html (accessed 20 July 2009).

Waspada Online 2009, 'Hukum Jinayah tak bisa disandingkan dengan HAM', 2 November, available at: www.waspada.co.id/index.php?...hukum-jinayat-tak-bisa-disandingkan (accessed 20 December 2009).

Index

For Product Safety Concerns and Information please contact our EU
representative GPSR@taylorandfrancis.com
Taylor & Francis Verlag GmbH, Kaufingerstraße 24, 80331 München, Germany

www.ingramcontent.com/pod-product-compliance
Lightning Source LLC
Chambersburg PA
CBHW050443280326
41932CB00013BA/2224

9 780815 362401